EVEREST GRAND CIRCLE

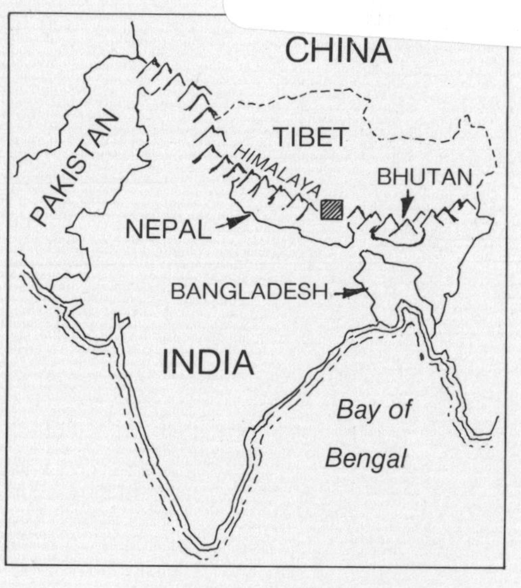

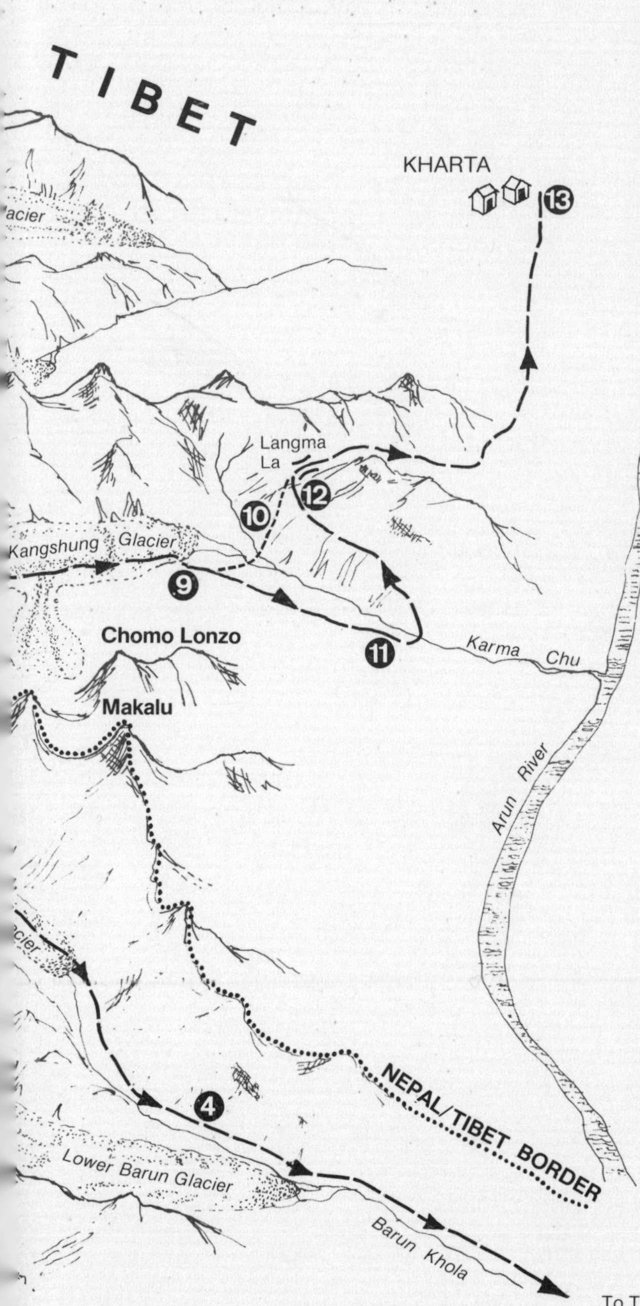

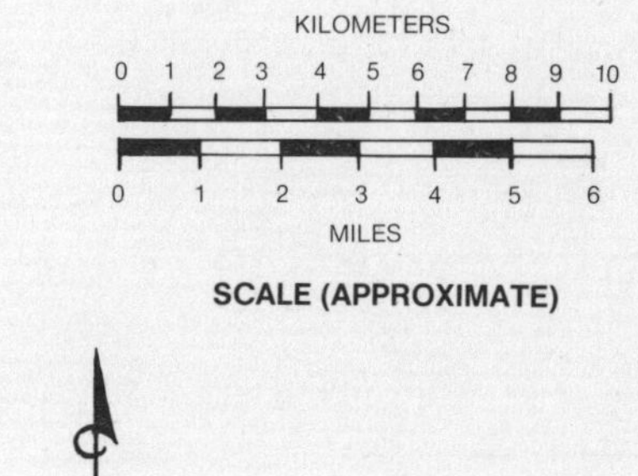

1. Pumori Base Camp at Gorak Shep
2. We part from Sherpas
3. Sherpas not at meeting point; we head down valley without food
4. We meet solo Frenchman
5. Rongbuk Base Camp
6. Ski to Lho La
7. Ned and Jim climb unnamed peak
8. British Advanced Base Camp
9. We lose trail
10. Trail that we missed
11. We meet Tibetan lumbermen
12. Tibetan porters meet us
13. We meet Chinese liaison

EVEREST GRAND CIRCLE

Everest Grand Circle

A Climbing and Skiing Adventure through Nepal and Tibet

NED GILLETTE & JAN REYNOLDS

THE MOUNTAINEERS

Seattle

NED: *To Jan, for being the other half on both halves, and much more.*

JAN: *To Ned, whose kindness, confidence, and patience have guided me through many doors that I might never have opened, left to myself.*

The Mountaineers: Organized 1906
". . . to explore, study, preserve and enjoy the natural beauty of the Northwest."

Published by The Mountaineers
306 Second Avenue West, Seattle, Washington 98119

Published simultaneously in Canada by Douglas & McIntyre, Ltd.
1615 Venables Street, Vancouver, British Columbia V5L 2H1

Manufactured in Japan

Edited by Sharon Bryan
Designed by Elizabeth Watson

Color photos by the authors
Map by Marge Mueller

Cover photo: From Pumori Advance Base Camp, looking across at the Everest Massif in the late afternoon.

Library of Congress Cataloging in Publication Data
Gillette, Ned, 1945-
Everest grand circle.
Bibliography: p.
1. Mountaineering—Nepal. 2. Mountaineering—China—Tibet. 3. Skis and skiing—Nepal. 4. Skis and skiing—China—Tibet. I. Reynolds, Jan, 1956- II. Title.
GV199.44.N46G54 1985 796.5'22'095496 85-15253
ISBN 0-89886-111-X

CONTENTS

ACKNOWLEDGMENTS

We would like to thank the people who contributed to the expedition and the book.

First, the team members: Jim Bridwell, Steve McKinney, Craig Calonica and Rick Barker—our thanks for circling with us and thereby, indirectly, "doing the book."

There were many who worked behind the scenes to get us to the Himalaya. We mention them in the chronological order that they joined the enterprise. Gregg Hartley found a fine sponsor for the expedition—R.J. Reynolds Industries. John Shostak, Dave Fischel, Nat Walker and Betsy Annese of RJR gave their unwavering support. We retain a special affection for Betsy, our dear "Coach." Advertising executives Ken Angel, Dan Kellams, and Margize Howell kept pre- and post-expedition promotion light and easy.

The North Face of Berkeley, California, designed and built alpine equipment for us. Phoenix provided skis marked with serial numbers 000001 through 000004.

In Asia, many people helped us. Mountain Travel–Nepal served as expedition outfitter for the southern half of the circle. Liz Hawley and Lisa Van Gruisen introduced us to Kathmandu. We are grateful to Mr. Sharma, the mountaineering section officer of Nepal's Ministry of Tourism, for not asking too many questions. We are equally appreciative to the Chinese Mountaineering Association for granting us unusual permission to roam the north side of Everest. Our Sherpas—Anu, Angpura, and Phutashi, and our Chinese aides—Chang, Losan and Laba—gave us devoted support in the field.

Finally, the book. We are deeply grateful to The Mountaineers. The book is billed as a co-authorship; in truth, it should be a sept-authorship to acknowledge our editors. Steve Whitney masterfully knit our two voices together; Sharon Bryan, as "word doctor," prescribed phrase and consistency cures; Betty Watson, who designed the book, kept her wits about her after hearing we'd taken 12,000 photos during the course of the expedition; and Ann Cleeland, charged with final, overall editing, coaxed the monster manuscript into sweet surrender. Finally, our heartfelt appreciation to Donna DeShazo, the "chief guide" of Mountaineers Books. We thrived on her precise and astute encouragement, and her lasting friendship.

AUTHORS' NOTE

During the Everest Grand Circle, we learned how to divide and conquer—or shall we say combine and conquer—as we went along. Most decisions brought forth two, and sometimes more, viewpoints. Often we would agree to disagree, in this way becoming more mutually supportive. We've included two of those viewpoints here, let two voices describe the expedition. To this day each voice swears that it tells the *true* story.

Initially, we thought the book would be a series of anecdotes and remembrances dressed up with a smattering of culture and history. But we soon discovered that each memory had layers of fact and illusion, reality and reverie. Digging more deeply into them became a way of finding out who we really were and why we had done the things we did. After finishing the book we know ourselves, the experiences, and the places much better than we did when we were in Nepal and Tibet.

1

THE ACCIDENT

"Gan bei!"

Chinese toast

NED: 

The Chinese liked doing business with Jan and me. In addition to being successful on their mountains and prompt with our payments, we were easygoing and quick to joke with them. Often our willingness to laugh together as friends brought better results than lengthy official meetings. We learned this on our first trip to China in February 1980, when we taught cross-country skiing to youngsters. Our get-togethers at sumptuous banquets introduced us to our hosts' time-honored way of saying yes or no. They often presented a new idea as a pleasant aside during some large or small celebration—one usually fueled by plentiful alcohol.

Such an aside, made during a banquet in Beijing in the summer of 1980, initiated the process that led to our circumnavigation of Everest. The banquet marked the end of a successful expedition on which we were the first Americans in 48 years to climb in China. Galen Rowell, Jan, and I had skied from the summit of Muztagata, a 24,757-foot mountain located in the Pamir Range of China's Far West. At the time, it was the highest complete ski descent of a mountain ever done. It gave us a blue-chip rating with the Chinese Mountaineering Association (C.M.A.) and created the opportunity for us to be asked back to China for a future venture. The offer that would lead to a dream and its fulfillment came as an offhand question during an evening of almost slapstick good humor.

Jan and I and the other four members of the Muztagata expedition sat at a table engaged in rounds of toasts with our Chinese hosts. With us were Mr. Shih, head of the C.M.A.; Mr. Wong, the organization's second in command; Mr. Chu, our vibrant liaison officer; Madam Hu, secretary of the C.M.A.; and an interpreter. As leader, I sat on Mr. Shih's right. It was summer, when the formal attire of the Chinese—men and women alike—is an open-necked white shirt and dark pants. Our round table had been placed in a private dining room located upstairs over a busy restaurant. The clatter of everyday eating drifted upward. The room was undecorated except for two paintings of docile dragons. I mused that pre-Mao dragons doubtless had breathed old-fashioned fire. Waiters moved briskly in and out of squeaky double doors, clattering platters.

Initially formal and correct, the spirit which swept the company soon became delightfully rowdy. By now, we had been through enough banquets to gauge the potency of the three glasses set before each of us. The largest was for beer, the middle for sweet red wine, the smallest—an innocent looking, shot-sized bubble perched on a stem—for *mao-tai,* an evil-tasting clear liquor with a gigantic kick. East and West alike toasted mountaineering success, our bridge of friendship, the C.M.A., Beijing, Washington, international accord, Mr. Chu, skiing in China. "*Gan bei,*" or "bottoms up," was the refrain that followed each verse of the evening. The rounds of toasts created a merry momentum all their own. Waiters leaning over our shoulders kept all our glasses filled, but it was the little glass that always begged attention. A single quaff drained it. Instantly, it was refilled. Beer and wine were off limits for "gan beis." There was good-natured competition to offer more flattering and more humorous toasts. The catcalls of the company made it impossible to sit out even one round.

In this pleasant alcoholic haze, both sides stepped across the disciplined boundaries of Chinese etiquette. We were soon drunk as skunks. We toasted socialism . . . they toasted capitalism; we toasted their leaders . . . they toasted ours. We toasted trees and glaciers and digging a hole through the center of the earth to each other. The interpreter was going bonkers. It was hopeless. We all toasted the nasty misdeeds of the Russians. Mr. Chu rasped a song from atop his chair. Expedition team member Dick Dorworth responded in fat-tongued lyrics that were sieved through the baleen of his beard.

Soon our circular table lay strewn with the debris of our meal: carcasses of black dragon grouse and Peking duck, lumps of monkey-head mushrooms. Ruby puddles of wine stained the once-white tablecloth, dribbles of sauce decorated once-white dress shirts. Bones littered the floor. Cameron Bangs, our team doctor, stuffed the neck and head of the duck into his shirt pocket. A greasy, Bacchanalian emblem spread across his chest. As Cameron swayed, the baked duck beak turned left and right as if attentive to conversations. Its eyes, like ours, were glazed. As doctor, Cameron had prescribed a crutch for himself in the form of Mr. Chu, whom he leaned on heavily. We had nicknamed them the "whiskey brothers" early in the expedition. Now they were jabbering gibberish to each other, one speaking English, the other Chinese. Neither had the foggiest notion of meaning, but they were roaring with laughter, comrades in arms.

Sometime late in the evening Mr. Wong, his face temporarily serious, leaned toward me. "When will we see you next?"

I pulled myself together. "I should like to ski in Tibet," I said somewhat whimsically. I heard myself say the words as if from a distance, as if from somebody else's mouth. I hadn't, until this moment, thought of skiing in Tibet. I really wasn't serious, but Wong thought so. "*Ke yi.* That will be possible." Wong straightened and rejoined the festivities. I had the unsettling feeling that our exchange had been more than idle conversation. I was momentarily sobered by the possibility that I had committed myself to something I had no idea how to accomplish, but these misgivings were drowned out as the next series of "gan beis" rolled in like ocean breakers.

Wong was bright-eyed the next morning. And he had not forgotten about Tibet. I decided not to lose face by explaining that my reply had been nothing more than a jocular comment spoken in the heat of the banquet battles. So it was agreed that I would be back in the spring of 1982 to ski in Tibet. (No more permits were available for spring of 1981, so I had some breathing space.) I was committed, like a gambler whose chips had been shoved to the center.

◆ ◆ ◆

Once I was home, I began to formulate a plan for the trip to Tibet. Initially, Everest was not in the picture. It was on the maps of Tibet I began to peruse, but way down at the bottom, so I didn't pay it much attention. Besides, Everest had been done. People had been up it solo, without supplementary oxygen, and in the dead of winter. They had traversed it and skied down it. It seemed that any and all imaginative approaches to the mountain must already have been used. But the lure of Everest, the "nose-tip" of the world, survives like that of no other mountain. "There is no end to this Kingdom of Adventure," wrote George Leigh Mallory. Everest is a metaphor—a symbol of excellence, of the barely attainable.

But for the time being, I was not thinking of Everest. I had asked the C.M.A. for permission to "ski trek" in Tibet, and on that I focused. For six months after my return from China, I continued to interpret my mandate literally, narrowly. As I wrestled with vague plans tailored for Tibet to further my concept of adventure skiing—using light cross-country skis in the big mountains and remote areas of the world—I knew I would need to find a focus and stimulus for the expedition—an unusual route, perhaps a first. I also knew Tibet would be expensive. I needed a grabber, something to make the venture attractive to a sponsor. I studied maps, searching for an exciting yet logical goal. Suddenly, calmly, via a detour of the eye into the world's most spectacular mountain complex, it was there: Everest. It stood on Tibet's southern border. Nobody had ever gone around it. Could I not knit together a high-altitude, circular route that would weave through weaknesses in the mountain's defenses? It would be creative adventure on a grand scale. The Mount Everest Grand Circle was born.

Everest, the "third pole," the ultimate lodestone for mountaineers, was now my goal. While most climbers were seeking new ways to gain the summit, I decided to put a different twist into an expedition to Big E. I proposed to tackle it horizontally instead of vertically, thus attempting to become the first to completely encircle Everest. It was a new way of looking at an old subject, but going in circles was not new to me. I had taken the same approach to Mount McKinley, North America's highest peak, in 1978 by leading a 90-mile circumnavigation. It had been novel, challenging, and lots of fun. In jest, members of the expedition claimed that we had invented a new sport called "orbiteering."

Even in the excitement of my discovery, I saw immediately that the circle would have to be broken into two halves, one in Nepal, the other in Tibet, since at that time the border between the two countries was closed. Nepal was a buffer between India and China, and neutrality was more easily maintained by such closure. Westerners were forbidden to cross from one country to the other and back, and Everest stood astride the border. First, a team would have to journey by some still undetermined route from the southern escarpment to touch the border (the crest of the main Himalaya chain) to the east and west of Everest. Then the team would have to repeat the process from the north, in Tibet, reaching the border as close as possible to our earlier footsteps. Two halves making a whole seemed contrived, but the plan increasingly gained my fancy.

One question still nagged me: was crossing the border entirely out of the question? Could I not do the circle in one clean, tight sweep? As I focused on that possibility, my imagination took a quantum jump, and I conjured up a swashbuckling scenario. With permission from Nepal or China to operate in the general vicinity of Everest, I could slip up and over the border, moving light and fast around the mountain with a small team of guerrilla raiders. The Walter Mitty in me flew to the dream; the nostalgia flooded in for the time when the great overland marches of Hedin, Younghusband, and Stein had been possible. The rascal in me wished to skirt authority and overlook political boundaries. But the border was more than an arbitrary line; it was the crest of the main Himalaya. On the far side of the mountain we would be distant from supply lines—totally self-sufficient, without chance of rescue. The very madness of the scheme was a terrific lure.

We wouldn't have been the first to sneak across the border. Climbers both notable and unknown have done so, but most in a time when fewer mountaineers rummaged through the Himalaya, and governments had fewer regulations and spying eyes. From Nepal, Edmund Hillary had scooted over the Nup La on a nostalgic fling to visit the north side of Everest—the scene of early British attempts on the mountain. Woodrow Wilson Sayre had taken four against Everest in a clandestine foray across the border in 1962. Maurice Wilson, Earl Denman, and Klavs Becker-Larsen had made solo attempts, crossing the border without permission. Who could guess the number of other mountaineers who had done so?

Despite my flights of fancy, I knew major illegalities were out of the question. Too many people would be compromised. It would be an international embarrassment to my country, Nepal, and China. I would certainly be banned from future expeditions in both countries and maybe even blacklisted by other Asian countries. An illicit foray might tip the balance against the relaxation of permits offered to climbers for sensitive areas. And it would certainly prohibit any sponsorship, for such a sortie would have to be made in secret. And there was no point in simply asking for permission, since I knew it would be denied.

No, international politics demanded a wilderness installment plan. Our orbit, put together like two halves of a clamshell, would, I calculated, take four months and cover 300 miles. It would not be as pure or outrageous as I would like, but it would be legal.

2

PAPERS AND POLITICS

"You'll have to scale bureaucratic summits before you scale mountain summits."

Mr. Shih, Chinese Mountaineering Association

NED:  Mountains in Asia are not free to climbers as they are in North America and Europe. National governments consider them economic assets—not only is it necessary to obtain permission to travel on or climb them, but you have to pay a fee. In some ways it is more difficult to obtain permission from Asian governments than it is to climb.

The first permission required—and the one I had assumed would be the most difficult—was in hand. China had only recently been opened to climbing expeditions, and visits to Tibet were very limited. But the Chinese had promised us entry into Tibet for the spring of 1982, so I had only to shift the location of our ski trek to the Everest area. Confirmation of the change arrived on the usual C.M.A. stationery—which is no stationery at all. There was no letterhead, no fine paper. It was somehow refreshing, and the mark of a seller confident in the quality of his product—in this case mountains. The signature consisted of a stamp, purple and impersonal. In dealings with the Chinese the venture was dubbed the "Everest Ski Trek," so it had a name and therefore an identity, even though no specific trekking route had yet been agreed upon.

Second, with half of the budding expedition's miles now in Nepal, I had to secure permission from that country's Ministry of Tourism. Sill thinking of the project as a trek, I was not particularly concerned. Permits are little problem for trekking near Everest; thousands pass through the region each year.

Indulging in benign political skullduggery, I decided to tell neither His Majesty's Government of Nepal nor the People's Republic of China about the entire circular route, the grand game plan. They could get edgy if we talked about touching borders. I planned to talk only of passes and ridges to cross and areas through which to travel. After the expedition succeeded, I would be pleased to include everybody in my little secret.

But now it was time to include Jan. Hers was the third permission to secure, and in some ways it was the toughest. I knew this from past experience. We had done a long ski trip together in New Zealand, then taught Chinese youngsters to be better racers in Manchuria, then skied Muztagata. But it had taken her weeks to agree to go on the expeditions. This was not because of indecision, or any lack of wanderlust. But she is no sideline spectator. She wanted to make sure the expeditions were her style and that she could play a contributing role.

I recall our final dash to the summit of Muztagata, when she set the women's altitude skiing record. We had been climbing upward from our high camp for more than nine hours, and it was almost dark. We were cold and exhausted. Jan, who had never before been above 12,000 feet, was now at twice that altitude. We had gone up fast, too fast to acclimatize properly. Galen Rowell and I had goaded each other, and the climb had turned into a long sprint. At the end we were very tired and dehydrated, with headaches, nausea, tunnel vision, blurry thinking—the usual fare at high altitude. But we were still in control. Near the top, Galen asked Jan, "How're ya doin'?" Her response was to lean over and, with a graceful near-curtsy, vomit on his skis, then climb on with a sharp, "If you're going, so am I."

I didn't know how Jan would react to enlarging the Tibet ski trek idea into a circle of Everest. She asked about the level of technical difficulty and danger, reminding me that she had started climbing only a little over two years before. Since my research was incomplete, I couldn't be specific about the route through the mountains of Tibet and Nepal. That bothered her; she didn't want to get in over her head. But she listened. I expected to wait out her usual lengthy period of deliberation, but much to my amazement, she gave a prompt "yes." She still had doubts and there were unanswered questions, but she was in. "So far, everything I've done has been by the seat of my pants," she said, "Why not this?" We were partners for our fourth expedition.

But somehow her clean, quick acceptance unsettled her. Previously, deliberation had ensured safety and success; thus she now advocated risking nothing more on the expedition than was absolutely necessary in order to make it around. We talked about the make-up of the team. I explained that mountaineer Kim Schmitz and I had talked generally about a ski trip in Nepal during 1980 when we were together on a traverse of Pakistan's Karakoram Range. My vague agreement with Kim was that each of us would pick a companion for any Nepalese ski junket. The Everest trip fit that mold, and I wanted to keep my word. I sensed that this arrangement made Jan feel somewhat left out, since she was a pickee, not a picker, but she let it pass. She wanted to know a schedule. "If we are locked into spring for Tibet, when will we do Nepal? Before or after?"

"I think we should do it before, during the winter," I answered. "It'll mean we do the two halves closer together, so it will seem more like one piece. We'll stay low enough to avoid the worst of the winter gales. If we do that, it can't be that cold." Everest is on the same latitude as Florida. Oddly enough, there is less snowfall in the high Himalaya in the dead of winter—December and January—than at any other time. A great deal of snow falls in February and March, which increases avalanche danger. I wasn't sure when we should ski in Nepal, since not much skiing has been done there. I guessed that earlier would be better, but that we'd have to stay high, up closer to the snowline.

"High enough to be on snow and low enough to be below the worst of the wind," Jan summarized. We talked on and on, planning and trying to knit together all the variables. Jan had one stipulation. "Just don't go pulling one of your usual moves of upping the stakes. I know you too well. You can't say no to a new idea. Let's keep it a fun trek."

◆ ◆ ◆

We had to determine the specific route we would follow in Nepal and

Tibet, as well as its proximity to Everest. There were several choices, and we could make it as technically difficult and dangerous as we wished. In other words, we could establish our own rules of the game.

Although there was scant up-dated information on the north side of Everest in Tibet, there was a good deal of literature from the seven British attempts on Everest between 1921 and 1938. I put together a route that largely followed in the footsteps of the original 1921 British Reconnaissance. That expedition pioneered the approach to the most logical route up Everest. I felt at ease basing my plan on data more than a half-century old; it was but a blink of geologic time. I was much less easy about gaining the blessing of the C.M.A. for an unusual route, and one that would take us far from a base camp and the eyes of a liaison officer.

In contrast, there was plenty of current information available on Nepal—not on the winter conditions, but on geography and government regulations. At first it seemed we should move from east to west around Everest on the Nepal leg. On the east side of Everest we could ski up to the border on the Barun Glacier, which curved north around Makalu, the fifth highest mountain in the world. On the west side, three passes provided access to the border: the Nangpa La, a trade route into Tibet still used by Sherpas, was off-limits to foreigners; the Lho La was dangerous but had the advantage of being close to Everest; the Nup La was the pass Hillary, then Sayre, had used to enter Tibet illegally. The Nup La was not attractive, being several miles distant from Everest and approached through a complex icefall.

I wrote to Colonel James Roberts, an emeritus expeditioner and Nepal Himalaya expert, for advice. "I would choose April for this crossing," he wrote back from Kathmandu. "February is midwinter and you might have serious problems. . . . Of course, if you come in April (or possibly in March—really, I can see no alternative to these months for skiing) there will be no snow for skiing at lower altitudes in the Khumbu. Depending on the year, skiing may be possible above 16,000 feet."

I had written to him in confidence about the overall plan to circle Everest. He continued on about getting up to the border. "Now the problems. The Lho La, although loose and unpleasant, can indeed be climbed. . . . However, it is the way up the West Ridge of Everest and I don't think a permit will be possible for people not actually climbing Everest. . . . The same applies for a visit to the *foot* of the Nup La [permit for Gyachung Kang required]. . . . I must say this is a rather ponderous and expensive way to go about things. . . . You need not of course climb the two mountains but you would have to pay the royalty, etc. I think that Pumori might be a better choice than Everest or Gyachung Kang and might be a mountain you would like to climb. This would give access to the border and hopefully you can reach the same point from the other side."

Pumori! Of course. It is a beautiful 23,442-foot pyramid standing on the border just west of Everest. The climb to the summit would be a classy way to touch the border and begin the Mount Everest Grand Circle. I was excited. Pumori would guarantee that the circle was a real mountaineering challenge. I had been on too many long ski trips when we, even though among the great peaks, were relegated to speeding through the valleys. Now we had a mountain to climb, one on which the expedition would turn. But when should we fit in Pumori? My thoughts had been directed toward skiing in the winter. Why not continue the same line of thought and climb in the winter? It was an awesome proposition. No Americans had ever climbed a major Himalayan peak in the winter. A new route in winter! The expedition continued to mature. So did my assessment of conditions we would be likely to meet in the Himalaya in winter. Few expeditions had wrestled the big peaks during the sun's lowest ebb, and fewer still had succeeded. As the old challenges of Himalayan climbing were giving out, there was a budding movement to explore the high peaks in winter, and we could be part of it.

The 1950s were the golden age of Himalayan climbing: out of the 14 giants over 8,000 meters, 13 fell via the easiest route. Edmund Hillary and Tenzing Norgay scaled Everest in 1953. Where was the next challenge?

Techniques developed on the sheer granite walls of Yosemite and the rock and ice faces of the Alps were soon adapted to the Himalaya. In 1970 Chris Bonington led the first climb of a great Himalayan face—the 12,000-foot South Face of Annapurna.

With the barriers of altitude and terrain falling fast, it was inevitable that the weather would be the next challenge. Traditionally there had been two climbing seasons in the Himalaya: one just before the summer monsoon, the other just after. Although autumn presents more settled weather, early mountaineers favored spring, which is warmer. In 1979 Nepal officially opened a winter climbing season, during which the cold is numbing, and jet-stream winds of over 200 kilometers an hour descend onto the tops of the highest peaks.

The Poles were first to take up the winter challenge. In 1973 they climbed Noshaq, a 24,580-foot peak in Afghanistan's Hindu Kush. The following year they attempted Lhotse, 27,923 feet high, and failed, but learned to work in the atrocious conditions. In the winter of 1979-80, they succeeded on Everest—the highest mountain in the hardest season. On February 17, the last day of their climbing permit, the summit bid began a half-hour before sunrise in a severe storm, with the temperature minus 50 degrees Celsius. "It was very hard," the summit team said from the top via radio, "If it was not Everest, we should have given up at the beginning of the route."

◆ ◆ ◆

Jan was less than enthusiastic when I broached the newest modification of adding Pumori to the plan. I had been thinking on my own, forgetting that Jan and I were now equal partners in this venture. She voiced misgivings about the difficulty of Pumori. "If an accident occurs on Pumori," she observed, "it could well cancel the remainder of the circle, and that's our main goal." In her mind the sensible thing was to get the circle done in as safe and simple a way as possible. Pumori did not fit in, but she was willing to consider it. She had one question: "Why do you want to climb it?" I gave her a lot of reasons, all of which fell flat. As she persisted, I flung a final retort at her, one that erupted from my gut. "Because it's a beautiful peak and I'd love to be on it in the same way I wanted to be on El Cap. It's beautiful."

JAN: I never realized Ned had obtained permission from our Chinese friends to return to China until he began to talk to me months later about going skiing in

Tibet. At first I was delighted by the idea, but after years of working with Ned, I knew a light-hearted ski jaunt would hardly be his entire plan. Ned's projects are like a dry sponge dropped in a puddle of water. As the information is absorbed like water, the plan increases in magnitude at an alarming rate. Besides, I knew that this developing expedition had to offer a major challenge for Ned to justify throwing himself into it. A relaxed vacation just isn't his style.

Although I was quietly flattered that Ned had begun to badger me about being part of this ski trip, I retained my nonchalant veneer. I wanted to wait until I had that gut feeling that his plan had matured fully. Only then, if it sounded feasible, would I commit myself to the endeavor. So, I bided my time directing a ski school in Vermont while Ned continued to incubate his plan. Months later, as I had expected, Ned's ski trip had fermented into a vintage expedition: the Everest Grand Circle.

I was upstairs fussing with my plants when Ned came bounding up the stairs from the office. He held a map in his hands and his eyes were alive with excitement.

"Jano, I've got it! We'll ski around Everest. As far as I can tell, no one has seen each face of the highest peak in the world. I've found a route we can follow. Look. We won't just ski in Tibet; we can ski in Nepal as well."

Ned carefully laid the map down on the counter as if it depicted directions to precious buried treasure, and traced a route around the peak with his index finger. Ned's route looked excitingly possible. My internal smile spread across my face. I was no longer listening to Ned with detached judgment, but found myself being drawn in by the unusual concept and the power of Ned's enthusiasm. Without thought, on pure impulse, I said yes. I agreed to be a full partner and share responsibility for making this thing go. Once again, Ned's coaxing confidence had made an arduous adventure sound like child's play, and my curiosity overcame my hesitations.

◆ ◆ ◆

Ned and I decided to split expedition preparation equally between us. While Ned wrestled with politics and papers, I waded through the planning of menus, ordering food, clothing, and equipment, organizing everything as it arrived, and paying bills. Since both Ned and I were the hub of the wheel that would roll around Everest, I thought it was only fitting that I might have some say in the selection of the other team members. But my opinion didn't make a dent in the reality of the matter. Ned was as possessive as ever about this aspect of the expedition.

Something didn't settle quite right inside me. Until now I had been "invited along" on Ned's expeditions, but this Circle demanded equal effort from both of us. Yet it was obvious my voice wouldn't carry as far. I would have ignored the whole team selection process if I hadn't been convinced that Jim Bridwell, whom I'd met and worked with in California, would be perfect as our climbing leader.

I liked Jim because he was serious about his climbing, yet he treated life as a great joke. He had a wide-ranging sense of humor and endless patience. I'd heard of Jim's past history as the King of Climbing in Yosemite, where the only thing that mattered was what you climbed and how you climbed it. Jim had been known for pushing the limits and for developing innovative techniques.

He was also known in those days as brash, arrogant, and difficult to work with. But the Bridwell I met wasn't a suntanned, boyish rock king. He had just returned from the first alpine ascent of the 5,000-foot East Face of the Moose's Tooth in Alaska. I met a strong, unassuming man with versatile climbing skills, who had no qualms about working with women.

When I first suggested including Jim, the person I described didn't correspond to "the great bird" Ned remembered from Yosemite. Both had lived there ten years earlier, and Ned had been put off by Jim's flamboyant style. I could see Ned would have to be cajoled a bit to let go of his impressions. I wasn't sure it was worth the effort, since the team had already been selected, so I let it go.

◆ ◆ ◆

Weeks later, when Ned again came up the stairs with the map in his hand, his step was deliberate and he had a defensive glint in his eye. He wanted to ski Pumori as part of the circle. The peak's declination lines were so close together that I broke into a cold sweat just looking at them on the map. I couldn't understand why he wanted to climb the peak, and I couldn't even imagine any of us skiing it. I was also irritated that he was tampering with the original circle plan when we'd agreed to keep this thing simple.

Again, Ned's persuasive powers went to work. His first tack was to assure me that I wouldn't have to climb if I didn't want to. But we both knew that if any of us were to attempt Pumori, I wouldn't be satisfied to be left behind. So I still wasn't at ease with the idea or persuaded that the climb was necessary. But when Ned finally blurted out his deepest reasons for wanting to climb the peak, I finally relented. "Okay," I said. "Let's do it!"

NED: Once again, it seemed the hardest part was over. Jan had wanted to be convinced that I was including Pumori out of love for the endeavor and an appreciation of the mountain. We still had to obtain a peak permit from Nepal. The official winter climbing season included only the months of December and January. Our initial plan to ski over the high Nepalese passes in spring was now outdated—whatever the snowfall, we would be there in the dead of winter, because of the time limitations on a climbing permit for Pumori. Cross-country skiing was suddenly a secondary consideration. To be fresh for Pumori, we decided to reverse the Nepal leg, and start on the west side of Everest. We were ready to head around Everest except for the small matter of money.

Willie Sutton, when asked why he robbed banks, quipped, "That's where the money is." For the Everest Circle, we didn't yet know where the money was. Fund-raising has been a major hurdle for every Everest expedition, beginning with the first reconnaissance to the north side in 1921. Then money was raised by private subscription, including a contribution from King George V, and contracts with the press.

Strangely, we were unconcerned. We had a novel plan, and had built a good record of fulfilling promises to past sponsors of our expeditions. But the world is full of good people with good ideas. We sent one of a number of proposals off to our friend Gregg Hartley, a marketing expert in the ski business. Six weeks later Gregg called to say he'd found a prospect: R. J.

Reynolds Industries, a Fortune 50 corporation that was advertising a product on an expedition theme, was interested in the enterprise.

Jan and I had been climbing and skiing in the Far West, but on separate trips. I located her, then together we flew to New York. There, with Gregg, we waited at a fashionable restaurant to meet the executives. Jan looked smashing in a new dress. I wore a suit. In walked the executives, sporting polo shirts and casual jackets. They had dressed down as far as we had dressed up, each side bent upon putting the other at ease. The dinner proceeded with topsy-turvy spontaneity. It was downright riotous—so much fun that, toward the end, I became concerned that no business had been conducted. But it had, and three months later we had our sponsorship. It was the first time that an American corporation stood as sole sponsor for a major mountaineering expedition.

◆ ◆ ◆

There is more risk on an expedition than that relating to falls and frostbite; permission and sponsorship must dovetail. Before funding was confirmed, we had to obtain permission from the governments of China and Tibet. Otherwise we risked embarrassment with the sponsor if the plans should fall through. Yet failure to raise money after permissions were in hand, and subsequent trip cancellation, promised certain unofficial blacklisting by the Asian government bureaus.

Confirmation of sponsorship came through in September. We had been assured by our contacts in China and Nepal that all was proceeding normally, but I felt uncomfortable not having official signed protocols in hand. We had time on our side in dealing with China, since we would not be there until spring, but we were scheduled to leave for Nepal in late November. I fired telegrams, telexes, and letters off to Bobby Chettri, my contact at our outfitter, Mountain Travel-Nepal. He soothed my growing concern with each turn of a calendar day. Pumori would, he felt sure, be open to us even at our late date of application. Winter, a season newly opened to climbers, was not requested much.

In early October, I heard from Bobby that "permission [for Pumori] should be forthcoming soon." I felt uneasy with his use of the conditional verb. Bobby said that he could not agree to send the Sherpas assigned to our expedition over the high passes between Everest and Makalu during the winter, and that they would staff only Pumori Base Camp. We would be on our own after Pumori, in our swing around the southern flank of Everest. If we required a food cache at Makalu Base Camp, the Sherpas would have to take the lower and less risky route. This did not concern me. I preferred that we be on our own going over the passes because fewer people made for a simpler, bolder style.

I replied to Bobby that, with such short time, there could be no mistakes, no misunderstandings. We must have Pumori and we must have the subsequent trek over to Makalu, since the whole circle would be compromised without them. I couldn't forget that many an expedition had been sunk by the obstacles of bureaucracy, including the first serious plan by the British to climb Everest in 1907. The Secretary of State of India, an Englishman, shot down the proposal at the last minute out of spite for one of the expedition patrons, the former Viceroy of India.

Permission for Pumori was finally confirmed in October. Permission to then trek eastward to Makalu was left tentative until we arrived in Kathmandu. The government could understand the climb of a mountain, but not a high traverse in the dead of winter. The government wanted more information, and safeguards for the liaison officer who would be assigned to us, before okaying any pioneering. We would go to Nepal wondering if politics or possible bad temper of the Minister of Tourism on a particular morning might jinx the circle.

On the other hand, we would not go to Tibet at all unless we first signed a protocol with the Chinese in Beijing. A trip to Beijing is expensive, so a special trip to sign a protocol is to be avoided if possible—yet signing cannot be done through the mail. Fortunately, Kim Schmitz planned to pass through Beijing in October, as a member of another expedition to climb in China, so I asked him to negotiate the protocol. I gave him a written set of points and questions to cover with the C.M.A., and authorized his signature on the protocol. I made it absolutely clear that he was not to speak to the C.M.A. of the circle concept because of sensitivities concerning the border. The Tibet half was to be referred to only as the "Everest Ski Trek."

I was humorously dismayed when Kim delivered the signed protocol to me six weeks later. There, billboarded, was the "Mount Everest Grand Circle." If the Chinese ever suspected, they never let on.

◆ ◆ ◆

Before leaving for China, Kim had asked Steve McKinney, a long-time friend from Squaw Valley, California, to be the fourth member of the expedition. At 28, Steve held the world record in speed skiing, 124.34 miles per hour. He was a steely-nerved daredevil, phenomenally strong, but only a moderately expert climber. I felt a bit uneasy because I did not know him well. Accepting him on the team went against the first principle of choosing a successful team: realistic knowledge of ability and substantial friendship between members. I was also concerned about Kim's and Steve's dedication to the project. Steve needed to train for speed skiing, and Kim would be participating in an energy-sapping expedition that was scheduled to return a week prior to our departure.

In November, I received a letter from Kim, still in China. He wrote "I think Pumori will be too cold—it's not that great a climb—this climb is and I can barely get my gloves off. Anyhow, I did sign form [Chinese Protocol] and plan to go on rest [of Everest Circle] depending on your arrangements but I do not feel dealing with Pumori in winter is worth beans." His withdrawal left us without a lead climber on Pumori—a problem, considering the moderate proficiency of the rest of the team.

Jan had earlier suggested that Jim Bridwell would be a fine addition to the team, but I had not taken her seriously. I had known Jim slightly when he was the kingpin rock climber in Yosemite during his, as he put it, "irresponsible, swashbuckling years." I couldn't imagine myself on an expedition with him. I thought of him as a hard man, brimming with macho. Yet he was without doubt one of the world's great climbers. Soon after I received Kim's letter, Steve called to say he had spoken to Jim, who was enthusiastic about the Pumori climb. I asked for a couple of days to think it over.

There was no doubt in my mind about his climbing credentials; but would he fit in with us? I talked it over with Jan, and finally left it up to her. She was delighted to make the decision—at last she would get her choice of a team member. She was absolutely certain Jim and I would get along well.

I called Jim and welcomed him onto the team. Straightforward from the outset, he said he wanted to do only Pumori, not the entire circle. I agreed—that was where we needed him. He would be climbing leader, I overall leader. He merrily confessed to having little high-altitude experience. I confessed my moderate climbing proficiency. We laughed and the bond was formed. Together we would be off on our first trip to the Nepal Himalaya.

◆ ◆ ◆

Throughout all the permission and personnel juggling, Jan and I were hard at work designing and accumulating the scores of large and small items with which to outfit the expedition. In the extreme wind and cold we would be likely to meet, clothing and tentage would be critical. We talked with designer Mark Erickson and product manager Tom Mann of The North Face in Berkeley, California about our requirements, and they helped provide us with their best equipment. A hundred years ago, Arctic explorers struggled for hours to thaw their buffalo sleeping robes with body heat in order to slip inside. We would at least be spared similar hardships.

As we collected piles of gear for our four-person team, Jan took over the nasty job of chief coordinator. It was a collecting frenzy: double plastic climbing boots with closed-cell foam inners, double leather cross-country skiing boots, ice axes, ice hammers, 9-mm rope, 7-mm rope, webbing, ice screws, deadman anchors, snow stakes, carabiners, crampons, jumars, cross-country skis (they would arrive at J.F.K. Airport the same day we flew to Nepal), climbing skins, ski poles, gaiters, plastic long underwear, overboots, sleeping pads, high altitude meals and snacks for 40 days, cooking stoves, lighters, pots, fuel containers, water bottles, down booties, running shoes, snow shovels, repair kits, first aid kits, headlamps, batteries, mitts, gloves, socks, hats, silk balaclavas, face masks, dark glasses, goggles, sun cream, toothbrushes, nail clippers, drinking mugs, spoons, backpacks, duffel bags, books, writing tablets, tape recorders, cassettes, eight 35-mm cameras, 200 rolls of 35-mm film, 16-mm camera, 16-mm film, air tickets, visas, traveler's checks, and lots of cash.

I wondered, as I always do in the clutter and frantic pace of such a departure, if there was not some way to keep the process simpler, cleaner. Could you, as Shipton and Tilman claimed, organize an expedition on the back of an envelope? I suppose. But I would need hundreds of envelopes.

Most mountaineers train for an upcoming expedition on rock crags and ice slopes. Jan and I hit the promotion trail for our sponsor. We worked out on staircases leading to newspaper offices, balanced on high stools in front of radio microphones, sweated under the glare of television lights, dodged questions flung like rockfall. In November, we spoke at a press conference in New York to announce the Mount Everest Grand Circle. I was superstitious. I did not feel easy about announcing a kind of success before we had done what we were aiming to do. Here we broadcast our primary goal of circling Everest. Until now we had hushed the circle concept, especially when dealing with the governments of Nepal and China. What would happen if either heard of our public announcement? Would they put two and two together? We trusted our luck.

3

KATHMANDU

"We're going to be continually walking off the edge of our assumptions."

Steve McKinney

NED:  We arrived in Kathmandu on November 30. Used-up Datsun and Toyota taxis, none of uniform color, jammed the paved path in front of the airport. Their drivers darted about as if the business of attracting fares were a Wild West roundup. Dust swirled in the air, lifted by hundreds of sandalled feet. Steve, Jim, Jan, and I—first-timers in Kathmandu—unsuspectingly stepped into the corral of untamed Asian capitalism. The drivers pressed about us. "Here-a taxi. Best-a price. Which-a hotel? Thirtee rupees. Taxi. Taxi." We didn't yet know the street value of a rupee, to say nothing about "which-a hotel." Fortunately, a representative from Mountain Travel-Nepal had been sent to shield us from such excesses. He mounted a simple rescue by escorting us to a well-groomed taxi, which promptly set off for the city with all four of us aboard. He stayed to look after our dunnage.

Our driver was skillful at the wheel, his confidence that of a newly licensed American adolescent. We shot down alleys banked by tiny shops jammed shoulder to shoulder. Shoppers spilled out of stores and directly into our path. We dodged bicycles and rickshaws, tractors, and other bruised autos. Our driver leaned on the horn as if mere volume alone could part the masses—of which we, remarkably, now formed a part.

"It is an unfortunate time to be in Kathmandu," the driver commented. His English was good. "The Starr beer factory is on strike. It is the first strike ever in Nepal."

Tiered pagodas and spiked temples lined our passage. Kathmandu was our looking glass, our point of transition, into another world. "What a place of contrasts," Steve said, hanging out the window to get closer to the place. "We're going to be continually walking off the edge of our assumptions."

"Yes," the driver said, punctuating his speech with determined, athletic yanks on the steering wheel. "The beer strike." He threw both hands in the air. The car, its wheels out of alignment, careened toward a little boy squatting over an open sewage gutter. The boy leapt aside without stopping to pull up his pants.

We entered a crowded market square. A group of soldiers, equipped with nightsticks and woven bamboo shields, stood along one side. Soldiers in paradise? "Some Nepalese would like to see things change," explained our driver. "Yesterday there was a march to protest the shooting of a Communist leader. They chanted 'demm-aw-craa-cee, demm-aw-craa-cee.' Tourism has brought more than new ideas. Ten years ago there were no beggars here—each family took care of their own unfortunates. Now the beggars come up from India."

Late that afternoon we checked into the Nariyani Hotel and then headed for the dining room.

JAN: My eyes surveyed the table. The others were bent over their meals as if in prayer, but in fact, they were falling asleep. Ned's head began nodding down slowly, then jerked up in surprise. Jim seemed to move in slow motion, and Steve, who is never still, laid his head in his arms on the table. They were all exhausted, but for some reason I felt wide awake.

As I toyed with my food, I realized that our relationships to each other had stabilized. We had easily passed through the early, awkward stage of sizing one another up, like children on a playground. During trip preparation in Vermont, it had become apparent that we could live happily together, not just tolerate each other. And, to my delight, humor and laughter dominated our conversations. Even Jim, the eldest of us, had shown me that he approved and even encouraged my sense of foolishness by being more ridiculous himself.

Ned and Jim were a human yin and yang combination. Money and politics appealed to Ned's keen business sense, and he handled them as if he were a trained banker or lawyer. Without the burden of these logistics, Jim was free to think about equipment, routes, and weather—the areas he knew best. Each was the other's perfect complement. I'd often find them discussing exceptional people, exotic places, and adventures that had been done and that remained to be done. They sparked ideas in each other.

Steve and Jim, both from Squaw Valley, California, were old friends. Steve respected Jim's knowledge of and experience in the mountains and quickly complied with his direction. Steve was eager and amiable, yet somehow aloof. I always wanted to penetrate his cheerful exterior but could not. Of my companions, Steve was the toughest for me to read.

We all respected Ned for creating the dream of the Circle, and for turning it into reality. His was the voice of authority; he called the shots.

As for me, I suppose I helped provide relief from some of the pressures and tensions of the trip. I was always happy to listen, and aware of how everyone was feeling. Also, since I had shared organization of the expedition, I knew what we had for equipment, where it was, and how it worked. This helped me to feel necessary, not incidental or peripheral.

All four of us were vaguely aware of each other's weaknesses, and accepted them. The range of our personalities was broad enough so that when we combined as a team, we were quite strong and resilient. Among the four of us, someone was always primed to be momentum's catalyst. I treasured the mutual respect growing between us.

The next morning we woke ravenous. As we waited for our breakfast, the soft, eerie, Indian music playing in the dining room was punctuated by a staccato, high-pitched version of "The Yellow Rose of Texas" . . . from Jim Bridwell's watch. All eyes turned to Jim. Jim gave us a sheepish grin. "I don't know how to turn the damn thing off." He never did figure out how. Every morning, from sea level to over 20,000 feet, we heard "The Yellow Rose of Texas" at eight o'clock sharp.

Bellies full, we loaded two small taxis with our remaining bags and headed out through town with the Mountain Travel-Nepal courtyard as our destination. My cabby was thrilled with the idea of showing us the town, and his driving displayed his enthusiasm. A taxi just ahead of us carried our skis crosswise in its open trunk, and I winced when I saw an unsuspecting Nepalese on a bicycle come within an inch of being decapitated by their protruding metal edges. On our first taxi ride I hadn't been able to see out past all our gear. But now as we sped along, I peeked out through the smudged window at the city.

Kathmandu (from *kath*, "wooden," and *mandu*, "house") was bustling with buildings of a mud-brick and wooden variety, put in at all angles and sizes. It was a city of nooks and crannies—brown, cream, and yellow buildings seemed to sprawl without plan or pattern. Their most charming features appeared above street level—beautifully decorated upper stories with decks and open windows, and sod roofs sprouting orange pumpkins on green vines. But I had to laugh when I saw a tourist gawking up at an open window get a garbage shower accidentally dumped over his head. Anything goes in Kathmandu.

Originally, this central valley was called *Ne-pa-lo*, and later Nepal. The people outside the valley didn't consider themselves Nepalese, but separate tribes. As Nepal began to grow beyond the valley and absorb outlying tribes, the largest cluster of wooden houses in the valley was named Kathmandu. Myth and fact agree about the origin of the Kathmandu Valley. According to myth the valley was a deep, pure lake, until the god of learning wielded his sword and cut a deep cleft in the circling mountains, draining it. Geologists agree that the valley was once completely under water, for shells and fossils found in its subsoil are of types common to lake basins.

We eventually made it to the courtyard, bodies intact. Since everything in Kathmandu happens in the cluttered street, cars barrel right down the middle to avoid limping dogs, wobbling bicycles, and men and women lingering to talk. Whenever we met another car—head on, of course—our driver would swerve left and I'd hide my eyes, expecting the worst. But to my amazement, the other car would pull to its left and we would be safe once again. I had forgotten that the British gave Nepal its rules for the road.

NED: Our outfitter, Mountain Travel-Nepal, became the first trek outfitting agency in Nepal when it was established in 1965 by a retired British Army officer, Lieutenant-Colonel James Owen Merion Roberts—who was "tough as old boots and a hard whiskey drinker" (Unsworth, 1981). He was a climber and mountain explorer who was well-versed in the complexities of Nepalese government administration—and the same James Roberts I had written for advice on our Everest Circle route.

Kathmandu's electricity is not turned on during the day, so the hallways and stairs inside the Mountain Travel-Nepal building were dark, and I felt my way along gingerly. In an upstairs office I met Bobby Chettri, and could finally attach a face to all those telexes and letters. Although he was Nepalese, his mannerisms and expressions were as American as mine. He joked that he had learned his English from *Playboy* and *Mad* magazines.

"Everything is under control," Bobby assured me. "You know, we outfit many expeditions each year, and dozens of treks. In our country, even though it is small and closed in so many ways, there are always ways of doing things. Don't worry—Pumori is all set. But you must pay a visit to the Ministry of Tourism to obtain permission for your trek over to Makalu from the Khumbu."

"Obtain permission? You mean confirm."

"Well . . . no. We still are not sure if they will allow you to cross over. The winter is a very unusual time to be on the high passes. But I'm sure you will find Mr. Sharma at the Ministry very receptive. You must ask him."

I had hoped that Bobby might somehow have nailed down final permission. I recalled Galen Rowell telling me that the great Italian climber Reinhold Messener was once forced by a minister in another country to wait twelve days before he was allowed to leave the capital city to climb a mountain for which he already had permission. "Technicalities" needed to be worked out, the official said; in fact, the delay was simply a demonstration of his power. Such stories made me uneasy. We were here to undertake a project for which we still didn't have complete written permission.

Bobby ushered me out into the open-air courtyard that serves as a staging area for expeditions. At the far end was a Himalayan-sized pile of barrels and cartons, each stenciled "1981 American Medical Expedition—Everest." These were the remains of an unusual mountaineering expedition, the chief objective of which was to study human functioning at extreme high altitudes. Scientific measurements were even carried out by the five who reached the summit. There, most of the available oxygen is used simply to stay alive, so little is left over for work. The medical rationale for the experiments was that a climber on the summit who has removed his oxygen mask has an oxygen pressure in his arterial blood that is one-quarter that of a person at sea level: the problems are similar to those faced by patients with severe lung or heart disease.

Diagonally opposite the pile of gear stood a solitary figure who was introduced to me as Rod Jackson. He was setting off the next day to do field research on snow leopards in northwestern Nepal. This was extraordinary because government officials are sensitive about the untamed area on the northwest boundaries, and permits are next to impossible to obtain. In the early 1800s, Mustang and Dolpo were provinces of Tibet. Now that Tibet is controlled by the Chinese, the Nepalese want to avoid any border incidents which might provide an excuse for the Chinese to move back into the provinces. In addition, bandits still operate there, and stories abound of illegal trekkers who never returned. The simplest solution was to close nearly half the country to foreign visitors.

While we were talking, a small man padded up to us. In a gentle, authoritative voice he said to me, "My name is Anu Sherpa. I am your *sirdar.*" I shook his hand, then introduced myself too enthusiastically. He would be the equivalent of the foreman for our trip.

Anu continued in the same calm voice. "I have purchased many things for Base Camp, but there are still many things to buy." He showed me a long list written in Nepalese. "It is possible to acquire money for these things?" I replied that it was, as long as he interpreted the list. Halfway through his roll call of food, pots, stoves, baskets, tarps, and dark glasses for the porters, I stopped him. I was satisfied that everything he wanted was necessary, and promised to provide the money the next day.

The next morning I went to the bank. In addition to the money for Anu, there was the second half of the $842 peak royalty to be paid, as well as a $500 fee to permit us to shoot 16-mm movie footage. There were also the odds and ends of climbing gear that Jim had purchased in Kathmandu. I needed a big wad of small-denomination rupees for the trek into Base Camp—to pay porters, buy food in trailside tea houses, and purchase whatever knick-knacks caught our fancy. The bills I received were old and worn thin as tissue. They smelled like unwashed hands.

The bank I went to was upstairs in a wing of a 100-year-old Rana palace that had seen better times during less democratic days. Government offices now had squatters' rights where nobility once slept. The vast facade was white, anemic after 30 years of neglect. Inside it was very dark and musty. Clerks struggled to see their own figures. There was more light on the ceiling than on the desks, and I could see the ornate carvings above from which paint drooped, dog-eared. The room mourned for the past splendor of the Ranas, but the squinting clerks probably did not.

The Ranas who ruled Nepal from 1846 to 1951 as hereditary prime ministers controlled Nepal as if the country were a private family enterprise. A system of heavy taxes, debt, and tenure imposed by favored, wealthy families relegated Nepalese farmers to the perpetual servitude of medieval peasants.

When I returned to Mountain Travel-Nepal and left the money for Anu, an employee took me aside. "Your liaison officer is here. Too bad, he is a city boy."

He was worse. He was sullen and surly and, from the outset, made it obvious that he didn't give a damn about our expedition. A liaison officer is assigned to each expedition by the government. Some are good, some not; ours was a bad apple. He puffed out his chest at me and introduced himself as Puru. "You have a sleeping bag for me. Let me see it." After examining it with pompous thoroughness, he said, "I need goose down."

"It is goose down," I replied.

"Of course," he retorted. "I will need it when I am on the mountain."

After a frigid conversation, I joined the other team members, who were sorting gear in the courtyard. They had met Puru, and I commented on our bad luck in drawing him. "He's probably afraid," Jim observed. "We'll badger him and keep him so busy that he won't think about where he is. No way that guy has climbed more than a set of stairs in his life. My prediction is that he'll be at Base Camp no more than one day—if he makes it at all."

JAN: About four that afternoon, after beginning to pack our equipment into yak- and porter-sized loads, Jim, Steve, and I slipped off to explore while Ned was at the bank. We headed directly downtown to the markets vending wares that span the centuries. It is possible to find anything to buy or barter here, from Hong Kong's microchips to bats' eyes and nirvana dust used by Tibetan shamans in their tantric magic.

Steve, to my surprise, was the most voracious shopper of us all. He bought everything in sight. Every now and then, as we ambled down the streets, I would catch Jim's wink that indicated, "Looks like Steve's been taken again."

We meandered down Thamel Street, where tiny, crowded wooden stalls lined either side of this rough street offering typical tourist fare—shirts embroidered with dragons, yak-wool jackets, thick colorful rugs, turquoise and silver jewelry, and more. But Thamel was also the street where mountaineers hung out. Here we met climbers from around the world, bartering their used expedition clothing and equipment for trinkets to take home to family and friends.

When we each went our separate ways briefly, I discovered how creative shopping in Kathmandu can be. I chose my own stones and drew pictures of earrings which were then quickly fashioned and set by an eager-to-please jeweler. At another stall, I made a paper pattern and then a tailor sewed up the material I chose into a perfect fit. Shopping in Kathmandu was hardly the bore it was at home.

Later on that afternoon, as I turned away from some knives I had been considering, I spied Steve waving from the doorway of a nearby shop. He was sporting a brand new T-shirt with "Kathmandu" written across the chest, and turning his new prayer wheel. He showed me these treasures while I flagged a cab and yelled to Jim. Somehow, even before Steve slipped into the car, he managed to purchase a day-glow painting of purple mountains and green men. As the taxi began to push its way slowly through the crowd, a small boy about nine years old ran up to our window shaking something wrapped in paper at us, shouting what sounded like "yak bone." In a flash, Steve had handed some rupee notes out the window in exchange for the carved statue. Jim sat across the back seat from me in the taxi holding a bundle in his lap. As our climbing leader, he had the job of selecting and purchasing our technical climbing gear. But because he is a fairly relaxed sort, he waited until we were here in Nepal to buy some basic necessities, like rope for fixed climbs and extra jumars (mechanical camming devices for ascending ropes). It was obvious from the grin sprawling across his face that Jim had been dickering for awhile.

"I got some rope today," he said. "I got a real deal."

"What did you get?" Steve asked casually, as he admired his yak-bone artifact.

"I bought a 600-footer so I can run it out if I want."

"Great," I quipped, suppressing a motherly instinct to caution him.

"Yup, 600 feet and it's polypropylene."

Well, "polyprope" rope has one real advantage—it's light. It's just like a water-skiing rope. But one disadvantage is you don't want to take a fall on it. "And I got a real deal," Jim added. "I got it secondhand." We couldn't help it: we all burst out laughing.

Jim had taken many risks in his life, and it was plain to see that by being with him the rest of us would too. I knew Jim wasn't kidding. As it turned out, he would run out all 600 feet with no protection, thereby risking his neck to save ours!

That is the crux of expeditions: the chemistry between team members that permits success to raise its head. You have to trust one another, to accept that a job done in some other way than yours isn't necessarily doomed to failure. It's difficult to be that trusting in a life-and-death situation, but doubt can destroy any team. Jim was in command of the climb, and we accepted his decisions.

NED: I was apprehensive about the scheduled meeting at the Ministry of Tourism because we still had not obtained final permission for the high traverse from the Khumbu to Makalu that constituted most of the distance of the Nepalese half of the circle. I hoped that a diplomatic presentation would turn the trick. We spent the next day and a half waiting for the meeting, organizing and modifying our equipment, and talking over our plans with Anu.

On the morning of December 3, Steve and Jim accompanied me to the Ministry. I instructed them not to mention our plan of circling Everest or our desire to get up to the border, since I feared that might put an end to all our plans.

A battered taxi conveyed us to the Ministry at an unusually moderate pace. The vehicle's horn was out of commission—a condition more dangerous in Kathmandu, our driver assured us, than the loss of brakes.

I imagined the Ministry of Tourism occupying an entire wing of a large Rana palace—maybe even the entire palace. Tourism is, after all, Nepal's major source of foreign exchange. So I was shocked when we arrived at the Ministry's doorstep. The building—a small, rough, dust-slathered, one-story brick structure—could hardly have been less imposing. It seemed deserted, but a faded, hand-lettered sign directed us down a flesh-colored hallway to the office of Mr. Sharma, the mountaineering section officer. A curtain divided his office from the hall and we stooped to enter the low doorway.

Mr. Sharma was a small, exceedingly polite man who wore his multihued Hindu cap at a jaunty angle. He shook hands all around, then leaned back in his chair. I thought I detected a glint of humor in his half-closed eyes. There was a poster of Pumori on the wall. "It is a beautiful mountain," I commented.

Dispensing with niceties, he said, "What allowances have you made for the comfort of your liaison officer? It will be very cold in a winter Base Camp." I described the kit we had brought for him. "Exactly what route do you plan to climb on Pumori?"

"We will not know precisely until we are at the mountain," Jim answered. "We will try a new route. If possible, we would like your permission to climb on the general east face of the mountain." Mr. Sharma agreed, understanding that we would need some flexibility. He spoke firmly and carefully.

We covered several subjects, all of which went smoothly. Then I broached the question we had come to ask. "In order to see more of Nepal after Pumori, we ask the Ministry's permission to depart from the mountains via a trek to Makalu and then down the Arun River."

Without hesitation, Mr. Sharma answered. "I would not recommend such a trek. No, it is much better for you to stay in the Khumbu. The high passes are no place for a man in the winter. It is not sensible."

McKinney, who had said little until then, stiffened. "You must let us go!" he cried. "We have to go. We have to get around Everest!"

The room was momentarily silent. My vocal cords seemed paralyzed. Mr. Sharma simply said, "Everest? I thought you were climbing Pumori?"

I found my voice. "Mr. McKinney means that, to climb over the high passes to Makalu, we will have to detour around Everest. The important thing is to see more of Nepal. It is our first visit."

"But what of your liaison officer? He will not wish to accompany you on such a . . ." Mr. Sharma allowed a half-smile to cross his lips, ". . . a caper."

We offered more reassurances and, despite his hesitations, Mr. Sharma finally granted permission for the entire route we requested. He kept any suspicions he might have harbored private and off the record. Although it was his job to enforce regulations and avoid any embarrassment for his country, he also had a genuine desire to help mountaineers accomplish their goals.

JAN: Liz Hawley first came to Kathmandu as a correspondent for a news service and succumbed to the lure of the city, making it her home. She was intrigued by the nearby mountains and, through the years, became an expert on the Himalaya in Nepal. Now climbers from all over the world stop in at Liz's upstairs apartment to pore over her extensive mountaineering library and to catch up on the latest gossip about the most recent expeditions.

When our disheveled troop arrived in the early evening, Liz had a candle lantern on the stairs to light our way. She sent one of the two Nepalese working for her to greet us, while the other scurried around pouring us cold beer and setting out dishes of popcorn and cashews. It wasn't long before Jim became absorbed in a photo of Pumori in a well-thumbed book, while Ned and Steve browsed the shelves. I was much more interested in Liz's version of life in Kathmandu.

Liz began by telling me that the sporadic, unpredictable means of communication put time into special perspective. She shrugged her shoulders as she turned her back to me to look out the window on the dark night. "I'm absolved of worry when my messages go undelivered, because it's beyond my control," she explained. This laissez-faire attitude that pervaded the work world of the city was, Liz felt, "a necessity for maintaining sanity." Kathmandu seemed to be a city for those who are patient and flexible.

Liz told me that, despite its slow pace, Kathmandu is woven with an undercurrent of excitement, since it is the gateway to exotic jungles, high peaks, and other settings for adventure. Even at cocktail parties, rumors were continually circulating about yogis who ate themselves piece by piece, or the latest sighting of tigers in the Terrai.

"Even though I'm supposed to have the route worked out," Jim revealed, "this is the first real picture I've seen of Pumori." Liz gave her understanding grin, poured us more beer, and switched from stories of Kathmandu to tales of previous ascents of Pumori.

4

KHUMBU

"Ladies first."

The Men

JAN: 

As we sat in the airport, I tried to shift my thoughts from the pleasures of Kathmandu to the very different ones of the high country. I savored my last bit of Walkman music as I watched the anxiety grow on my teammates' faces. Our plane to Lukla, the gateway to the mountains perched at 9,000 feet, was late. And perhaps it wouldn't fly to Lukla at all today, as was rumored through the partially constructed airport. Accepting the inevitable comes easily for me, but I knew why the others were so eager for us to be on our way. This was the fifth of December, so if the onset of the winter monsoon began at its usual time, it would be nipping at our heels by Christmas.

Since I could do nothing to improve our odds of getting up and down Pumori before winter storm season, I refused to worry, since worry is wasted emotion—it has no positive effects, and only wears one down. So I continued to sit and observe, catching a few favorite tunes before handing over my Walkman to an appreciative Nepalese, a Mountain Travel employee who agreed to look after it for me while I was away.

At last, hours later, we took off in a De Havilland Twin Otter and flew east along the southern escarpment of the Himalaya. Our plane could seat 19 people, but we had it pretty much to ourselves. The ceiling, which was duct-taped together, was typical of the plane's interior and exterior appearance.

Airports with lax, unorthodox procedures, pilots without uniforms, and shabby pit crews are unnerving, to say the least. I surveyed the interior of our plane in search of light seeping through cracks, and tried to size up our pilots as I watched them—through the missing cockpit door—get ready for takeoff. I figured this should be as good a ride as any I'd had at the fair.

NED: The name Himalaya derives from Sanskrit—*hima* meaning "snow" and *alaya* meaning "abode"—"abode of snow." The range stretches as a crescent-shaped rampart for 1,500 miles, an uninterrupted barrier separating the torrid plains of India from the chill plateau of Tibet. The Greater Himalaya, together with the Karakoram Himalaya, boasts all 14 of the world's 8,000-meter peaks; over a thousand peaks rise above 6,000 meters.

Geologists trace the origin of the world's great mountain ranges to the collision of huge sections of the earth's crust. These sections—called "plates"—are rafted about on a hot, semifluid rock layer called the mantle, which lies tens of miles beneath the earth's surface. As mountain ranges go, the Himalaya are young and brash, still flexing their tectonic muscles. Beginning about 50 million years ago, with the break-up of the supercontinent of Gondwana, the Indian Plate began to charge northward—at a rate of about four inches per year—and smacked into Eurasia. The collision crumpled the earth's crust and shoved it skyward, creating the Himalaya. Caught between the two colliding plates, slices of sea floor were thrust upward so that when climbers struggle to the top of Mount Everest, they are treading on marine limestone. The subcontinent of India has already bullied its way 1,200 miles into Eurasia, and it is still going, although at half its initial speed. Mount Everest is pushed higher each year.

Flying over lush valleys of thick, green vegetation, we passed the deep gorge of the Sun Kosi where it cut directly through the range. It is one of several rivers that are older than the mountains, and were strong enough to hold their courses as the mountains rose. We were flying at a height from which we caught a glimpse of the bleak Tibetan Plateau through the Sun Kosi's gorge. It is the highest land mass in the world—the lowest point is 12,000 feet. The Himalayan chain—the planet's greatest wall—controls Tibet's weather, blocking monsoon rains from the south. Scientists say Tibet is rising about an inch every five years—so fast, in fact, that some villages have been abandoned as a consequence of the changing climate and lowering water table.

JAN: The pilots had been gambling that the weather would clear enough for us to land in Lukla. They were right, and as we made our approach I could see green winding rivers, terraced fields, and swelling hills. I could also see the nose of the plane dip down as I peered into the cockpit. All that was visible through the gritty windshield was a steep hillside, and we seemed to be flying right into it. There had to be an airstrip under us—somewhere. We dove down, and at the last minute I saw what looked like only 200 yards of gravel strip that ended at the hillside. When we landed, it was as if we were a can thrown on to the ground. The brakes were applied full force as we lurched and screeched to a halt, just yards before the looming hillside.

The sighs of relief in the plane hissed like air rushing out of tires. When I stepped to the door I saw much scurrying and confusion. Through the crowds of watching and some waiting locals, and through the ambling yaks, I could see a shining face. It was Anu, our sirdar, a sharp, muscularly tight fireplug of a man. His face radiated excited charm and his grin could calm anyone's worry. He dressed with a Western sense of style—he knew what was cool. He was as attentive to us as a mother cat to her wobbly kittens.

Anu hastened to attend to our bags, immediately setting them apart from the other freight. Within an hour, our equipment, including our skis, had been distributed among the Sherpas and we were off on the trail. Anu had hired his buddies to be our porters for the trek into Pumori Base Camp. They appeared shy but attentive as we all worked together packing and securing gear. Occasionally, we'd pull out extra gear and clothing for their personal use, which obviously pleased them. Western clothing has high status among the Sherpas.

We had a superior lot of Sherpas to work with: cheerful, selfless, and proud of their jobs. There were six in all, but Anu's main men were Angpura, general handyman, and Phutashi, the cook, both of whom we met for the first time only at our first night's trail camp. Phutashi's skin had been pitted by chicken pox, and his lower jaw protruded beyond his top jaw. He was shy but very proud, especially of his patchwork English. Throughout the entire trip, Phutashi wore the same pair of blue and gold houndstooth check polyester pants, alternating only the tops he wore with them. He was not as suave as Anu, but was extremely sensitive and giving. Phutashi spent long hours in the steamy, dark cook tent, making delicious meals out of what appeared to me to be nothing. It was Phutashi who would rouse us gently in the mornings and it was Phutashi who unceasingly offered assistance.

Angpura looked like the Cheshire cat. His face was pumpkin-round and he grinned perpetually. His English was poor to nonexistent, but he nodded in response to everything we said, whether it registered or not. I never once saw Angpura lose his temper. I didn't see how we could have a bad time with Anu and his gang on our side.

Trekking in Nepal gave me the illusion that we were part of the aristocracy (of backpacking) because our Sherpas treated us like royalty. Each morning we were awakened by a soft voice offering us sweet, warm tea as we lay muffled in our snug bags. Then breakfast was not only cooked for us, but served to us as we packed only our own personal goods for the day's trek. I was quietly astounded to see that it seemed to please the Sherpas to serve us well.

NED: We walked into a culture where everything moved on foot or hoof. Time decelerated accordingly. We ambled along a trail that was newly widened and improved. Terraced fields of brown stubble lay untended after the fall harvest beside huts with white walls and gray roofs. We carried very light packs filled mostly with camera gear. We were unburdened in every way, trusting Anu's organizational expertise in handling the ponderous logistics of moving baggage to the foot of the mountain. Such an attitude would have begged trouble in most other Asian mountain areas that boasted a nomadic heritage of preying on hapless caravans during centuries past. Not so in the Khumbu. The Sherpas are small, hardy, selfless people who make Nepal the most enjoyable country in which to trek or make an expedition. As sirdar, Anu's salary was thirty-eight rupees per day (about three dollars). Each porter received 25 rupees. A clever sirdar has the opportunity to make a lot of money if he is rewarded with much of the expedition equipment at the end of the trip, or makes deals with local vendors of goods and services.

Prior to 1947, Nepal was a closed country, and there were no treks or expeditions from which the Sherpas could make a living. For 300 years, since the Sherpas migrated into the Khumbu from eastern Tibet (Sherpa means "man from the east"), these mountain clans had been traders—middlemen between the Tibetan Buddhist kingdoms to the north and Indian Hindu kingdoms to the south. Trade was an economic necessity, since the Sherpa homeland was at such high altitude that crops and animal husbandry were insufficient to sustain the communities. The Sherpas carried goods for barter over the crest of the Himalaya. Grain, butter, paper, sugar, snuff, dyes, and Indian finished goods went north, where they were exchanged for salt, wool, fat, and goat meat. Everything was carried on the backs of yaks. Profits accrued largely from the great difference between the price of salt and grain in Tibet and Nepal, and many Sherpas became wealthy by local standards.

Before the modern era, Sherpas were interested in passes over which to trade, not peaks to climb. In those days, they gave little notice to the great peaks which towered into the clouds at the head of the Dudh Kosi. In the summer they pastured yaks in *yersas,* or summer hamlets, as high as the grass grew. There was no reason to go farther; they were not climbers. There was no need to expend energy without economic return. They were drawn to the Bhote Kosi Valley and the Nangpa La at its head because it led into Tibet. There was no money in peaks. Not yet.

JAN: I could hear the familiar creaky squeakings of my swaying pack and smell my salty sweat. I was at once excited and anxious: excited to be strutting out on the superhighway of the high country, the trail to Everest; anxious about how I would respond to the challenges that lay ahead. I am forever wondering if I'll measure up to my self-inflicted tasks. I am a survivor, though everything of note that I have done in this world has been by the seat of my pants. Ned's blind confidence in me has pushed me through many doors. For instance, I had never been higher than 12,000 feet before Ned enticed me to join his expedition to ski off 24,757-foot Muztagata in the Chinese Pamirs. Out of six climbers, Ned, Galen Rowell, and I skied off the summit. Though I didn't know it at the time, I broke the women's altitude skiing record, which had been held by a Russian.

All the local people I passed on the trail greeted me with warmth and charm. They all smiled and repeated the same word—*namaste*—which I figured meant hello. I liked to say it just as a Sherpa would approach, then listen for him to echo the word back to me. I felt very comfortable in this strange land, welcomed by those who lived here.

A few miles down the trail we came to our first Sherpa tea house and slipped inside to escape the snapping coolness of the day. With pointing fingers, Bridwell illustrated the way he wanted his eggs cooked. I settled for just tea and let its heat warm my hands. It was dark inside the stone hut, and wisps of smoke from the open fire hung in the air. As I stepped outside for some fresh air, I tripped over a playful pup. I scooped him up to play with. He liked the teasing and the attention, and returned it with affectionate bites. He stuck with me until it was time to move down the trail again.

"Can't I keep the pup?" I asked Ned. "He'll be such fun at Base Camp." I was teasing, but Ned looked uneasy, and Bridwell remarked, "So is this where the division starts?" He didn't see any humor in my question. I assumed he was referring to a division between the men and the woman. I was embarrassed that he thought I was serious, and immediately put the puppy down. I tried to turn the whole incident into a big joke. "You're just afraid he'll get more attention than you do," I fired back at Jim.

Jim's remark opened my eyes to possible difficulties that I'd never considered before. It had always been easy for me to be "one of the guys." I suppose Jim was afraid my being a woman might cause problems, though he had never before indicated any concern. Perhaps my asking for something as foolish as keeping the pup made him think I might not be serious or hard enough for the climb when the time came. This was as serious as the male-female issue ever got on the expedition. Actually, it became a source of humor. On perilous portions of the trip the men would look at me with devilish glints in their eyes and tease, "Ladies first."

NED: Trailside merchants had set out baubles, religious mementos, bangles, knives, snuff bottles, pots, and a hundred other items for sale on rugs laid on the ground. Often we would be stopped by shrill, pleading voices speaking in clipped English: "Hello. Tibetee. Tibetee—very old. Silver. Very good. Okay. Hello. Hello."

I bumped into Steve bartering with one merchant for a "priceless" trinket. Puru stood next to him, and warned, "They are only made to look old. You must be careful. If there is business, there is mischief. That is the law of business." Then he turned and walked off alone.

After playful inspection of the goods, Steve and I walked on together. He began talking about Einstein's theory of relativity, and the fact that when an object approaches the speed of light its internal clock slows. "If I had a twin," he said, "who rode a spaceship toward a faraway star, he'd age more slowly than I would on earth. Speed skiing's the same."

"It is?" I asked dubiously.

"Sure. In the mind. In the mind." With his huge hands, he shaped a universe in the air, then went on. "The faster my body travels when I'm speed skiing, the slower my mind seems to work. It seems like an eternity to decide on, then take, an action. In reality, it happens almost instantaneously. At the peak of speed, there is no sound, no vision, no vibration—no thought at all."

"No thought at all? At 125 miles per?" I asked, still unconvinced.

"Static," he stated.

"No giddiness? No fear?" I asked.

"You might feel fear just before the run. You might feel fear afterward. But not during the run. There's not enough time. But you're totally aware—aware of another dimension of yourself that is totally in control. But at first you can't see it. Some Eastern and mystical writers see it. I've read their books."

He stopped in the middle of the trail and started the next sentence, not with words, but with a grimace that froze his face for several seconds. His mouth gaped, his eyebrows lofted sharply. I could sense his mind pacing at the speed of light, now almost stopped, as Einstein would have it. Then the words burst out. "I've seen it many times. Part of me was draining a lot of energy. You know, the kind of thing when you talk to yourself, worry, hope for things that aren't there. Letting yourself veer off into the future or the past decreases what you can do now. For me, the speed of skiing is my concentration on the present. I go skiing and climbing and hang gliding because it's the only way *I* know to move into that moment of calm. It's sensual. It's a way to cleanse myself and look at things in a new way."

As we talked we pulled up alongside Puru. As usual, he was moping. With each shuffling step onward and upward, he mentally retreated another notch from our project. I was impatient with his whining. I couldn't subscribe to British expeditioneer Lawrence Wagner's philosophy, as reported in 1969 by Eric Shipton, "that it was a great advantage to include one member so universally disliked that the others, with a common object for their spleen, would be drawn together in close comradeship."

Steve, more accepting, listened as Puru spat more words: "I hate to be here. It is not from choice, not my job. It is duty. Nobody wanted to go in winter, so it came to me. I was on the bottom of the pile."

Steve and I moved on, talking. We were from very different backgrounds.

He had stormed the speed skiing circuit and been first to break the 200-kilometer-per-hour barrier in 1978. At that time he had been a long-haired, bearded, mustached California hippy in baggy dungarees who had dropped out of high school and the stringent discipline of the U.S. ski team. I'd come out of the Ivy League and stayed on the ski team for the Olympics.

We caught up with Jan and Jim at the tea house. It was dark inside, and the air heavy with smoke. The stooped, blackened proprietor inserted sticks into the fire through a side opening in the adobe stove. A sooty teapot and omelet pan occupied two holes on top. A cryptic menu advertised tea with milk and sugar for one rupee, one egg omelet for five rupees, pancake with butter and jam for the same price, wild peach wine for ten, and sleeping space for three rupees. We ordered glasses of *chang*, thick, white beer made from fermented rice or millet; and a glass of *rakshi*, clear, distilled spirits from rice, potatoes, or grain.

When we had finished our drinks and were leaving, we stopped to speak to a tall Japanese who worked in a skeleton of wooden beams that would one day be a hotel. A sign, Chumao Sherpa Hotel, had already been hung over the doorway. The man told us that the money donated by foreigners had run out, so the building had stopped. "I must borrow," he moaned. "Many problems, but . . . it is our life." Then, thinking of us, he said, "Many trekkers up too quickly. If headache, go down. If lose life, cannot try again."

After walking two more hours, we crossed the Dudh Kosi just beyond Ghat and climbed to a little grassy plateau, where we discovered that the Sherpas had set up camp. Food and service awaited us that we normally associated only with the luxury of city hotels.

Phutashi, our cook, and Angpura, our mail runner, shook our hands, then hugged us. As he was pouring our tea, Phutashi congratulated me on the beauty of my daughter. I immediately corrected his erroneous assumption about Jan. Phutashi's face first went blank, then crumpled with laughter. He laughed at himself, and he laughed when I explained that for her to be my daughter I would have had to become a father at age eleven.

JAN: We reached the entrance of Sagarmatha Park in the early afternoon. I thought it strange at first that a land so remote and charming would find a need to set aside tracts of land as a national park, but it wasn't long before I realized why.

Sagarmatha, meaning "goddess of the Universe," is the native name for Everest. The park includes 480 square miles of the Khumbu district, and was principally the idea of Sir Edmund Hillary of New Zealand, who, along with Sherpa Tenzing Norgay, was the first to stand upon the summit of Everest.

In 1951 Hillary, as a member of a British team, made a reconnaissance for an Everest attempt and reported the Khumbu region as being lush with giant rhododendron trees and littered with juniper bushes—so much so that the team began hauling juniper up to the Khumbu Glacier to burn. In 1952 a Swiss expedition did the same, and though 400 porter loads of their juniper remained stacked up on the ice, Hillary's next expedition hacked up another couple of hundred loads to be sure they had enough. And so the trend was set. As Galen Rowell reports, Hillary himself admitted, "We were the ones who started cutting it out. . . . Now the juniper has virtually been wiped out. The whole area up there is just a desert now, which is all eroding." The delicate balance of the high mountain ecosystem had been upset. Perhaps the area could have weathered the disruption of an extra handful of expeditions per year, but the Sherpas, the native people of the Khumbu, fell into a new industry, which furthered the damage.

When China firmly grasped struggling Tibet in the early 1950s, Tibet was virtually closed to all foreigners and Sherpas were forbidden to trade with Tibet. With Tibet closed, the Sherpas were in desperate need of commerce to survive in the Khumbu. Enter the mountaineers. Nepal opened her tightly latched doors to the western world for the first time in 1950, and when Tibet closed her borders, mountaineers scurried to Nepal, on the south side of Everest. Hiking tourists who called themselves trekkers followed the mountaineers into this mysterious kingdom. This created a new source of income for the Sherpas, who hired themselves out as guides and porters.

Trekking in the Khumbu has boomed to the extent that each year the trekkers outnumber the Sherpas more than three to one, and Western tourism is now the foundation of the Sherpa economy. The effects of the change have been widespread. One of the more obvious is the dwindling supply of wood. The Sherpas had been successful woodlot managers left to themselves, but when the demand was increased substantially by expeditions and trekkers, as well as by Tibetan refugees, a lush forest was chopped to bits. And what precious little topsoil there was began washing out to sea with each monsoon's rain. To compound the problems, as the wood disappeared, yak dung was collected and dried for fuel instead of being left to replenish the soil's dwindling fertility.

Hillary foresaw some of these problems, and pushed for Sagarmatha Park in hopes of minimizing them. The laws governing the park went into effect in 1974, and the area was officially declared a national park in 1976. The Sherpas' feelings were mixed about this Western concept of a park being imposed upon them. They understood the need for regulation and management, yet they defied the laws. This was their home and they felt they should be free to chop as they wished. As a result, park officials have found it frustrating to try to apply Western management concepts to an Eastern culture.

The Sherpa culture has also suffered from some of the changes. Their closely knit communities have been disrupted by the long absences of many men on treks and expeditions. Traditional education, handled by Buddhist lamas and monasteries, has to some extent been supplanted by new schools that emphasize secular education. The Sherpa culture that had developed facing East was all too suddenly turned West. Heavy traffic and foreign values came so quickly that the Khumbu in particular resembled an adolescent child struggling to keep up with its own growth spurt, tripping over its own feet and unable to control its changing voice.

NED: After paying a fee to enter Sagarmatha National Park, and showing our government trekking permits to a Nepalese ranger, we started toward Namche Bazaar. At the far end of the village of Jorsalle, Angpura waited in front of a two-story house. With a bonnetlike cap on his head and a wicker basket full of fresh eggs, he reminded me more of a schoolgirl at Easter than a tough Sherpa.

As I neared the house, I could hear guttural rumblings rising and falling. "The lamas are praying for a dead man. You may see," he said.

Instantly, I was alert. This might be a chance to step inside a culture we had merely been striding through as if it were a museum.

I stepped through the first floor doorway into a very dark stable. I heard lowings and grunts on either side. As I felt my way along the wall, groping for the stairs, my hand sank into an unpleasantly soft mass—my nose rather than my eyes told me what it was. My right foot found the ladder and I lurched forward, my Nikons bumping the rungs. I hauled myself up, leaning back to protect the cameras. At the top I banged my head on the edge of the floor opening, then finally rose up into the center of a family of Sherpas. I was slightly dazed and confused, but still a photographer with a mission. I was surprised to find Jan, Jim, and Steve already there.

I nodded politely to the male Sherpas, who sat together, and then to the women, who were dressed in long, dark, sleeveless wool tunics, bright blouses, and striped aprons. On their necks and ears hung exquisite jade, coral, and silver jewelry. They smiled briefly in acknowledgement.

I turned next toward a dozen slack-faced, red-robed monks. I nodded; they nodded back, in rhythm with their baritone chanting, beating drums, and clanging cymbals. A hundred flickering butter candles set on a gaudy, makeshift altar cast a flickering strobe effect over the scene. One monk blew a bone horn, then rocked back in laughter. I noticed another trimming his fingernails with stainless steel clippers. To appreciate where I was, I realized I had to toss aside all my preconceived notions of what a funeral should be.

I lifted my camera and bent my head toward it as a way of asking permission to photograph. The monks smiled and nodded in the same way I had seen parents grant children their wish. I set up my tripod, awkward under my load of camera gear. My mind focused on exposure and composition and I shot several frames. When I lifted my eye from the viewfinder one of the monks made a motion to me as if he were rubbing paper money between his thumb and forefinger. I contributed 40 rupees, then took a couple of additional photos. Meanwhile, Jan, Jim, and Steve had retreated outside. I was ecstatic, but in a divided way. Through my photography I had both gained and lost the experience. I knew the photos would be superb. But I had witnessed the ceremony as a series of 35-mm stop-action frames which kept me from immersing myself in the experience and being part of it.

JAN: As we joined up with Angpura, we could hear strains of music coming from a nearby building—heavy drumbeats punctuated by horns. Our curiosity overcame any hesitations we had, and we slipped off the trail and up the dark stairs of the building, uninvited. Someone whispered something about this being a funeral. I knew almost nothing about Nepal or its customs, so my imagination began conjuring up images of dead bodies and tantric rites as I tiptoed into the room at the head of the stairs. My eyes were struggling to adjust to the blackness. The only thing clearly visible was a candlelit altar at the far end of the room, but after a few moments I began to see many smiling faces. To my surprise, the occasion didn't appear solemn in the least. Standing there in the midst of it all, I had to say something, so I repeated the only word I knew, namaste, which I had learned is a Sanskrit word meaning "I salute you." The group grinned and nodded, repeated the greeting back to me, and continued with the ceremony as if I weren't there.

Below the pyramid of candles on the altar were eight-inch-high rice mounds that looked like little snowmen. Some of the Sherpas were drizzling red dye over the tops of the rice. Others were printing scrolls, drinking chang, and following the lamas' chants.

I drew out my camera slowly and leaned against a support beam to brace myself for a photograph. Then I moved over to watch the Sherpas who were printing, and I was offered a drink. I couldn't see any of my teammates, and wondered what had happened to them as I faded into the background of the ceremony.

Before long, Ned came bumping and banging into the room. In his hurry to set up his tripod, he bumped a carefully sculpted rice mound. A Sherpa looked up and motioned him to move. Then came the rapid-fire photographs. The lama, still with a smile, stood up and held out a hand to Ned, gesturing for money. When the lama asked Ned for payment, it seemed to me a symbol of the disruption of traditional Sherpa values and economy. Sagarmatha Park itself, which came into existence to preserve what tourism was destroying, was another example of Western interference. Suddenly, I felt intrusive and out of place. Although the people in attendance seemed pleased to have us take part, I crept quietly out and started alone up the trail leading to Namche Bazaar.

NED: Jan had already started hiking toward Namche Bazaar. Steve and Jim were talking with a dignified Sherpa named Sange, who told us in English that he had been sirdar on many expeditions. He owned the house in which the funeral was held, so I asked him about what we had seen.

"For my father. He was eighty-eight. After his wife died, he became a lama and hid himself in his own monastery."

Sange pointed at the cliffs that rose high above. A stone hut hung from the mouth of a cave, reached by a catwalk of sticks and boards. He suggested we climb to it, and we started up. Toward the top of the steep trail, a small, domed beehive structure stood on a flat shelf.

"Here we burned my father five days after he died," Sange said. "Now there are 10 days of mourning."

He told us that the head lama of Thyangboche had slept with the cadaver for two nights before the cremation. "What will be done with your father's ashes?" I asked.

"After one week, the head lama will inspect the ashes," Sange explained. "He will see the next life. Maybe another lama, a man, a woman, a goat, person from another country. If my father is to be an animal in his next life, he will see those tracks. If a high lama, then much good will have been done in past life." He paused, then shaped his hands like the wings of a bird. "Some men coming again, some men go up. If not born again, finally free."

"What do you think your father's next life will be?" Steve asked Sange.

"Maybe one, maybe another. I am ready for the party. On full moon day, all people come. I give them rice, butter, curry soup, buffalo meat. They drink all chang and rakshi."

"It sounds like a marriage," Jim said, chuckling.

"Same," Sange agreed with a smile. "The cost is maybe 30,000 rupees." After descending, we shook hands and said good-bye. "Here is my card," he offered. "Maybe you need best sirdar for next expedition. Also, I have restaurant in Kathmandu. It is Kamel Pokaree. You visit."

JAN: By myself, heading toward Namche Bazaar, I felt pleased to be traveling on the trail with Ned, Jim, Steve, and the yak caravan all behind me. Anu had run ahead to Namche, his home, to ready things for our stay in his mother's house. I strolled alongside the Dudh Kosi (Milky River), crossing over near its intersection with the Bhoti Kosi, or Tibetan River. I picked up my pace, thinking the others would soon catch me and then blow right by on the last, long 3,000-foot uphill stretch for Namche. I didn't want to be left trudging too far behind them, getting discouraged. Besides, I had hit my stride and was being carried along by the rhythm of it.

I was lost in my own dream world, drinking in the sounds and smells of a place foreign and fascinating. Before I knew it, the hill was behind me and Namche Bazaar spread before me like a grand amphitheater on a slope that falls away to a cliff, and then down 3,000 feet to the Bhote Kosi River. The wooden balconies of the village houses were dotted with blossoming flowers. The stone walls contrasted pleasantly with the white-washed brick. Strings of prayer flags hung like clothes on a giant clothesline over roofs of wooden shingle held down by large rocks. More lines of prayer flags were strung up the climbing hillside. Inside the semicircle of the terraced homes stood the classic Buddhist *stupa* with its omniscient eyes. These stupas, or shrines, are representations of the contemplating Buddha. Namche Bazaar has become such a large village because it rests at the confluence of two major routes: to the northeast, the trail to Everest Base Camp; and to the northwest, the trail to the Nangpo La, a 19,000-foot pass leading into Tibet.

Then it dawned on me. I didn't have a clue as to the whereabouts of Anu's house; nor could I ask directions intelligibly. I decided to wander through the village of about 140 houses to browse the open-air stalls and paw through the trinkets spilled out on the vendors' blankets in the streets and sniff Anu out. As it turned out, all I had to do was mention Anu's name and people in this small town could point out his house.

But getting to Anu's house wasn't as easy as it appeared to the eye. Actual streets were minimal. The village was so steep that most homes were terraced on rock embankments to hold them up, leaving little or no room for walkways. It was difficult to assess just what level you were on in relation to which level you wanted to get to on the other side of town. I found myself climbing up and down terraces, almost falling twice making my way over loose rocks from one level to another. I laughed to myself, thinking how foolish I'd look having a "climbing" accident before I'd even reached the Himalaya.

The first story of Anu's home was a barn for the livestock, which created rising heat for the humans living above. I met Anu upstairs, waiting with a pot of tea. I was surprised that Ned, Jim, and Steve weren't yet there, considering the time I had spent rambling through the village. Steve arrived soon after I did, but by the time Ned and Jim straggled in, it was dark. They were both exhausted, and shortly after dinner, Ned threw up. We were at 11,290 feet, and these were the familiar early effects of high altitude. Who will be affected, and when, is unpredictable. I was faring quite well with my pulse at about 60 after our day's total rise in elevation of 4,000 feet. But regardless of how many times you've felt strong at altitude, there's no guarantee you won't be sick the next time around.

Ned, Jim, Steve, and I slept in a room adjacent to the main living quarters, which was a well-kept Buddhist monastery. The temple walls were a frescoed panorama of brightly colored creatures—some vicious and some benign. As we were ushered into the room, through a small door built up one step to trip evil spirits, Steve began reciting Coleridge's poem "Xanadu."

We unrolled our sleeping bags, but before we lay down we roamed around the room, peering at the murals in the wavering candlelight, perhaps hoping for instant enlightenment. Ned wondered about one figure in particular, a four-armed wild thing holding a tiny, helpless human in its grip and squeezing the life out of it like toothpaste from a tube.

But I was too tired to look or to speculate any more, and I fell asleep as soon as I lay down.

The next morning we were awakened by Mama Anu, as we affectionately called her. She went to the chest-high altar, on which stood a large Buddha and other small figures. In front of them were 7 large silver cups and 14 smaller ones. Chanting softly, Mama Anu wiped the cups and filled them with water for the good spirits to drink. Then she rotated five times, a three-foot-high prayer wheel set into the altar, so that a bell rang delicately each time the wheel made a complete turn. Anu came in behind his mother with a ladle of burning incense to "cleanse our souls." Anu's family, like those of the other Sherpas I met, were neither proud nor embarrassed about their firm beliefs. Their only concern was to share them with us.

Anu asked if we'd mind waiting a day here in Namche while he hired some high-altitude porters, and we all assured him that it wasn't a problem. I think everyone was relieved to have a day to rest and acclimatize. It was spitting snow as we left to browse through town and shoot some 16-mm movie film with our new camera. Steve had wandered off somewhere alone, while I tagged along behind Ned and Jim, who were soon deep in a discussion of camera mechanics and scene sets.

During the filming we became a part of a scene that made me feel sad and confused. As Jim was filming Ned and me walking the streets of Namche, a blind woman approached us, begging, with a swarm of children around her. When the children put dung in her hand, she bit it, spit it out, then threw it. The children laughed and put some kind of corn in her hand, which she ate. Then she began to claw at us, pulling at our clothing. I was at a loss. Officials at the Ministry of Tourism had instructed us not to give to beggars, since that only leads to more begging. Yet the native children had obviously fed the woman before. I had no food to give, but she kept clutching at me. I couldn't bear to just walk away. I dug into my pocket, pulled out a rupee, and quickly pressed it into her hand, hoping a small amount of money would do the least amount of damage. Again, I felt haunted by guilt for disturbing the culture.

When Steve rejoined us that evening, he, of course, had been shopping. But this time he really had something to show for his efforts—a meteorite. It was black and extremely dense, heavier than anything of the same size I'd seen before. It looked like a cloverleaf the size of my palm. Steve didn't know if the vendor had known what he had for sale or not, because he had asked so little for it. After we tired of trying to imagine how the meteorite ended up here on the outskirts of the Himalaya, we dozed off. I had carefully arranged my bag on the floor in front of the Buddha, taking care to have my head close to the idol because Anu told me I must not have my feet there.

At about midnight, I found myself half-awake. A prayer I had heard an old woman chanting as she circled the large stupa in Bodnath, outside of Kathmandu, was running through my head. Its repetitions were hypnotically calming. The next thing I knew, I seemed to be outside of myself, watching as I stood in the center of tremendous turbulence, held there, repeating over and over again, "I'm in a vortex." Yet I was also caught between two strong forces trying to pull me in opposite directions out of the turbulence. I began desperately repeating, as loudly as I could, "I'm for the forces of good, not of evil." Then I became the base of a vee of light extending up past the Buddha at my head. I vibrated rapidly, and something was drawing me up.

Then I began to hear dogs barking. I was confused and frightened, but after a few moments I started to get my bearings . . . I was in a monastery in Nepal and Ned was beside me. I turned to Ned and gently tucked my arm under his for comfort. To my surprise, he gave a sharp yelp and said, "What is *that?*" I assured him it was only me and asked him if he'd heard me talking or yelling in my sleep. He said he hadn't heard a peep, but that when I touched him it felt like an electric shock.

I couldn't get back to sleep and after a while I crept out of the monastery, across Anu's family's living quarters, and down the stairs to the barn. As I stepped through the door and into a beautiful moonlit night, all the dogs suddenly stopped barking.

The next morning I was afraid that if I mentioned what had happened, the others would think I was crazy, and I'd lose all my credibility as a serious member of the team. But finally I just couldn't hold it in any longer. For some reason, I thought Jim would be the most understanding. I asked him what a vortex was, and he described it as something that draws everything around it into its center. Then I asked him if he knew what the woman had been chanting that I had unconsciously picked up in Bodnath. "It's *Om mani padme hum*, the jewel is in the lotus," he answered. Of course, Jim wanted to know what I was getting at, so I told him of my experience.

Jim didn't seem particularly surprised by the events I described. "You were accelerating in that space between half awake and half asleep," he offered. Steve jumped in: "You should have gone with it. You were close to levitation." I was getting more confused than ever, and decided to drop the subject.

Early that same morning the monks began blowing the rough horns that sounded like motorcycles starting up. Later I learned from Anu that the monks play these horns from 10 to 15 days of the year to chase away evil spirits. I didn't tell him that I felt as if I had done battle with evil spirits the night before, but my experience had been too vivid to ignore. I left Namche Bazaar with a strong respect for the few Buddhist practices I had seen, which no longer seemed totally foreign.

NED: Anu's parents had been divorced for 15 years. His father, remarried, still lived in Namche, but across town. His mother, who had become fervently religious, had not remarried. Even though he had two older brothers, Anu was head of a household of women—grandmother, mother, and two sisters.

Anu's father often spent time at the house. When I shook hands with him, he held on limply. His left hand continued to manipulate his beads and his "namaste" was like a murmured prayer. Anu later told me that his father was wealthy and owned many yaks. Twice each year his father drove 20 yaks northward up the Bhote Kosi, then over the glaciers of 19,000-foot Nangpa La and into Tibet to trade. Before the 1950s, there was heavy traffic over the pass: yak hooves wore deep grooves in the ice. Only yaks were taken across because the Sherpas held to a curious superstition that any ponies taken would die making the trip, and the owner as well. The round trip to the Tibetan village of Tingri took three weeks—more if the weather was bad. As Anu's father walked behind his animals, his hands made hundreds of round trips on his beads.

"At all other times my father is very happy to rent his yaks to expeditions," Anu said. "He charges highest price."

I asked Anu if we were using family yaks.

"Maybe some. Special price." He grinned.

We spent two nights in Namche. As we left, Mama Anu draped white linen scarves around our necks for good luck. We headed north for Thyangboche, walking amidst a cacophony of grunts, whistles, and chants from the Sherpas who pushed our 24 poky yaks.

We hoped to see Everest from our route, which contoured high above the Dudh Kosi. But although we walked in comfortable sunshine, clouds cloaked the highest peaks. Soon we arrived at the junction with a trail that led to Gokyo. At the head of this valley, off our course and beyond the Ngojumba Glacier, stood Cho Oyu, the eighth highest mountain in the world at 26,750 feet and Gyachung Kang, 25,990 feet high. To the east of these peaks lay the Nup La, a pass at 19,400 feet. We had once considered touching the border at the Nup La in order to start our Grand Circle. Others before us had used the pass as access to the border.

In 1952 Edmund Hillary, with fellow New Zealander George Lowe, had crossed the Nup La on a clandestine six-day, 50-mile lark around to the north side of Everest. They had been prompted by a romantic desire to visit some of the famous places of the early expeditions.

Hillary had approached his brazen jaunt as an expert mountaineer. But the man who followed in his footsteps 10 years later, Woodrow Wilson Sayre, a bespectacled 43-year-old assistant professor of philosophy from Tufts University, was an unlikely candidate to achieve the most outrageous feat of guerrilla mountaineering in modern times. In one way, his inexperience was an advantage: he was not bogged down by precedent, so everything seemed possible. Yet it was his inexperience that stopped him in the end.

When Sayre led his four-man party up the Gokyo Valley in the spring of 1962, he had in hand official permission from the government of Nepal to try a first ascent of Gyachung Kang. But it was all a smoke screen to avert suspicion. In reality he was headed over the Nup La into forbidden Chinese Tibet to try nothing less than an illegal ascent of Everest.

They toiled for 33 days at altitudes of 17,000 to 21,000 feet to break

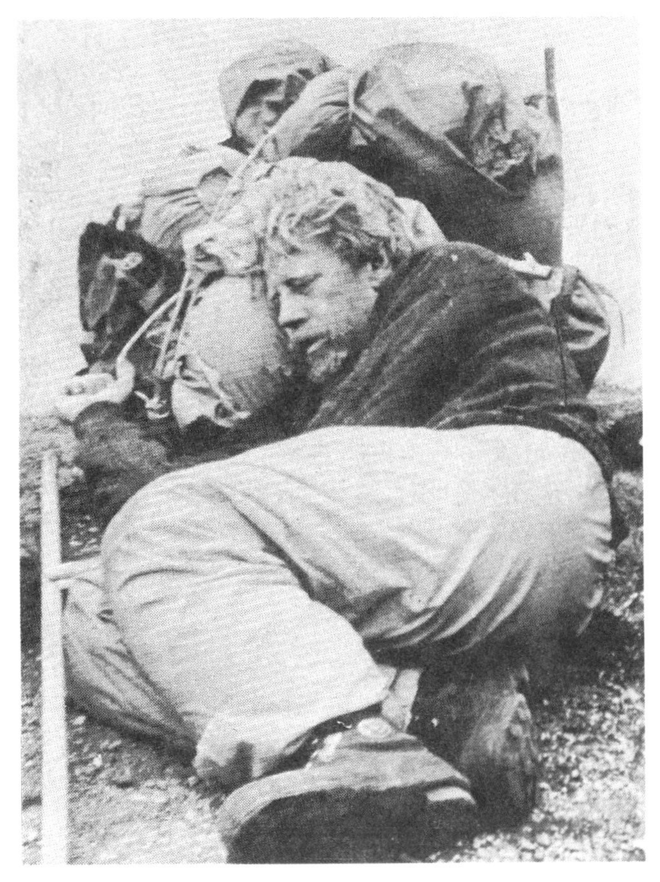

Woodrow Wilson Sayre rests at trailside, exhausted from falling several times and carrying heavy loads. Reprinted from his book, Four Against Everest.

through to the foot of the North Col. Each man moved 120 pounds of food and gear in relentless relays. Vulnerable and half-exhausted, yet in no way dispirited, they then managed to make a gutsy climb to the North Col, at 22,916 feet. At that moment, Sayre felt superhuman, believing he could do no wrong. In the euphoria, judgment lapsed. Descending that evening for the last loads, Sayre and one companion fell 150 feet, then dropped over a 40-foot precipice. Miraculously, they landed in soft snow, dazed but relatively unharmed, then survived a bivouac without sleeping bags.

Although badly shaken, Sayre, during the next three days, pushed to 25,500 feet on the Northeast Ridge before admitting he was beaten. Now, as Sayre took his first steps of retreat after his hopes of the summit were extinguished, the real problems began. The team had extended themselves too far. Energy evaporated; it was replaced by an incredible carelessness and a frantic desire to be off the mountain. The descent was harrowing, and was marked by four more long falls. Astoundingly, nobody was seriously hurt. Sayre arrested one plunge of 300 feet by grabbing the corner of a tent as he shot past! Exhausted and half-starved, they staggered back to Nepal. They had spent 47 days on their attempt, which Everest scholar Walt Unsworth summed up as "brilliant folly and an epic of Himalayan endurance." Looking up the trail to Gokyo, I could not help but admire Sayre's iron-willed tenacity.

Moving on past the entrance to Gokyo, Jan, Jim, Steve, and I walked together down to the Dudh Kosi, then Jan simply ran away from us on the long climb to Thyangboche. I never heard the starting gun go off.

Jim caught sight of her banking around a switchback above us. "She's just bending over backwards to show us she's not holding us back," he offered.

At the top of the hill, at 12,600 feet, we passed under a stone gateway and onto a grassy saddle. Before us were the red and white buildings of the Thyangboche monastery, home of the reincarnated lama who is religious leader of Solu-Khumbu. It is a relatively new building and its origins, oddly enough, are tied to the potato.

Although Buddhism had been prominent in the area for over 300 years, the construction of monasteries, nunneries, and new temples has taken place within the last 50 to 80 years—since the introduction of the potato. Anthropologist Christoph von Fürer-Haimendorf theorized in 1964 that a more plentiful food supply eased economic pressures enough to allow monks to withdraw from the working population and into monasteries. The source of the Khumbu potato, he wrote in 1964, was probably, "the gardens of European settlers in Darjeeling and the garden of the British residency in Kathmandu."

All but three caretaker monks were in lower villages during the cold weather. In the little hotel, we bought a quart of beer for 45 rupees and saw several young trekkers listening to Walkman tapes.

The clouds that had earlier obscured the big peaks were lifting. The great wall of Nuptse and Lhotse, all of it over 25,000 feet, filled the valley to the north. The mountains were ruddy in the sunset, and seemed a long way from the grass on which we lay sipping sweet tea. Had the lamas been there, I believe they would have chuckled at our love of climbing mountains, even though they themselves undoubtedly took great pleasure in looking at them. Thyangboche was a superior site for worship and contemplation.

I turned my head toward a squat, heavily bearded Italian fellow who, towing two handsome blond women, chugged out of the monastery courtyard. He was very excited. Looking north along his outstretched arm, he exclaimed, "There! On the behind! Everest! Stupendioso!"

I turned to look north again. The black pyramid of Everest, suddenly clearing, loomed over the Nuptse-Lhotse wall. It looked menacing, polar, and almost totally inaccessible. From where I stood I had no sense of size or height—only a vague sense of the mountain's immensity and superiority. From the south, Mount Everest was, as Sir Francis Younghusband wrote, "a singularly shy and retiring mountain" (Howard-Bury, 1922). Had I not known which peak it was, my eye would have passed it over in favor of much shapelier mountains nearby.

This was my first look at the peak that had captured the imagination of the public and the ambitions of mountaineers ever since its discovery. Anais Nin wrote in 1966 on the metaphorical significance of Tenzing's ascent of Everest: "Just to satisfy one's ego? Not at all. It gives courage to others. You can choose to question the motivation of the application of it, but you cannot question the example of courage and endurance. I read it as a metaphor. It seemed to me that all of us are trying to climb Mount Everest. That we risk wounds, falls, precipices, frozen feet and hands, snow blindness."

At the beginning of the nineteenth century, the Andes of South America were thought to be the highest mountains in the world. Since Nepal and Tibet were closed to outsiders, calculations of the height of the distant peaks of the Himalaya, which looked more like clouds than mountains, had to be taken from stations on the plains of India. In 1809-10, Lieutenant W. S. Webb calculated the height of Dhaulagiri to be 26,862 feet. (Today it is listed as 26,811 feet.) Initially, geographers outside India derided the figure, but before long, Kangchenjunga was proved to be even higher—28,307 feet.

Between 1845 and 1850, the Great Trigonometrical Survey of India, still working from south of the Nepal border, undertook a series of triangulations on all the great peaks. Since few local names were known, each peak was designated by roman numerals. In 1852, recordings logged in the field from six observation stations at an average distance of 111 miles from Peak XV—a relatively unimpressive peak—gave a computed height of 29,002 feet. The world's highest mountain had been discovered. Later, the true height was calculated to be 29,028 feet.

Everest was named for Sir George Everest, who held the posts of Surveyor General of India and Superintendent of the Great Trigonometrical Survey from 1830 to 1843. His most noteworthy contribution was the measurement of the meridian from Cape Comorin to the Himalaya. He subsequently was able to calculate the length of the earth's axes.

Many argued against the name "Everest" and in favor of one of the local traditional names, of which there were several. The Tibetans knew the mountain as Chomolungma, which means "goddess mother of the world." The Nepalese called it Sagarmatha. But the cartographers of the Survey of India liked the idea of honoring their Surveyor General, and continued to use the name Everest. Eventually a compromise of sorts was reached. Today, most maps label the massif as Chomolungma, and the specific peak Mount Everest.

To my ears, the local names used by generations of natives, or names improvised from Tibetan, well suit these mountains. The names are rooted in the place. I like Changtse better than North Peak, Lhotse better than South Peak, and Nuptse better than West Peak. Pumori means "Daughter Peak." It was named in 1921 by George Leigh Mallory, after his infant daughter Clare, far away in England, as he viewed the peak from the Tibet side.

◆ ◆ ◆

After camping at Thyangboche for the night, we strolled along an enchanted path among twisted juniper and silver birch hung with pale green lichen, and above terraced fields lying barren and unworked. *Mani* walls—piled stones carved with Buddhist prayers in Tibetan script—divided the trail. Sherpas always leave the etched rocks to their right, so that on their return they will have made a circle—another circle of the wheel of life.

We were on our own circular pilgrimage, or *gnaskor,* which in Tibetan means "going around places." The Tibetan concept implies a journey taken in no hurry and without a specific goal or destination. Circumnavigating Everest would demand that we be more single-minded, but it was my hope that our forthcoming experience would be spiritually rewarding as we immersed ourselves in the Buddhist way of life and in the pristine wilderness beyond the communities. We knew that, at the end of our orbit of Everest, we would be changed from the people we had been.

The ultimate gnaskor for both Mahayana Buddhists and Hindus is the pilgrimage around sacred Mount Kailas, the "jewel of the snows." The glistening mountain rises to 22,027 feet on the southwest edge of the Tibetan plateau, and has some of the same significance that Mount Olympus had for the ancient Greeks. Kailas is believed to be the home of the god Siva and the center of the spiritual world. One circuit—36 miles—washes away the sins of one's life; 108 circuits ensure Nirvana.

Lake Manasarowar, the "Lake of the Mind," lies at the foot of Kailas. It was shaped by Brahma, the creator, and bathing in the waters is believed to be a life-giving ritual. Four great rivers flow from the near vicinity of the lake: the Indus, the Brahmaputra, the Karnali, and the Sutlej, radiating life to India and Tibet. Even the Ganges, according to myth, arises from Kailas.

On the trail in Nepal, we trekked gradually higher during the course of the day and camped beyond the last tree at Pheriche. We pitched our tents on summer pastures ringed by walls of rounded stones. The Himalayan Rescue Association stations a doctor here during the trekking seasons of spring and fall to aid climbers and trekkers who encounter altitude sickness.

The hamlet itself lies in a broad, flat-bottomed valley. At the edges, jagged peaks angled abruptly upward. No longer were we tucked away in cozy, water-cut defiles; we'd broken out into expansive alpine regions. Sometime past, in a colder time, the Khumbu Glacier, not even in sight today, had inched down here. The place reminded me of Alaska, where I had served my expedition apprenticeship during ten trips. When I imagine mountain wilderness, I picture Alaska's immense expanses and snowy mountains, so Pheriche's similar appearance made me feel welcome here halfway around the world.

While waiting for dinner I sat on a pile of round stones that had tumbled from a pasture wall. Jim joined me and we talked of Alaska. He had recently climbed Kichatna Spire, a 3,000-foot spike lapped by glaciers, which he described as "the most miserable climb of my career . . . steep and strenuous and pouring down ice water." Soon afterwards he had returned to tackle the 5,000-foot East Face of the Moose's Tooth. He had climbed in the thirty-below cold of late winter so that the unstable rock would be frozen together.

Bridwell is a self-taught climber of high standards and serious thought, a superb athlete and self-indulgent rowdy. During the decade of the seventies, he made Yosemite his personal arena. Often the object of controversy, and sometimes slander, from other climbers, he had perservered longer and maintained a higher level of motivation than any of his peers. For total number of routes climbed, he was unmatched. At 38, he was going as strong as ever, in spite of the epics he had endured and the fast life he had led. He was a climber through and through.

Our conversation progressed from Alaska to Yosemite. "I went to Yosemite because I loved the big outdoors," he explained. "But I found a lot more. In the early years in Yosemite, climbing was an adventure, not a sport. Climbers were avant garde, at the edge. We were escaping from ruts, routines, mediocrity. But I did a lot of thinking about equipment and technique in

Yosemite. That's what set me apart. To me it's critical to continue advancing, learning, expressing yourself in new directions."

Then we shifted to talking about his new direction: using the speed climbing techniques developed in Yosemite in remote mountain ranges where vulnerability is highest. He had climbed Cerro Torre in Patagonia—6,000 feet of vertical rock—in a day and a half. On the descent a storm hit, and he fell 130 feet to the end of his rope. Against the odds, he survived.

"People don't look at me and say, 'My, how normal you look,' " Jim said. "You know why? Too many lines on my face! From too many days looking up into the sun, or over my shoulder at the storm clouds—of being terrified. But you have to deprive yourself to learn, to move ahead."

JAN: We spent another three nights en route to our base of operations for climbing Pumori and beginning the Everest Grand Circle. Our final night on the trail was spent in Lobuche, a small summer settlement at 16,000 feet. My sleep was punctuated by bouts with an altitude headache. Ned was restless too, and I could hear Jim and Steve rustling around in their tent. The Sherpas, however, were having a grand time singing, stamping their feet, and dancing into the early morning.

The next morning, when they asked why I hadn't joined them, I was sorry that I hadn't danced away my insomnia with them. I decided to bridge the gap between Sherpas and sahibs by joining a Sherpani I had watched and admired, a working porter in our caravan. I shuffled over and nudged her, grabbed a load, hoisted it on the nearest yak, and motioned for her to tie while I lifted. She got the idea immediately, laughed, and we set silently to work. Like many Sherpanis, she had a handsome, full face, beautiful honey-colored skin, and large teeth that filled her wide smile. She wore a long black wrap dress, with a hand-woven striped square pinned like an apron at her waist with a silver clasp. One thing that intrigued me was that she and the other Sherpas wore the same clothes day in and day out, regardless of any change in temperature or weather, while we were constantly taking off or putting on layers.

As the yak caravan began to move out for its last day of bearing our burden, Saile, the Sherpani, waved to me to come along. I stashed my cameras away and eagerly joined them. As I herded the yaks down the trail, I remembered how proud I had been as a little girl to herd all our cows up to the pasture gate for my father. I knew special calls I'd learned from Gusty and Charlie, our hired men. They'd chuckle to hear my young voice repeat them, but it sure brought the cows from the far corners of the pasture.

Saile taught me her calls, and we giggled as I mutilated her language. After a distance, she slipped her hand into her dress and pulled out a harmonica. When she finished her tunes, I lifted the instrument from her hands and belted out "Swanee River," "Oh, Suzanna," and a few other American classics. Again, she was laughing with delight. The Sherpa sense of humor eases tension as well as hard work. Earlier on the trail, a small girl struggling under a giant basket of wood slipped in the mud and fell flat under her load as she looked up to see us coming. I ran down the hill to help what looked like a bundle of wood with two spindly legs sticking out from under it. When I got there I heard no angry cries or sobs, but gales of laughter bubbling out through the mud!

During this last day, my legs held strong but my lungs wheezed in the thin air of almost 17,000 feet, as I pushed and shoved yaks over the uneven moraine. One of Saile's yaks became stuck, but I had to keep mine moving or be stuck as well, so I reached Base Camp ahead of her. I pulled out a green figured silk scarf that I'd bought in India, and when Saile came trotting in I offered it to her. She snatched it and pressed it to her chest, glowing with pleasure. We set about unloading the yaks, again in silence. The day was done. Saile gave me a warm "namaste" and climbed the moraine leading out of Base Camp. Before she slipped out of sight, I saw her silhouette at the top of the moraine, her arms waving with big, broad sweeps. I felt a twinge of sadness at saying good-bye to a new friend and to my last bit of female companionship. I hadn't taken any photographs that day, but I came away with even more valuable memories.

5

PUMORI BASE CAMP

"Nothing at home but sit around. Cold there too. Better here. Work and earn money. Your money, my pleasure."

Phutashi

NED:  The morning of December 11, which dawned clear and chill, was the first time I heard Sherpas groan. They had drunk rakshi and danced far into the night. They took twice as long as usual to round up the yaks grazing on the stubbly hillsides surrounding Lobuche, then load the animals.

Lobuche was the last Sagarmatha National Park facility on the trail to Everest. The rest house and campground were run by Pasang Norbu, who sported a gold tooth, and his wife, Chagum, who inhaled snuff as she cooked. They had five children. The oldest was a very pretty 18-year-old daughter. Anu was nowhere in sight as we began to organize our departure, so while we waited for him to appear, I talked to Pasang. He had gotten the job because he had worked as a carpenter on a project financed by the New Zealand government that built the structures, then stayed on. He paid the Nepalese government 20,000 rupees a year for the right of operation, but estimated that he would gross twice that amount.

When I asked Pasang if the number of trekkers coming to see Everest would continue to increase, he replied: "Yes, for three, maybe four years. After three years, Tibet border will probably open, so more trekkers there."

Anu finally appeared, grinning, followed closely by Pasang's eldest daughter. At ten o'clock our little caravan headed out on the last leg to Base Camp along the west side of the Khumbu Glacier. At first we walked along a grassy moat marked by scores of separate yak trails, then across bare moraines where the trail was indistinct among the rocks and the way was marked by cairns. The Sherpas shouted and whistled behind the yaks as they plodded along at their drowsy pace.

Just beyond Gorak Shep, we broke over a high moraine. Everest and Nuptse dominated the view to the northeast; Pumori, much closer, reared overhead to the northwest. Lhotse was hidden from our vantage point by the Nuptse wall. Looking down, we spied an irregular patch of sand beside a small, frozen lake. Anu informed us that this was the traditional Base Camp for Pumori. We descended, and the yaks were quickly unloaded, then herded back to Lobuche. Throughout the afternoon we tended to the business of setting up our small sleeping tents and the big oval community tent and sorting our mountaineering gear. Our skis were set aside until after we'd dealt with Pumori. The Sherpas rigged a large tarp over an alcove in the rocks and set up a cooking facility in which they stored slabs of buffalo and yak meat; sacks of potatoes, flour, sugar, and pancake mix; bags of coffee, tea, and dried milk; piles of cabbages and carrots; eggs; and a carton of ketchup bottles. The wind whipped the strings of faded prayer flags that previous expeditions had hung between boulders. It also tugged at and blew away every piece of equipment that was not tied down.

But it could not budge our liaison officer—nor could we. He sat sullenly in the lee of a rock. He was unhappy and wanted us to know it. During the entire trek into Base Camp, he had never pitched in to help anybody else. He hadn't even been willing to pack his personal gear in the mornings; instead, he ordered one of the Sherpas to do so. Often Steve had been so disgusted with Puru's rude commands that he had packed the L.O.'s gear himself. That night Phutashi served a delicious meal. Puru scowled at the plate as it was handed to him, left the food half eaten, and stalked off to his two-person tent—which he shared with no one. That night five Sherpas slept in the other two-person tent.

Nobody slept well. The moon was full, flooding the camp with bright light. From the open door of Jan's and my tent, I peered out at Pumori. The mountain seemed to be waiting. It looked cold and unreal, and seemed very distant from my life.

In the morning I felt as if I had the flu, but it was only the altitude of nearly 17,500 feet temporarily setting me back. Puru had a permanent setback. He felt poor, he said, and, not surprisingly, announced that he would retreat to lower elevations. As if to fulfill some vague sense of duty, he stated, "I will report to the Ministry that you have established Base Camp and are following regulations." Escorted by a Sherpa he fled to Namche, where he spent the entire expedition under the wing of Mama Anu. His month-long rakshi and rum binge grew to be a substantial expedition expense. His hasty departure, which Jim had predicted back in Kathmandu, was welcome, since it removed the single source of negativism and friction from the party.

I lay in our tent all morning. Angpura, grinning broadly and nodding with concern, kept my cup filled with hot tea. My head throbbed whenever I raised it, so I didn't. Even when I was lying down, my view of Pumori from the tent was stunning. I felt better toward afternoon, and rolled out of the tent to aid the others working on gear. They were adjusting the fit of crampons on our climbing boots—a mountaineering "Rubik's Cube" comprising plates, ribs, screws, and nuts which we had put off fitting as long as possible. Steve spent all day adjusting his—with time off for eating, talking, and daydreaming. It was an easy day and we needed it. By Christmas we were to find that we could have used several more days of acclimatization.

JAN: "This is the sandbox of the Himalaya," Ned laughed as he bent over, sifting the fine material through his fingers. Actually, the consistency was more like fine ash. We'd settled our camp on a small oasis of glacial silt surrounded by the vast expanse of moraine. It wasn't long before I realized this moon dust was inescapable. It was in my hair, teeth, clothing, and sleeping bag. But once I made peace with the stuff and accepted it as a part of my new habitat, it became unobtrusive—and perhaps gave my diet the bulk and fiber it had been lacking.

We set up a large canvas cook tent for the Sherpas, a big dome tent for dining, and two smaller domes as beach cottages for Jim and Steve and for Ned and me. While we were setting up the big dome tent, a strong wind picked it up and blew it over a nearby lake as if it were a child's balloon. Ned, who ran after the tent, stopped short on the frozen snows and yelled a warning as Steve sailed out after it. "Look out, Steve, or you'll become the S.S. *McKinney*." The thin plate ice cracked and chipped under his feet, but the heavier sublayer held. I thought Steve was either fearless or foolish, but with Steve it was next to impossible for me to tell which.

But he did rescue our dining hall, which we hurried to anchor with a kerosene heater, appropriately dubbed "the great American Buddha." We huddled around its warmth in gratitude. It was December 11, our first night in Base Camp.

Dinner was delicious, but at that altitude our bellies became excruciatingly bloated with the food and tea. Satiated with Phutashi's Sherpa stew, and its accompaniments, we all nodded off in the warmth of the heater. When we woke up later, after our Buddha had burned out, we had to drag ourselves through the cold night to our respective tents.

The next day, I was pleased that Jim asked me, instead of Ned or Steve, to go route hunting with him. I'm sure Jim knew how important it was for me to feel essential, not just along for the ride, because although he was demanding, he was also sensitive to our various personalities.

After a two-hour hike over the moraine, Jim and I decided on a glacier-striated peninsula of rock at 18,000 feet as the site of our Advance Base Camp. From there, we had a clear view of Pumori. I hazarded a guess at the route. Jim listened to me work my way up the mountain, then patiently pointed out my mistakes and explained why he would vary the route at critical points. Jim described his route as "splitting the line between disasters" because the avalanche danger was tremendous on either side of it. In fact, our route might be impossible any other time of the year because new snow could make it lethal. When we had first seen Pumori from a distance, I had been caught off guard by its beauty, and a bit intimidated. But as Jim and I looked at the mountain pitch by pitch, it lost some of its forbidding magnitude and began to seem approachable. There was a dark shadow at about 21,000 feet that looked like the only reasonable place to camp. We optimistically planned to climb the peak using only one camp.

NED: Pumori was first climbed in 1962. An expedition led by Gerhard Lenser climbed the far eastern spur to a saddle, then followed the northeast ridge to the summit pyramid. Since then a dozen more teams had climbed it, but none in the winter.

From Pumori my eye was drawn to a rubbly knoll—the tail end of the South Ridge of Pumori—that bulged above Base Camp to the west. The 18,000-foot knoll was known as Kala Pattar, meaning "black rock." It seemed an unlikely formation to have a name of its own, but it was the trekkers' Mecca, the end of many a puffing pilgrimage, for it presented a superb view of Everest. It was also historically significant. From there, 30 years before, Edmund Hillary and Eric Shipton glimpsed for the first time the route by which the highest mountain on earth would be climbed.

On September 30, 1951, Shipton and Hillary climbed to Kala Pattar as

Eric Shipton. Reprinted from his book, That Untravelled World.

members of the first official team to reconnoiter the southern approaches to Everest. As they climbed higher, the prewar route across the border on the north side in Tibet stood in full view. To his eager listener, Shipton pointed out Camp V, Camp VI, the yellow bands, the second step, the great couloir—places made famous during the early struggles.

"Almost casually I looked toward the Western Cwm," Hillary wrote in 1955, "although I didn't expect to see much of it from here. To my astonishment the whole valley lay revealed to our eyes. A long, narrow, snowy trough swept from the top of the [Khumbu] icefall and climbed steeply up the face of Lhotse at the head of the Cwm. And even as the same thought was simmering in my own mind, Shipton said, 'There's a route there!' And I could hear the note of disbelief in his voice." Like a vision, the key to Everest had appeared.

By the time Hillary returned to attempt Everest in 1953, Shipton, who believed in small, self-sufficient parties, had been replaced as leader by Colonel John Hunt, whose experience was with large military-style expeditions. When Hillary and Sherpa Tenzing Norgay finally stood atop the great prize, Hillary wrote, "I turned and looked at Tenzing. Even beneath his oxygen mask and the icicles hanging from his hair I could see his infectious grin of sheer delight. I held

John Hunt (left), Edmund Hillary (center), and Sherpa Tenzing Norgay, Mount Everest, 1953. Reprinted from Everest—A Mountaineering History, *by Walt Unsworth.*

out my hand and in silence we shook in good Anglo-Saxon fashion. But this was not enough for Tenzing and impulsively he threw his arm around my shoulders and we thumped each other on the back in mutual congratulations."

Returning to the South Col, Hillary greeted his old friend George Lowe. "Well, George," he said, "we knocked the bastard off."

◆ ◆ ◆

The next morning was cold. I got up early and, shivering, ducked under the cook tarp to join Phutashi, who was readying breakfast. He poured my cup of sweet tea. "Why did you decide to come with us in the cold of winter?" I asked him.

"Nothing at home but sit around. Cold there too. Better here. Work and earn money. Your money, my pleasure." He laughed.

During breakfast a Sherpani walked into camp and delivered a small foil-wrapped package addressed to me. I opened it to discover brownies made by my sister, Debby, in San Francisco. She had sent them with a friend coming to trek in the Khumbu. He had carried them to Lobuche and given them to the Sherpani courier. I took a bite—they were still moist! With the Sherpas, we gobbled the entire batch in a few minutes.

Afterward Anu, Angpura, and the four of us started up to the foot of the route that Jim and Jan had eyed the day before. We carried 40-pound packs, and the weight made the two-mile trek difficult. We Americans lagged behind the slender Sherpas, who skipped lightly across the terrain. After half an hour we topped an ancient moraine, and before us lay an exquisite view of the entire East Face as it rose to the Northeast Ridge. It was from here that Jim and Jan had determined the course of the new route by which we would try to climb Pumori.

The face was steep and festooned with great seracs that hung menacingly above the lower slopes. Several faint ridges plunged down from the Northeast Ridge. They were composed of milky turquoise ice that ran down from the crestline in chevron patterns of long flutings, and streaked by stark dark rock. A massive ice bulge extended all the way across the top of the face, and the bottom was guarded by distinct bands of rock. A large icefall poured down from the juncture of the East and South faces. The route, which Jim had named "sapphire bullets of pure love," followed the vague ridge to the right of the icefall. We all agreed that it looked impressive. Anu and Angpura chattered and gestured excitedly. A little ice avalanche broke down the far side of the ridge. "There," Jim said, pointing, "and it's also safe. See how the slide tracks away from the route? And that hole in the ice two-thirds of the way up—see it? That could be a likely spot for a camp." He paused, lipped his cigarette, then continued. "The quality of excitement in a new route is so much higher. It's all the unknowns. The engineering of a new line is art."

We continued on, working our way gradually upward by contouring along slopes of yellow-brown grass and lichen and across loosely anchored scree. Swinging around a rocky buttress and into its chill shadow, we lugged our loads up a long gully filled with giant boulders—where we flushed mottled brown birds—then traversed to our right and onto a rocky slope. As we rested, rocks banged down from above into the top of the gully we had just left. The scree lying in the gully attested to the fact that rockfall was common. It was a place to hurry through.

We discussed the location for our Advance Base Camp. We needed a spot safe from rockfall and icefall, but also one as high as possible for easiest access to the route. We continued up over fractured rock for another 150 vertical feet to the very edge of the snow and ice. Unfortunately, there was no level spot here; the slope was angled and dotted with tablelike slabs of rock. With the Sherpas doing most of the work, we hacked out a level platform in the snow and ice and pitched one of our narrow assault tents. We cached our gear inside, then left for Base Camp. A little way down I turned and looked back at the tent. I was uneasy about the location, which was too vulnerable to falling debris from the steep slopes above. It would be adequate for a cache, but not for habitation, and I resolved to find a safer spot when we next returned.

During the walk back Anu broached the subject of joining us on the climb. He said the idea had occurred to him earlier, as we stood listening to Jim describe the route. He had attended the Sherpa mountaineering course, and felt confident of his ability. We had grown to like him and trust him, and he had performed on the expedition with devotion that went far beyond the basic duties of the job. But we had not obtained permission or taken out any insurance with the Ministry of Tourism for any Sherpas to go above Advance

Base Camp, and so had to say no. If Anu had been hurt going high, we would have been legally and financially liable.

Just as climbing expeditions had reshaped Sherpa life, so the Sherpas in turn had influenced the character of most major climbing expeditions. They were the workhorses. Until recently, when it has become the mark of a stronger and purer style to climb unassisted, it was virtually unthinkable to mount a Himalayan expedition without Sherpas. They were professionals, working for money, in the same way that a European Alpine guide is a professional. They supplied the logistical support necessary to put the lead climbers from foreign countries on top. They also put themselves on top—often on first ascents, as of Everest itself. When Tenzing reached the top of Everest in 1953, it was his seventh expedition to the mountain. He was 19 when he signed on as a porter on his first Everest expedition in 1935. Other Sherpas had strength, technical expertise, and spirit equivalent to Tenzing's. The trait that set him above the rest was his single-minded determination to succeed.

As soon as we returned to Base Camp, Anu announced that he had business back in Lobuche and asked to leave, promising to be back at first light the next morning. Angpura and Phutashi smirked when they overheard Anu's request. I was mystified, but said okay. We learned later that Anu was sweet on Pasang's daughter; the eight-mile round trip was no barrier between the two love-struck hearts.

The next day, for acclimatization, we made the two-hour hike to Advance Base at 18,200 feet carrying light packs. While there we double-checked our climbing gear and moved the tent 100 feet lower onto a rocky promontory. Not only was it safer from rock and icefall, but there was a reasonably large, flat area from which to operate. The sun, which had been shining since we arrived at Base, except during an occasional snow flurry, moved behind the shoulder of Pumori about two o'clock in the afternoon. The temperature immediately dropped, and we headed down to Base Camp to sleep. The next day the four of us moved to our Advance Base, set up a second tent, and established it as our operations center.

JAN: We spent three days working like busy ants carrying loads over the cairn-studded path to our Advance Base Camp. Our route followed above the white, jagged teeth of the glacier moving out from under the tumbling Khumbu icefall. The icefall looked almost too spectacular to be real, and seemed more like a painted backdrop for a Hollywood set. Sometimes we hiked together, chatting, and other times we traveled separately, to listen to our own thoughts and enjoy the peace of our own isolation here at the top of the world.

On December 15 we performed a small dual ceremony before leaving Base Camp with our last loads. As Anu lit the juniper branches which he'd carried in to burn for our good luck, Ned secured the yak-bone carving he'd bartered for in Kathmandu between two rocks facing Pumori. We hugged our Sherpas good-bye amid the sweet smoke, and they grinned like children when they gave us the "thumbs up" signal as we moved away.

Jim's tendon had been bothering him, so he stayed below while Ned, Steve, and I headed up over an icy patch in the moraine, shod only in hiking shoes, to move our camp out of avalanche danger. I was surprised that Steve appeared tentative crossing this icy section, since I had thought of him as fearless. I was comforted to know he was as human as I was.

At our new camp it was a shock to begin organizing, cooking, and caring for ourselves, because the Sherpas had done such a wonderful job for us for so long. I could see tension growing as we took on our new duties. Now that we were on our own, Ned's sense of urgency had increased, and he was impatient with Steve's relaxed attitude. Ned was irked that Steve slept in or lay in his bag listening to music or smoking when things could be done to help out the group. I could feel the friction and, in hopes of defusing the situation, defended Steve. "Ned, remember, this is Steve's first expedition and perhaps he isn't quite aware of all the little things that need doing. Just give him time. Let's cook dinner for everyone in our tent tonight."

I missed our Sherpas as friends and the convenience they provided us, but I liked the idea of finally working together with just our tight society of four. I also wanted us all together in one tent for dinner for another reason. I finally piped up when we started eating. "I don't think I'm going to be able to climb, you guys." Ned looked at me. "What . . . ?" "It's my boots. I didn't realize it until today; I've noticed that up here over 18,000 feet, I swell so badly that my feet fall asleep within minutes." I hadn't said anything earlier, but I had watched Jim hack away at his inner boots with his ice axe to release pressure points on his foot, so I knew he had had similar problems. But my condition was so extreme that I would have to shave away most or all of the insulation of the entire vapor barrier inner, rendering it useless. I had used ski mountaineering boots on Muztagata with no problem. Perhaps it was the cut of these climbing boots that shut off my circulation.

"Who knows, maybe I retain more fluid, maybe that's why I get so swollen. But how can I climb without my boots? It's winter out there you know," I said, trying to lighten up the announcement with a little humor, even though I was devastated that I might not be able to climb high. But I hadn't been able to come up with a solution.

Jim spoke up. "Phutashi has a pair of climbing boots that the American Medical Expedition left for him. I'll bet he'd lend them to you."

"Yes, I thought of that but they're big on him. They're probably larger than a size ten and I wear a six. Just think, each step would be a brand new surprise. Are my crampons in contact with ice and snow or not? It sounds a bit chancy to me. Balance would be difficult at best."

We licked the mushy, freeze-dried beef stroganoff from our plastic spoons in silence for a while.

"Why not try your cross-country boot inners in your climbing boots?" Jim suggested, as he stirred the glop in his plastic cup.

"That just might do it!" I exclaimed. "My cross-country boot inners are much thinner than these vapor barrier inners, so they'd give my feet room to swell. I could double up on overboots to make up for thinner inner boots, and maybe my toes will stay intact. Why didn't I think of that? Jim, you're a genius," I teased. "Either way, I've got to go back to Base Camp tomorrow to retrieve my cross-country inners or Phutashi's boots. I have no choice."

"Just as well," Ned said. "I've got a list of things we've forgotten. Jim, Steve, and I will start the route, and you get the gear and your boots straightened out."

I was pleased that there might be a relatively simple solution, but disappointed that I would miss the first day of real climbing. The others would set the first couple of pitches while I returned to Base Camp.

The next night, when we all met at Advance Base Camp, we exchanged stories about our day over goopy dinners. I had opted for my cross-country inners, a thin synthetic booty. They provided minimal insulation, but with them my feet fit into my climbing boots. I had also been able to find all the small, forgotten necessities at Base Camp. Steve wasn't feeling well, and seemed a bit distant; Jim was convinced we needed more rope; and Ned thought Jim's route was beautiful. Suddenly Steve perked up.

"I saw a bunch of rope at the medical station in Pheriche. I think it was left over from the medical expedition on Everest. I'm willing to go back and retrieve it." We figured Ned, Jim, and I could haul our gear from Advance Base Camp up the newly fixed lines the next day without Steve, and decided it probably was best if he fetched the additional rope. I wondered why, after his first day of real climbing, Steve was anxious to be away from the mountain, rather than on it.

NED: On December 16, while Jan was tending to her boot problems, Steve, Jim, and I made our first foray onto the mountain and scaled 1,200 feet. From our tents, we climbed back up the fractured rock to our initial cache site and clamped on our crampons. Carrying two 165-foot, 9-mm perlon ropes and one 600-foot, 6-mm polypropylene rope, we traversed a quarter-mile long slope of low angle snow and ice to the end of a band of rock. The debris of three separate snow avalanches cluttered the slope. In between lay bare ice. Now and then a single stone or ice pellet whistled down without warning from above the rock band, and I made a promise to myself to start earlier the next day, when all the debris would still be frozen in place. Below our path, a second rock band fell away onto the glacier, which was covered with gravel and spotted with depressions filled with green ice. The traveling was not difficult enough to demand a rope, but we could have been hurt or killed by falling debris or by tumbling over the cliff below. We judged that, in this situation, a rope would have increased the risk, by slowing our progress through the danger zone. It would be a bad place in the event of a major avalanche, but there is little snow accumulation in the winter. At any other time of the year, our approach across the traverse to the start of the climbing would have involved far more risk.

At the far end of the traverse, under the ridge we would climb, was a spot safe from rock and icefall. We roped up among a thousand fragile ice stalagmites that shattered at our every move. Jim led over the *bergschrund* or gap between the ice and the rock wall that continued east from the end of the rock band. Its maw had been twisted into grotesque shapes by sun and ice movement. Steve and I moved up to it, then I led the next pitch of several rope lengths for a full 500 feet. I scrambled over a small rock outcrop at the base of the ridge and continued up along its left side on a moderate slope of hard snow. Toward the end of the pitch I moved right and anchored into the blue ice at the edge of the ridge. A rocky prong of gneiss and black slatelike rock stuck out of the ridge a few feet away. It looked comfortable, so I crossed to it and sat down while the others jumared along the rope.

Since we were still poorly acclimatized, we lounged at the belay for half an hour and debated whether to continue. There was hardly any wind and the sun shone through a high, scudding layer of clouds. Somehow Jim's conversation wandered to the subject of his parents having been married and divorced three times—to and from each other.

I still felt strong and decided to lead up another 250 feet. Moving back out onto the ice, I diagonaled up and left in order to stay mostly on hard snow. But icy runnels scored the snow and the lead demanded a good deal of climbing on the front-points of my crampons. I thoroughly enjoyed my progress on the clean snow and ice. I placed two ice screws as anchors and rappelled down to Steve and Jim, leaving the rope in place. The sun had long since disappeared from our side of the mountain, and it was cold. We used the remaining ropes to slide down to the bottom, then hustled across the traverse to camp. Phutashi had come up with Jan and had hot tea ready. After serving it, he said good night and hurried back to Base Camp.

We retreated into the tents and into our sleeping bags. Jan told us about her successful solution to her boot problem, and we described our satisfaction with the terrain on the beginning of the route. Then, while the two stoves worked, we lay silently gazing across the Khumbu to Everest, Lhotse, and Nuptse as they slowly turned crimson in the sunset. To our right, a mass of gray clouds filled the lower valley; perhaps it was snowing at lower elevations. The obelisk of Ama Dablam stuck up above the clouds. To our left rose Lingtren and Khumbutse. They were separated from the West Ridge of Everest by the Lho La, a low point of 20,000 feet in the border ridge.

Lying there, I thought of, Klavs Becker-Larsen, a Dane without climbing experience, but with plenty of guts and faith, who in the spring of 1951 had tried to use the Lho La as secret access to Tibet to climb Everest—alone. Failing, he crossed into Tibet via the Nangpa La, the ancient Sherpa trading route. He failed to reach the summit of Everest there too, but he had become the first westerner to visit both the north and south sides of Everest in the same season.

◆ ◆ ◆

On the morning of December 17 we decided we needed more rope, and Steve volunteered to descend to Pheriche in hopes of purchasing a few coils. Jan, Jim, and I carried food, stoves, fuel, and one tent up as far as we had climbed the day before. We cached it all in a duffel bag that we left hanging on the top two ice screws. Once again Phutashi was waiting for us when we returned to Advance Base Camp. He had come up from Base Camp to make us hot tea.

The next day Jim and I headed up to extend the route. Jan offered to accompany us, but there was no need for more than two. From our previous high point, Jim led four pitches up steepening gray ice to a spot where the ice slope was cut off by cliffs and ran into the ridge. He climbed quickly and with little protection, making long run-outs of over 100 feet. Chunks of ice from his axe placement pelted me, and I took refuge under the duffel that hung there. Then, leaving the duffel in place to be hauled up another day, I followed the pitches. I was amazed to find that what I had thought to be a smooth ramp of ice turned out to be an extensive series of steps that varied in height from six inches to six feet. We called it "the staircase." At the base of the upper ridge, a section which promised to be one of the cruxes of the climb, we anchored the rope to a sling placed over a natural post of ice. We backed it up with an ice screw, and left our excess hardware hanging from it. Then we rappelled down. Jan, who had been watching us throughout the day through her telephoto lens, greeted us with hot drinks. We were very tired, and it was obvious that we were not yet acclimatized. Even so, it had been a splendid day of climbing.

The next day was a prime day of sun, moderate temperatures, and little wind. While we rested, Anu and Angpura arrived with the extra ropes that Steve had fetched from Pheriche. We asked where Steve was.

"Steve had a very bad night. He is sleeping at Base Camp." Anu answered.

"What do you think the weather will do?" I asked.

"There has never been a winter like this," Anu said. "No snow. Last year the snow was knee-deep in Namche in late December. This winter—very good for climbing. But, very bad for the people. Really a drought. No potatoes or barley growing."

"What about the weather for the next few days?" I pressed for an answer.

Anu paused, then said, "The lamas at Thyangboche say that, according to prayer books, since it did not snow yesterday we will have one more week of good weather in Khumbu."

"Just for us, eh?" Jim said. "That's direct contact."

The next morning we strung the new ropes on the lower part of the route. They were caving ropes—okay for fixing in place, but too heavy and with too little give for leading and holding a fall. We retrieved our climbing ropes, working rather listlessly since we still weren't fully acclimatized. Still, with the winter storms probably close at hand, we felt we had little choice but to make a push for the summit starting the next day. When we returned to camp, Steve was there.

JAN: At last, on December 18, I began to "climb" Pumori. I had volunteered to lead the first pitch, which was a long, sloping traverse of ice ending in a bergschrund. Jim and Ned laughed, explaining that it wasn't worth roping up for, that they hadn't bothered the day before. If someone fell on the traverse, he'd probably pull the others with him over the cliff at the edge of the slope. Also, rocks as well as little snow sloughs had been washing over the traverse periodically. It was best to go across solo and fast.

I paid close attention to foot placement on the traverse. One slip here and a climber could plummet off the cliff high above the moraine floor. It took a few arduous moves to get over the bergschrund and then up a clean snow slope of 55 degrees to a rock outcropping we called "the perch." When the three of us were across, we sat on the perch eating frozen gorp and gazing over at Everest and into the Khumbu icefall. As I listened to Ned and Jim exchanging facts and rumors about the many Everest expeditions before us, I was delighted to be right where I was in the world at that moment.

Jim had an idea: he would set up a pulley system at the top of the next pitch above the perch to haul up the loads. Ned wanted to climb the following pitch along with Jim, so I waited on the perch until the system was rigged and rappelled down, hauling our heavy load of stoves, fuel, ropes, tents, and food up to Jim and Ned for them to secure at our high point. I continued on down to Advance Camp alone. Although I dreaded the final solo traverse, just as a student would a final exam, I didn't have any problems.

No loads were to be hauled the next day; instead, Jim wanted to go up and string the route higher. Ned went with him, leaving me at Advance Camp to sort gear and organize details. I wasn't insulted, since I knew that three climbing would be slower than two. There was little wind, and I could hear Ned's and Jim's voices faintly as they worked high up on the route. It was difficult for me to listen to their voices filtering down through the thin-walled tent from the perils above as I sat warm and cozy, cleaning our stoves. I couldn't help worrying about them, and I was eager to be climbing myself. But I knew there would be plenty of work for me later, and I knew it was important to conserve my strength for when it would be most needed.

I had just stepped out of the tent to photograph the two men climbing when an avalanche started below them and cascaded down beside our route, across our icy traverse, and on over the cliff. The mountain was alive. I realized I looked at Pumori as if it were an animal, sometimes benign and sometimes menacing. The avalanche also reminded me of just how dangerous the traverse was.

So far Pumori had been fairly docile during our brief visit. It was only two o'clock in the afternoon now, but the sun was already going down, and the cold creeping in. I was delighted to see that Ned and Jim had begun their descent, and began brewing some tea to warm them when they reached camp.

Jim and Ned didn't want to move the next day, regardless of the good weather and the fact that each day was precious because winter storms were near. Understandably, they were tired and wanted a full day of organization before we left Advance Base Camp for good to ascend the peak. The day passed lazily and the sun was so warm midday it allowed me to strip to the waist and warm my core in its rays. Unlikely weather.

That evening, Steve had some stories to tell about Pheriche. He had been interviewed by Radio Nepal. He had reported that it was 35 degrees below zero, Fahrenheit, on the peak, that the wind was blowing 70 miles an hour, and that Base Camp was at 21,000 feet. He was after rope, his story went, because when he was rappelling off the peak a rock chopped his rope, leaving the rest of us stranded above. Therefore, he absolutely must obtain more rope.

Steve explained, "I had to do something. There wasn't any rope at Pheriche, as I had thought there would be. So I needed to convince someone we needed more rope desperately."

"Never underestimate the power of a lie," Jim said in a booming voice, and then laughed.

"I really just embellished the facts a bit," Steve said in defense.

Jim continued to laugh. "We all know the experience is never as good as the story, anyway."

"Oh, no," I moaned, as the possible consequences of Steve's story began to sink in. "Radio Nepal—that means the Ministry of Tourism got your story about us being stranded, and it will probably show up on the AP or UPI wire in the U.S., and then in the papers. My poor parents!"

But Steve's saga continued. He had gotten drunk with the Sherpas at Pheriche, danced with them, and shared their Japanese *Playboys*. Steve found it amusing that the whole family—mom, dad, and the kids—looked at the pornographic magazines together, very matter-of-factly. The next day Steve had backtracked to Thyangboche with his newfound Sherpa friends to get rope, then had trekked back to Lobuche alone. But when he began traveling over the moraine toward Base Camp, he was engulfed by a whiteout—the same clouds we had been dreamily admiring below us.

Steve was following cairns, but they were leading him to Everest Base Camp. When the clouds parted for a moment and Steve saw Nuptse above, he realized his error and tried to scramble over glacier and moraine in the direction of Pumori. He hit some "desperate" climbing and backed off. Finally, at about midnight, exhausted, Steve crawled under a rock to sleep.

In the morning Steve hiked over the first rise and saw Lobuche below! Somehow he had circled back to his start. When he walked down and into the bunkhouse, there was Anu snuggled up with Pasang's daughter, sleeping.

Steve looked worn and bedraggled as he recounted his adventures, yet his eyes sparkled as he admitted, "I wanted an epic on this expedition, but I thought it would come in the form of a storm." I was relieved to know Steve's "epic" was over, and that we didn't have to go through it with him. Much of the rope he had returned with, however, was caving rope—too thick for jumaring, and heavy for climbing with. So we were still short of the kind of rope we needed.

This meant that the route wouldn't be entirely fixed, that the ropes would not be permanently placed all the way down the route, which frightened me a bit. There would be no established route of escape. I knew that we would probably be fine anyway, and wished my misgivings would go away. Perhaps people often become more superstitious during dangerous or strenuous endeavors because we are all hoping for an omen that will guarantee that everything will turn out all right, so we can be absolved of worry. I reminded myself again that worry is a wasted emotion.

6

PUMORI: THE FIRST ATTEMPT

"Gotta move, gotta move. Can't park our RV here."

Jim Bridwell

NED:  There was little to be done to leave our Advance Base, but it took a long time. We moved slowly, balking at beginning our commute up the ropes we had left on the mountain.

Because of obligations at home and a delay in departure, we had established Base Camp two weeks later than originally planned. It was December 20, so we couldn't delay, but there hadn't been adequate time to adjust to the altitude. We planned to climb to our previous high point and pick up the cached gear. From there we would continue up new ground to establish Camp I at 21,000 feet in a "hole" in the mountain that we had spotted through binoculars.

We estimated that the day's itinerary would take four to six hours, and that we would have little problem completing it during daylight, even on the shortest day of the year. The last thing we wanted to do was get caught by dark in winter temperatures before we made it back to camp. We would have to reach the hole or retreat back to Base—there was no campsite in between.

We warmed to the day's task only after Lhotse had shrugged the long rays of wispy sun onto us from its shoulder. While packing, we mulled over our chances of getting to the top while the good weather lasted. If the winter storms hit early, we'd have no choice but to pull back off Pumori and wait for a break in the storms. Even if they came when expected, we had but a few days of grace. From the records of the few expeditions that had climbed in the winter, we knew that they had run into atrocious wind and cold immediately after Christmas. Because of this we had decided to hurry our assault.

Once we had much of our gear cached a good way up Pumori, and had fixed ropes to that point, our plan to reach the top was short and simple. The whole climb should take three days: the first day to Camp I in the hole, the second to the top and back to Camp II, the third back down to the bottom.

In addition to the fact that we weren't acclimatized, something was missing—some spark, some overriding commitment to the climb. I had felt that spark before—in cross-country skiing championships, for instance, and with Galen Rowell, when he and I had climbed Mount McKinley in one day. I remembered the giddy confidence, the transcendence of normal limits, the direct tap into full strength of mind and muscle. But this morning, lethargy dominated. I didn't know it, but by dusk we would be in trouble, fighting for survival. Then we would find the spark.

We disassembled our tents, leaving one cached for our return, and packed the assault tent. The second assault tent was in the cache hanging up on the mountain. On the snow where the tents had been pitched, four separate imprints remained of shoulders, buttocks, and heels—body forms cast during the long hours of darkness.

We departed, one by one, scrambling up the blocky steps of tan rock that rose to the long snow and ice traverse. I disliked the traverse; feared it. The 3,000-foot East Face leered above; when it spat rockfall or snowslide, there was no place to hide. This seemingly innocuous slanting walkway was the most dangerous place on our route. We minimized the danger by crossing early or late in the day, when ice would help cement the base rock, and by moving as rapidly as possible. Still, before marching across, I'd say a word or two to myself about luck, murmur a prayer. I considered myself lucky, and this was a test of luck—it would be pure good fortune not to get tagged by a rock or ice tidbit whistling down. As the Buddhists and Hindus would say, a safe crossing was simply one's karma or destiny.

I had made three round trips across the traverse during the previous days, and I knew that it stretched a quarter-mile. This morning, as usual, I found it essential to force myself to focus on secure placement of crampon spikes and ice-axe ferrule. This was not real climbing, but it would provide access to real climbing. There was a tendency to look beyond toward steeper, more exciting ground. In itself the traverse was nowhere and nothing, just an insidious invitation to relax our concentration—especially since we crossed it either morning-stiff or evening-tired.

We moved across unroped; this was no place to stop and belay. Jim, with his sure, brisk promenade, was fastest. One hand cupped a cigarette, the other swung an axe as if it were a baton. Jim's mind must have been on a subject other than his immediate footsteps—maybe 1,500 feet above, figuring the new part of the route. As he stepped nonchalantly from hard snow to solid ice, he slipped. To me, not far behind, it seemed a yeti had jerked his feet by some unseen cord. Both legs veed high in the air, as if he were performing an acrobatic stunt. From this position, Jim stabbed his axe into the ice, rebounded and straightened, then landed lightly on his feet. He continued on, not looking back at me or down at the ever-steepening gully below. I watched ice chips from his crampon placements funnel over the cliff onto the glacier.

"Clever, a 'ten,' " I judged aloud.

Now he turned, a grin on his face, pleasantly cocky. "Still the nerves of a diamond cutter, eh?"

The fixed line hung at the far end of the traverse. It provided easy, safe access over ground already climbed. Sometimes starting on it I felt like a small, wild animal—naturally wary, but seduced by a line of food pellets. I had done some of the early leading and had enjoyed it immensely. But Jim had to and would do the harder climbing. Although this was his game, honed over the past 20 years of extreme climbing, he treated us like equals. We depended on him, but I knew we must limit that dependency. If Jim were knocked out of action, we'd have to get ourselves up or off.

Steve must have forgotten something back at camp, because he was only starting the traverse when Jim and I were finishing it. Jan was close behind us. Then Steve had trouble with a crampon. Finally, after we were all across, we took some time to redistribute the gear among our packs. The first fixed ropes were the ones Steve had fetched from Thyangboche. They were fat and white—so fat that we could hardly get the jumar on them, so white that it was hard to see them against the snow. We started up, the intervals between us determined by the distance to the first anchor. "Jugging"—or jumaring—is monotonous. I tended to put my head down doggedly, like a marathoner. Steve and Jan toured the ropes, chatting and teasing each other and taking in the splendid view. Jim decided that two of the anchors should be placed differently. We also shifted the position of one of the ropes so that it didn't fall over a sharp outcrop of rock. Time ticked away, but there seemed little urgency in the sunshine and still air of the morning.

Five hundred feet up, beyond the bergschrund and the rock band, we gathered on a little rock nose we called "the perch" for a snack. We sat against the mountain with our legs dangling, lounging in the cold sunshine. There was still no wind, although a sliver of lenticular cloud had appeared over Everest. It signaled that strong winds were forming at high altitude. We munched and took in the scenery and let more time slip by. I photographed the others. Nobody else had brought a camera, so posing was their punishment. Jan and Steve wanted to concentrate on climbing; Jim had broken his camera, then broken one that I had lent to him. Still lulled by the springlike day, we talked of Yosemite, where we had all climbed.

JAN: Jim and Ned had teased me so much about crossing the traverse unroped again that I was convinced one lapse in concentration was sure death, although I would never let them know their jests were affecting me. Since this was our final departure from Base Camp, our loads were heavier than they had been on earlier crossings. Throughout the traverse, I thought of myself as a grandma with a cane as I carefully picked my way over the ice, using my axe for stability. I was relieved to reach the bergschrund safely once more, but then my concern turned to Steve. He hadn't even begun the traverse, but was still back at camp organizing his personal gear.

Once Steve had caught up, the day progressed slowly but routinely and was uneventful up to the top of the pitch beyond the perch, where our big cache of extra gear had been hanging on the mountain since Ned, Jim, and I had hauled it up three days earlier. I figured it was about time I was gallant, and offered to wait with the haul bag while the others climbed. Then I would proceed on up behind the bag as it was hauled, to push and shove whenever it lodged itself in the mountain's irregularities. I felt good today, and I wanted to take advantage of it. Offering to escort the haul bag was my first opportunity to perform something extra. Besides, Ned and I work together most of the time, so I thought it would be good to work alone and let Ned and Steve climb together.

NED: As I slung on my backpack and jugged up away from the perch, I wondered if we had been too nonchalant, and if we would indeed be snug in the Camp I hole by dark. I was often fastest on the ropes, not so much due to technique but to a mental set left over from years of skiing in cross-country races, head down and pumping.

Monotonous hand-thrusts and footsteps took me up the increasingly steep slope for several hundred feet. The hard snow turned to bluish white ice. Anchored at the transition between the two, I stopped to check the anchors on the duffel bag of gear we had cached, then continued up the staircase, my crampons scraping against the giant steps and hummocks of ice that looked like Pumori's goose bumps. A corroded skin of ice had flaked away from the solid ice and hung like lacy spiderwebs and tiny beach waves. Sometimes a misplaced crampon defaced this natural art, and sent it tinkling away into the void.

My reverie ended as I came to the end of the ropes and the upper anchors positioned at our previous high point. This was at the beginning of the ridge leading to the hole, which lay an estimated 600 vertical feet above. I anchored myself to the ice screws Jim and I had placed earlier. I was glad to see that the equipment we had left here—ropes, ice screws, "deadmen," carabiners, and slings—were all undisturbed. Had I expected a midnight burglary? My stance was at an odd convergence of the staircase and a ridge. It was a ragged eddy of rock and ice, the only platform available. I hacked out a larger platform, but in no way was it designed for four. Above, the ridge bent up sharply. Standing was not restful, since the bulge bumped me out over the precipice. Squatting was no better because my legs tended to cramp. Sitting was, but the position allowed no work, and there was work to be done.

So I stood and used my axe to chop the platform bigger in order to have enough room to set up a pulley system to haul the bag. As I worked, I folded back the soiled cuff of my climbing suit and glanced at my watch. It read 1:50. I glared at the watch as if it had played a demented trick on me. "One-fifty! It's almost two o'clock!" My bare wrist felt the hardening chill of a day now in full retreat. My momentary stop also alerted me to another change: the air was beginning to come alive. Insistent swirls nudged against me—the wind was on the rise.

Suddenly, I was wrapped in shadow. The sun had passed over the shoulder of the mountain. Since we were on the east side of Pumori, the sun faded as if it were almost dusk. The winter sun had always been a charlatan, promising far more warmth than it gave. Even so, its departure left me prickly with foreboding—not for the sickening impact of polar cold, but for that which the shadow announced—night. At nearly 20,500 feet in the Himalaya in winter, blackness halts climbing and can usher in a forced standing bivouac. We should have been keeping a closer eye on the time, but we hadn't. The late hour caught me by surprise.

Jim arrived, the last strokes of his jumar bringing him through the line of shadow. For a moment, he appeared to be both yin and yang, passive and active. Then he stepped up onto my shadowy platform. Even though he had been jumaring, he was full of energy. I was too, finally. We both seemed to have shifted from passive response to active control for the first time since stepping onto Pumori.

The dreamy state we had lazed in throughout the day flashed back once, then was gone for good. In that flash it seemed as if I had penetrated *bardo*—a hallucination that Buddhists believe precedes reincarnation. Bardo is a Tibetan word meaning "between-two-existences." Tibetan Buddhism teaches that a person's last thoughts will determine the quality of reincarnation, and since a person never knows when he will die, it is paramount to live every moment as if it is the last. My pragmatic Western mind allowed no possibility of this being our last moment, despite the fact that we were getting ourselves into an unexpected pickle. This was no time to contemplate; it was time to act.

Jim quickly anchored himself. "Chilly. Remember the Kathmanduans telling us the winter sun is a cold sun and no good? I told them a cold sun is better than cold shade, and I was right." As he spoke, he threw his head back. He eyed the new terrain above, evaluating it and psyching himself up for the effort ahead. We sorted through the climbing gear and organized it.

Steve arrived, puffing. He tended to make hard work of climbing, but his natural strength saw him through. He extended a cheery salutation to us, but Jim cut him short. The belay ledge was too small to accommodate us all. With no-nonsense motions, he anchored Steve off to the far side so he was cantilevered out over the drop below. Steve frowned. He wasn't concerned about his airy repose, but about Jan. "Jan volunteered to be last," he stated, "so she could help with the duffel. There was no use arguing. She thought it was the best way to help."

I looked down . . . she was waiting at the intermediary stance, 600 feet below. Somebody had to shepherd the duffel over the obstructive ice ledges when it was hauled up. Steve was strong and could haul with power from here, so Jan had made the right decision. But she looked very small and lonely against the big sweep of the mountain. The rest of us had warmed ourselves during the last leg of the climb, and were comfortable in our one-piece insulated, windproof climbing suits. Jan had already endured a long wait. I could see her stamping her feet and hugging herself to keep warm. With the wind now cracking across the mountain, it was impossible to yell any words of encouragement to her. Or of advice. I wondered why she hadn't put on her down parka to stay warm during the wait. I turned to work with Steve, trying not to worry unduly.

It took us several minutes to rig a haul system amid the tangle of ropes, equipment, and our own legs. With a carabiner, we hung a pulley wheel on one of the ice screws. A jumar attached upside down on the haul-line acted as a brake so the load wouldn't drop between our upward tugs. "I can't work anything with my mittens on," Steve fretted. "Yuh," I agreed, "and you can't take them off for more than half a minute with the wind. The temperature must have dropped 30 degrees since the sun left—at least it feels that way."

While we engineered the haul system, Jim gathered the spare hardware—three deadmen, six ice screws, a dozen carabiners, and several slings. He hung it around his shoulder. "This place isn't big enough for all of us," he mumbled. I didn't see him go, but he slithered left off the platform, then climbed up to scrutinize the route. He had tied into the end of the haul-line, but had not requested any belay. I heard the frantic scrape of crampons, followed by a sharp "Damn!" It sounded like an alarm. Reacting reflexively, I grabbed a wad of rope, hoping one would be the right one to arrest our climbing leader—whom I expected to swoop by on gravity's rapid transit.

"Jumpy?" Jim chortled from above. "I knocked the lit tip off my cigarette on an ice nodule." Balancing on his front points, he lit up again and moved up a few feet. The rope he had tied into came tight against him. He looked down with a scowl. "I can't move up until you gentlemen get some slack for me in that haul-line. It's the only rope we have to climb on. Gotta move. Gotta move. Can't park our RV here."

JAN: As I waited, crowded on the stance by the bulky duffel bag, I looked up at the pitch the others had continued on up above me. It was steep, fairly solid 65-degree ice, pockmarked by fallen rocks that had heated in the sun and then melted unevenly into the ice. With plenty of imagination, the formation could be termed a staircase. It took Jim, Ned, and Steve more time than they anticipated to negotiate the staircase and fashion another pulley to haul the bag. Meanwhile, the wind had kicked up and the warm sun had disappeared. I was dressed only in my thinnest polypropylene underwear beneath my specially designed, insulated climbing suit. I had actually been hot while active and warm while waiting, until the weather changed so suddenly. Now I was cold. The belay stance below the haul bag was tiny and awkward for wrestling my pack off and securing it well enough to dig for more clothing. I kept rationalizing that Ned and Steve would have the pulley working soon, and that if I dressed for resting I would be sweating too much when I climbed. If I got too cold, I'd run the risk of becoming hypothermic. If I got too hot, I'd sweat away precious fluids and get dehydrated—and again run the risk of becoming hypothermic from the damp chill that would set in when the sweaty work was finished.

So I waited, pressed against the snowy slope, for over an hour. Where I stood, at over 20,000 feet, the atmospheric pressure was only half that at sea level, creating a drastically reduced air mass that is never thoroughly heated by the sun. The warmth that I had felt as I climbed was intense solar radiation piercing through the thin air. Consequently, when the sun went down or behind the clouds, the temperature dropped dramatically because the thin air mass had little capacity for heat retention. Even so, it didn't sink in that I was setting myself up for a potentially dangerous situation by not bundling up as the temperature plummeted well below zero, because I was so intent on watching the others climb the staircase. A wave of relief flooded through my frozen limbs when I got the signal to cut the bag loose and climb up behind it.

The staircase pitch was difficult because the increased angle demanded more strength. The effort was compounded by the fact that my energy had already been drained by the cold. Regardless of my work output, lugging my own pack and pushing the bag, my body remained cold.

I struggled to get the engine purring by pushing myself harder, but my body was still sluggish. I consoled myself that one advantage of frozen muscles is that they feel little pain or strain. Still, I tried to drive my body faster in hopes of rekindling my internal heat. Some of the steps in the staircase were giant ones for me, and I had to puff with all my strength to pull myself and both loads up and over. My competitive spirit egged me on to prove that this pitch could be climbed faster than Ned and Steve had done it, and my sense of urgency in the cold increased my speed.

NED: Steve and I, who had come here to be workhorses, turned to muscling up the duffel bag. I clipped a second jumar onto the haul-line, then attached it to my waist, so that I was able to use my body weight. At each draw I "fell" backward, out over the drop below. Steve cranked with his strong arms, and our repetitive exertions brought the sack closer and closer. We were soon sweating, since we hadn't taken time to remove our down parkas. We were preoccupied by the task of getting the bag—and Jan—up as soon as possible. All our actions were now dictated by the fading daylight. "I hate sweating. Be a block of ice when we finish," I complained.

"Sweating's" . . . grunt . . . "just too bourgeois . . . for you, Gillette," said Steve. "Spit out the silver spoon!"

Jan had come up alongside the load, kicking at it with her feet and chopping at it with her hands when it misbehaved and snagged on ice protrusions. Even though she was now close enough to shout to us, she didn't. She was disturbingly quiet, not even looking up at us. But I knew her dogged determination and pride; I knew that if she really needed help, she'd ask, so I wasn't seriously worried. My attention turned to Jim. He was the one who could climb fast enough to lead the team to the hole, and safety, and he needed every available minute of daylight remaining.

When we had hauled the sack three-quarters of the distance, I let Steve finish the job. Jim planned to use the free end of the haul line to climb on, and now that there was plenty of spare rope, I wanted to give Jim a belay. He had already climbed 30 feet above our heads to scout with no belay. It made me apprehensive to look straight up at the underside of his crampons and the 20 spikes armoring each foot. I needed to shift only two steps to the left to belay him, but a great spaghetti pile of ropes and slings and packs cluttered the ledge, and it was very awkward to move. I fought through the mess and wrapped the rope around my waist. Jim placed a long sling around a prong of rock, clipped a carabiner to it, and ran the rope through. Now my belay was effective. The length of the sling he had placed allowed the rope to run out away from the sharp edge of the rock.

"I can see a long way ahead. It's a long, intricate ridge of ice and rock. It looks like it'll go okay," Jim called down. His words, rising and falling in the eddies of wind, were full of confident anticipation. "I'm going to climb as fast as I can to the end of the rope. Can't stay here for the night. Just keep giving me rope. You won't be able to hear me. If it turns out well, three tugs on the rope means it's anchored off and you can jumar."

"Good luck, Commander," I shouted.

Above, Jim checked the ice screws and deadmen that hung at his waist. Reaching to the rock prong with both arms, he mantled, then brought his right foot upward, placing its crampon points an inch from his fingers. He stood up smoothly. Without hesitation, he drew both axes and moved easily up a short wall of ice. He accelerated smoothly, almost charging the vertical face. From my distant vantage point, he seemed to enjoy the climbing wholeheartedly now that he was on new ground. His years of alpine experience paid off here: he climbed instinctively, calculating how each move would mesh into the next for maximum efficiency and speed. In a few more moments he surmounted the ice wall and passed out of sight.

Earlier on the trip, Jim had agreed with me that on the rare occasions you feel totally connected to inner motivation and power, there are no limits to what you can do. You can almost literally rise above your own abilities. For him, his day-and-a-half ascent of Cerro Torre had been the ultimate moment of transcendence in the game of climbing. I knew the urgency of our present situation would bring out the best in him.

The rope snaked through my hands. It stopped, then started. Jim had left his pack on an ice screw beside me to rid himself of hindering weight. Soon the rope stopped again. Now I took in slack: Jim must have encountered a complication. Then I could feel him move up again, the problem solved. The suspense made me giddy. My toes ached with the creeping cold, and I shifted from foot to foot.

I looked at my watch: 3:45. We had been on the mountain nearly eight hours, and we should have been far higher. But we had started late and had, until now, moved at a leisurely pace. I couldn't recall what had eaten so much time. Little more than an hour of daylight remained, and we were committed on steep, unknown terrain. There was no space for a tent where we stood, and the ice was too hard for a snow hole. The wind cut. When I removed a mitten to take off the dark glasses I had forgotten I was wearing, my bare hand numbed quickly.

I felt restless—eager to do something, to be somewhere. But we on the belay ledge were here to wait. Instead of the fatigue I expected at the end of the day, I was charged with energy and an animal-like alertness. Here was adventure, self-made by our own inattention to time. Canadian Arctic explorer Vilhjalmur Stefansson had once said, "A successful expedition is a boring one because nothing goes wrong." But tonight, somehow, adventure was not unwelcome. Our early, plodding lethargy had been burdensome. Suddenly I was thirsty, but when I checked the water in my bottle, I discovered it was frozen solid. I had a tingling sense of anticipation and fear about what the next few hours would bring. At the same time I had an uncalled for feeling of complete confidence.

Minutes crept past. The rope drew through my hands with agonizing slowness. Control was the key—not letting ourselves get overly stressed, concentrating on the job at hand yet keeping a certain detachment of objective judgment. It was essential to monitor everything we did, since it would be easy to slip up. Jim, as he had started climbing, had noticed a half-open carabiner on the belay anchors. It was nobody's fault, but simply the result of the three of us squirming for position. He had said, "That's how accidents happen—a silly break in the concentration at the end. We gotta stay scared. No shaking hands until it's all over."

While Jim raced to get to the hole before complete darkness, Steve continued to wind in the haul system, and finally landed the duffel on the ledge. It had been exhausting for him to work alone during the last of the hauling, but there had been no choice if Jim was to have a belay. Jan was on her way to our stance at the base of the ridge and rested momentarily not far below, leaning face inward against the ice, her shoulders heaving. Perhaps 30 minutes had passed since we had last heard the reassuring smack of Jim's axe into ice and the scrape of his crampons on rock, last dodged the chunks of ice pelting down from his advance. His tether was 600 feet long, and it was our last free rope. This was the final spree of the night; there would be no time for a second lead. If Jim didn't get to the hole within the length of the rope, we'd be forced to bivouac wherever he finished.

The belay rope continued to be drawn through my double-mittened hands, telegraphing uneven but ongoing progress. I pictured myself playing a giant tuna on the line. Although the cold crept inward from my hands and feet, numbing my body and anesthetizing my face, the tuna idea seemed funny. It also seemed funny that, considering our arctic situation, we were in fact at the same latitude as Miami and Cairo.

In some ways Jim was the lucky one. He was working, his mind fully involved in the task at hand. I knew he would be relishing this alpine Russian roulette. Three weeks ago, in Kathmandu, he had said, "When it's critical, I can always do whatever is necessary regardless of the danger. But I do it as seldom as possible."

I wondered about the terrain on which Jim now stood. Perhaps two-thirds of the rope had run through my hands, and it had been 10 minutes since I felt any movement through the line. We could not shout to him—there was too much mountain between us, and too much wind. Suspense built as we waited for the signal, the three tugs, that would tell us the rope was safely anchored and we could move up. Like a fisherman with a drop line, I "listened" with hands that lightly caressed the rope. I discovered I was holding my breath, and panted to recover. If Jim were forced to rappel, I would feel faint, continuous vibrations. It would be the first news of a failed search, our appeal for asylum denied by the mountain.

During those 10 minutes the day had withered dramatically, and night had taken hold. I suddenly ran out of patience. "Steve, you belay. We've got to move. At least see if we can. Soon we won't be able to see a thing. We can't climb on Jim's rope while he's on it, but I can climb up enough to maybe see how he's doing."

I had grown stiff during the wait, but neither my physical condition nor my apprehension seemed to hamper me. I was still running on the confidence I had felt earlier. Without a belay but tied into the tail end of the haul line, I sidled to the left, as Jim had, then marched straight up to the prong of rock. I used single-arm swings to send my axe into the ice securely, precisely. The front points of my crampons nudged the top of each ice ripple. Instead of levering myself over the prong—a position from which it would have been dangerous to retreat, given the difficulty of the mantel maneuver—I worked right along a small ramp, searching for a vantage point from which to survey the upper ridge.

There was Jim, 400 feet above, working left under a wall of white ice. He looked a mile away, miniaturized by the scale of the mountain and the haze of dusk. The polypropylene rope that led up to him—a red tracer on the whiteness—was intermittently visible, but mostly hidden by outcrops and bulwarks of rock and ice. The way the rope wove intricately on Pumori's face told me that the route had not been easy to piece together. Jim had been forced to cross the ridge from one side to the other several times, as his line of ascent was cut off. As I watched, he began pulling up the remaining 200 feet of unused rope. That seemed odd, for there was no place for a tent where he stood. Had he decided to retreat? Was he pulling up the rope so he could use it to rappel back down?

"What's happening?" Steve barked from below, surprised at the sudden forfeiture of rope through his hands. "Bridwell falling in slow motion?"

When Jim had accumulated all the slack at his position, I could see him tie off the rope leading down to us. Then he turned, waved, and grabbed the rope.

"There it is. Three jerks," Steve confirmed, his oversized hands monitoring the strand.

I watched Jim start climbing again. Then I understood. He had acted out of concern and foresight for the team, for us. Now that the rope was anchored at the two-thirds mark, we could jumar. In this way we could start up while he continued to lead higher, and probably join him before full darkness. For this final plan to work, Jim shouldered great risk to his own neck: he now climbed without a true belay, and a fall with 200 feet of slack, plastic rope with no dynamic properties would be fatal—the rope would snap like a cotton clothesline.

There was an additional overall commitment. With all of us moving up, we would be forced to stay the night wherever the lead ended, whether we found a campsite or not.

"Take Jim off belay," I told Steve. I backed down to the ledge as Jan arrived.

JAN: "That pitch didn't take me too long, did it?" I hurriedly puffed the words out as I reached the edge of the ridge adjoining the staircase.

"No, Jano, you climbed that in good time. We couldn't haul any faster." Despite my cold and fatigue, Ned's reassurance pleased me. I was relieved to be at the base of the ridge he and Steve were anchored into. It led up to the hole, a dark spot on the mountain where Jim and I had hoped to establish our first camp when we had scouted the line of the climb from below weeks earlier.

"What took you guys so long? Where's Jim?" I wondered aloud.

"It was just the damn pulley," Ned answered. "Jim is stringing out all 600 feet going for the hole. I hope he's there. Why didn't you put on your parka while you were waiting?"

"Because I kept thinking I'd get going," I said sheepishly. Shivers punctuated my sentences, the words throttled by my cracked lips and petrified cheeks. "I knew you were working as fast as you could," I continued, "but it all seemed to take forever. I was down there freezing."

I looked around myself while Steve wrestled with the haul bag. I had been paying such close attention to what I had been doing that I hadn't realized that the daylight had turned to near dusk. I made a few moves up and sat down on the edge of the crowded belay stance. The end of the ridge was shaped like a dish, surrounded by snow mounds; it was as if the three of us were being held in the palm of an icy hand. The belay stance was so extremely tight for space that we had to synchronize our movements to keep from bumping one another off. To ease the crowding, Ned gave Steve the go-ahead to clip his jumar onto the ascending line and begin climbing.

"Leave Jim's pack and the duffel. Steve, take your own pack. Take the tent. You go first. Go like you've never gone before." Ned was talking climbing speed to the speed-ski king. "Jano, wait until Steve is past the first protection, then get on it."

Steve slung on his pack and started up. His strength made the weight of his pack seem incidental, but he lacked technique. I remembered hearing that when he started speed skiing, he got by on his raw strength and natural talent. Only after breaking his back in a climbing accident in 1973, then skiing in a body cast, was he forced into mastering standard skills, and he hadn't yet had to do that in mountain climbing. He would—Pumori served as his broken back of mountaineering. In 1982 he climbed Muztagata, and in 1983 he was a member of a large American team that was turned back attempting to climb Everest via the West Ridge.

I was sitting with my back towards the ridge, looking out and down thousands of feet, but craned my neck around to watch Steve. He took off almost at a run, his eyes wide and anxious. This was the most excited and intent I'd seen him.

"Does this mean you and I divide the gear here between us to carry up?" I asked Ned.

"Hell, no," Ned replied. "We just have to get up there before it's blind dark. There's no time to fool around and the extra weight will just slow us down. We'll retrieve this stuff tomorrow. What's the matter? You're shivering like crazy."

"I'm just a little cold, that's all. Help me get this pack off and I'll bundle up. I thought I'd warm up on the pitch."

Often Ned is oblivious to all else but the larger goal at hand, but he sensed right away that I was downplaying the severity of my chill. My strength was at a low ebb, and I was fumbling with my pack. I wondered if this was an early stage of hypothermia.

While I readied myself to jumar, Ned busied himself bringing some order to the jumble of gear still cluttering the ledge. He checked the contents of Jim's pack and the duffel that were to be left behind, to make sure we didn't leave anything critical, such as the stove or a pot. We couldn't count on retrieving the gear the next day, since a storm might move in. Ned added a spare rope to his pack—just in case—and also Jim's parka.

"You're tired. Finish one operation before you start the next," Ned said out loud to himself. I glanced over and, for the first time since arriving on the ledge, grinned, as if to say, "I've heard it all before!"

We both knew that time was of the essence, and hoped Jim had found someplace to camp. If he hadn't, we were all in serious danger. Once all the gear had been shuffled and secured, Ned and I started up the ridge, panting, and occasionally giving encouragement to each other. I felt very weak, and now my rate of ascent showed it. We climbed mostly by feel over the mixed rock and snow. Then Ned hollered to me. "Jan, you've got to tie in your pack and climb without it if we're ever going to get there."

"What? We're almost there. The hole's got to be just over the rise." As my protesting increased, Ned's yelling got louder. I finally gave in, although I hated to. We had only 200 feet to go, and I'm still convinced there was no need to leave the pack behind. I continued to move up at the same rate, feeling Ned had been overanxious.

NED: Although we were in the shadow of night, I could see the last faint rays of sunlight had turned the summit rocks of Mount Everest crimson, but lesser peaks had been swallowed by shadow. With mirage-like clarity, the highest point on earth seemed embraceable if we stretched out our arms—even as it stood six miles distant across the upper Khumbu Valley. While we watched, it turned to the cruel blue hues of winter. We were silent. The elimination of Everest's glow seemed to irrevocably shutter life and thicken the shadow in which we huddled.

As soon as Steve clipped by the first piece of protection, Jan left. "You've got to fly, Jano. Wait until Steve is off each section of the rope before you get on it." She was gone. Now I waited alone. The team was strung out on the one slender thread, heading toward a sanctuary still only imagined.

"Good luck," I said aloud to myself. I needed to hear it. I could feel that luck was with us, but I couldn't define it. Luck was mysterious. It was probability, yes, but something more; something wonderfully and frighteningly unscientific. A scientist could calculate the probability of a given outcome, but couldn't tell us if we would be lucky.

Then I started up. I remember little of the features of the terrain I worked through that night, only vague admiration for the artistry with which the route had been engineered. Each lead out was long, and the protection had been ingeniously placed to minimize rope drag. Jim had a master's eye. I followed the rope up gullies of ice, solid ice steps, big walls of ice, and styrofoam-like ice mushrooms. I followed it over delicate traverses and weird criss-crossings of the ridge crest.

I realized I was catching Jan. She was not moving as fast as she had when she started from the belay ledge. The cold had sapped her energy during the long wait, and I was catching her on each jumar leg as easily as the night continued to swallow us. I calculated that, at this rate, we'd never get to the end of the pitch before total darkness. I knew what had to be done, but waited until Jan had reached a notch where the rope crossed the ridge. "You'll move better without your pack. Let's leave it here. We'll get it tomorrow." I tried to say it considerately, but surely I was overbearing.

"If I'm going, so is my pack. No way I'm leaving it." Her reply was loaded with fatigue, the sharp words slow.

She began to move forward off the notch. I blocked her departure with sharp words of my own. "We have only a few minutes left before we won't be able to see *anything*. We've got to *go*. *That* means dumping your pack. The *priority* is getting *there*," I pointed up, "not staying *here*," I pointed down, "*tonight*."

"I can *handle* it," she shot back, then moved off right onto a traverse that led from the notch to an ice gully. Given her fatigue, it was difficult for her to spider sideways. I watched her struggle, then stop at the end of the traverse, 20 feet away. Her head drooped. I saw her lift it up to survey the steepness above, then it drooped forward again.

I worked my way across to her. I was impatient with her obstinacy, but I also felt compassion for her struggle, and I was impressed by her determination to pull her own weight. No more words were needed. I lifted the pack off her shoulders and she slipped out of the straps. Together we fastened it to the ice screw that marked the end of the traverse.

"Let's get on up to the hole," I encouraged. She nodded, grinned and stuck out her tongue in a final salute.

JAN: When I reached the end of the 600-foot rope Jim had just fixed, I felt like a train at the end of the track. I also felt very vulnerable. Sometimes seconding can be almost mindless, because the route of ascent is already determined. But now I was faced with the Hansel and Gretel syndrome. My path-marking crumbs had been eaten and it was pitch-black out. I bent down, peering through the dark for footprints in the deeper snow. I wobbled in the ones I found, and the steps that had made them were too long for my legs. I followed them along the ridge, relying heavily on a well-placed axe, then down a 40-degree-slope for 50 feet into the hole.

I could hear Ned calling for me, and I yelled back directions. There was really only one way to go—right, into the hole. To the left was the sheer face that dropped off straight down to our Base Camp.

I made out two struggling figures hacking out a tent platform on the steep slope I was descending. It still wasn't quite wide enough to place the tent. It's strange how your strength can return when you know someone else needs you. I fell to my knees and began digging and scooping with my arms to extend our plot. We worked together for some time in silence, as if words might detract from our efforts, until Jim said, exasperated, "We've been trying to set this tent up for half an hour." He and Steve looked exhausted in the dim light of Steve's headlamp. Ned and I took over, hoping fresh determination could do what frustration couldn't. The tent had been built so precisely and tightly that it was a fight to position the poles. We performed with the electricity of urgency, despite our fatigue. Although in sore need of water and warmth, we took time to secure the tent well, because the location of our campsite put us in a perfect position to slide, tent and all, down the couloir and over the northeast face of Pumori.

We had only two packs between us. Between Ned's and Steve's loads, we had one two-person tent, two sleeping bags, two headlamps, a stove, and almost no food—all the essentials for a wonderful evening in the winter-ridden Himalaya. Quite unexpectedly, Ned's and Steve's headlamps burned out almost simultaneously. I had a feeling Murphy wasn't going to sleep a wink all night: everything that could possibly go wrong did. Jim threw the two packs defiantly into the tent and ordered me in behind them to stretch out the sleeping pads. I did as I was told, hiding my indignation. First Ned had ordered me around, and now Jim was bossing me around. Besides, I thought, we needed organization, not a hogpile in the tent. I thought the packs should remain outside, but I said nothing. I was afraid making waves at this point might cause tempers to flare.

Then Jim changed his mind. "Pull Ned's pack back out and dump everything out to get the stove." I was dismayed. I knew that in the dark the pieces of our intricate mountain stove were likely to get lost in the snow. That would never do—a functioning stove was necessary for melting snow, and we were all terribly dehydrated. Jim had taken command of the situation, and Ned and Steve were stamping around outside, saying nothing.

Abruptly, Jim jumped into the tent, mumbling something about being cold. Ned and Steve followed. The tent was a disheveled, crowded, lumpy jumble—and completely dark. Jim and Steve had strewn the contents of Ned's pack all over the tent as they crawled in, and had pushed me into the back corner. I saw a bad situation getting worse.

At this point I lost it—or rather, regained it. "Look, Steve, why don't you and I change places, then you and Jim can stretch out and actually be semicomfortable in the back of the tent. Ned, you and I can sit close to the door. And give me that stove before you drop all the pieces." Steve and Jim relaxed, relieved of duty, and used the contents of Ned's pack for necessary padding over the cold, hard spots in the tent. They also located our only two sleeping bags and draped them over themselves.

I rescued the stove Ned had been punishing, but as usual, he instructed me how to assemble the stove and light it, despite his own failure. Although it was dark, I'd assembled the stove so many times that I did it by instinct and promptly got the thing going, then placed it outside. We then all settled back into whatever little niches we could find, congratulating ourselves for finding the only reasonable campsite for thousands of feet. When the snow had melted, I handed the pot back to Jim. He took a sip from the cold, gray rim and, to my amazement, shot forward and spat it out. Somehow kerosene had gotten into the pot and our water was slightly contaminated. Still, considering we'd had a hard day and were at 21,000 feet, it was imperative that we drink, so we took our chances with this batch of water and drank gingerly.

We lay down head to foot, like sardines, and covered ourselves with the two sleeping bags. Beneath me were plastic boots, fuel containers, and other hard, lumpy objects. We all twisted and turned, trying to settle ourselves into some comfortable position between all the shrapnel of equipment. Out of the darkness a voice boomed, "Steve, will you stop wiggling?"

"I have to. That way I know I'm alive."

My space was tiny, and decreasing minute by minute. Every time I turned over in search of comfort, Jim filled in my space a little tighter. I was miserable. Midway through the endless night, I asked Ned if he thought his space was any better and would he mind trading. He succumbed.

"I don't see how you fit here, Jano." "I didn't," I answered as I settled into luxurious space. "Thanks. Good-night." Still, I couldn't sleep. I felt absolutely envious when I heard Ned begin to snore.

NED: We nestled in our protected hole; the west wind roared overhead and spindrift sprinkled onto our tent. On an expedition, a tent means sanctuary, shutting out the elements and warming us in its comfortable cradle. That night, however, the storm seemed to rage inside more than outside. Crammed miserably together, literally on top of each other, we vied with one another for resting and breathing space.

In the morning we felt awful, as if we'd been on a week-long binge. The morning light which we thought would never come, finally came. We were numb, disgruntled, and semiconscious. We didn't move, but lay huddled under the sleeping bags. The "Yellow Rose of Texas" blipped out of Jim's watch, and the sun lit the tent, loosening a rain of frost from the ceiling. I hoisted myself onto my hands and knees, unzipped the door, and crawled out of the foul air onto the sparkling snow.

I stood swaying for a moment, then assumed a perch on a nearby chunk of ice, facing east into the sun. There were no clouds and no wind. The sunshine melted my memories of the night before with baffling ease. In those moments, I was filled with the serenity of solitude. A person is an adventurer in direct proportion to the shortness of memory. If you remember only the bad times, you never go back.

My reflective moments were cut short by grunts from the tent, and soon the others had all joined me outside. Our immediate need was to rehydrate ourselves, then retrieve the gear discarded during the previous evening's scramble. It was decided that Steve and I would descend to the belay position for the gear there. Jan would retrieve her own pack from the halfway point. We spent two hours melting snow and drinking coffee, tea, and Tang.

Steve, Jan, and I rappelled down the ridge from Camp I, then Jan retrieved her pack and started up. Steve and I continued rappelling all the way down to the belay stance, 600 feet lower, where we distributed the weight between our two packs. I enjoyed my day working with Steve.

"Speed skiing has nothing to do with what we're doing here," Steve said with a funny half-laugh.

"Yes, it does," I said quietly.

"Well, yes, in the confidence, mind set, and determination," he admitted. "You know, Ned, I can't get a hold on Pumori."

"What's the key to speed skiing?" I asked.

"Penetrating the wind at the right angle. I was the first to go renegade—without gloves. One day I realized that the seams were big resistance. I tossed them off just before my record run."

"Wind resistance or mind resistance?" I mused aloud.

He did not answer immediately, but heaved his pack easily onto his back. Clipping his jumar onto the plastic fixed line, he started up. He stopped and looked down. "I have a certain kind of strength." His brute strength was ideal for the task of retrieving our gear. Attached to the fixed line that was securely anchored, Steve became a powerful hoisting mechanism. He could carry however much weight I gave him, and not be slowed.

This time up we had the luxury of time and light for the pitch. Ravens played in the air, and I paused frequently on my vertical promenade, turning to gaze at the fantastic scenery. For an hour I was a mountain tourist rather than a mountain climber.

I now fully appreciated Jim's superb route-finding during the previous day's closing minutes. The ridge was not a simple structure, but flawed, broken, and uneven. Each time I pulled up over a headwall, turned a corner, or crossed a crest, a new technique was called for to climb a gully, sidle across a traverse, balance on an edge, scrape over rock, spread-eagle a dihedral, or heave up pure steepness. The route expertly followed the flaws in Pumori's barriers, yet the passage stayed on solid rock, snow, and ice. Near the top we moved under a great mushroom of ice, lacy and unconsolidated, that barred the way. I passed it and climbed the far side that had been the crucial lead for Jim the night before. The formation was vertical, and the entire structure seemed so delicately balanced that an overly enthusiastic whack with an ice axe might fracture and topple it.

JAN: While Ned and Steve went after our duffel bag, I retrieved my pack, which was dangling from the fixed line. I was the first one back to Camp I and crawled into the tent to ask Jim what he thought about the upper portion of the route. As we warmed ourselves with tea, the conversation eventually turned to his wife, Peggy, and his three-year-old boy, Layton. At Base Camp, Jim had showed me a picture of them. Now he told me that Layton was doing some of his first skiing, and I sensed that Jim was quite disappointed not to be part of it. Through the conversation Jim's voice softened, then he was quiet. Without a word he started rustling around collecting climbing gear, and the next thing I knew he was asking me to belay him on a tricky traverse that would lead up to our next pitch. I was surprised, because we hadn't expected him to string out the route until the following day.

We had only enough rope for Jim to go part way out on a tricky traverse. He untied from the rope and did some solo clambering to determine our line on up. I admired Jim's nerve, and never feared for him when he was climbing solo. I tied off my end of the rope when Jim anchored his end—now he could stay out there as long as he wanted and just jumar back to camp. When Ned and Steve appeared, they were as puzzled and curious as I had been to see Jim already out there.

A few days later, Jim confirmed what I had suspected: he was homesick for his family and wanted to do something to distract himself. For most people, hanging off ice unroped at 21,000 feet would have been a drastic measure, but to Jim it seemed just what he needed. Jim's is a dual nature: his leathery skin and chipped teeth give him a tough exterior, but that hides a heart as warm as any I've encountered. His sense of adventure raises havoc with his home life: when he's with his wife and child, he pines for adventure; in the midst of adventure, he longs for his family.

Fetching our supplies was draining but routine work, and by two o'clock that afternoon Ned and I were able to erect our tent. At least we wouldn't be as crowded as we had been the night before.

The next day, December 22, we opted to rest and eat rather than push for the summit. We hadn't quite pulled ourselves together yet and were having trouble getting our specially prepared food down our dry throats. A natural foods co-op had developed a protein mixture for us to eat on rest days, and a carbohydrate mixture for climbing days. We had learned through research that carbohydrates are metabolized very effectively at high altitude, so a carbohydrate diet should minimize the effects of altitude. It all worked well on paper, but in reality the altitude and dry air made our health foods so unpalatable that we just couldn't choke them down. Because we weren't eating much, our fatigue was beginning to manifest itself in flaring tempers.

NED: While Jim explored steep, new ground above the campsite, Steve and I dug a second platform below the first. Before long, Jim returned to camp. Jan and I then set up the second tent. Now we could properly term this Camp I. A 75-foot pinnacle of ice hung overhead, protecting the camp from avalanches. Several blocks of ice had broken off and littered the area in front of the tents, but the closest block rested 10 feet away. We hoped no new chunks would fall closer to our nylon shelters.

Jim returned from his scout. "I'm tired. Just not acclimatized. I thought I'd gotten over the hump, but it must have been the adrenalin rush from last night's climb."

We slid into our tents and began the task of melting snow and cooking. Since we were tired and somewhat nauseated, the tedious chore took as much determination as the climbing itself had. For all our high tech gear, we lived no better than a shanty existence—high-altitude hoboes crouched over peel-top food packets. Tangled atop our gear like nesting hens, we lay waiting for the pot's contents to boil. The worst part of it all was that some of the resultant mess had to be consumed. The daily, cramped toil of feeding, dressing, and toiletting—more than any other aspect of the expedition—wore us down.

We drank hot mushroom soup, tea, and Tang; then ate powdered potatoes spiced with powdered cheddar cheese and crumbled bouillon cubes. It should have tasted good, but even the best meals were not tasty at high altitude.

The next morning, nobody had much get-up-and-go. Our small band had lost much of the delicious surge of energy felt during the dark scramble two nights earlier. Jim decided that we needed more rope for the climbing he had scouted above Camp I, and I went back down to the belay stance at the base of the ridge for the second 600-foot length of polypropylene. I enjoyed the simple, hard work of my solo project, which temporarily counteracted my lethargy. In the afternoon Jim did more scouting, and secured ropes across steep, hard ice diagonally up and to the right of camp. When he returned he said, "The weather looks stable. We should go for the top tomorrow."

7

PUMORI: FAILURE

"Yes, it'll go! It's just a short push to the top."
Ned Gillette

NED:  Our two tents, like lobsters that had scuttled into a rocky cranny, were backed up into the hole on Pumori designated Camp I. It was December 22, and we were still tired and still struggling to acclimate to our 21,000-foot elevation. My heartbeat was rapid, a metronome that jazzed my body and mind. The others were restless, too. Even though it had been dark for two hours, sleep did not come easily. We continued to talk, planning the next day's summit attempt, as Jim was chalking strategy on the blackboard of the night.

Our problem was a common one: Should we go up, or down, or rest? Since we were not fully acclimatized, we might end up more easily and safely successful in the long run by descending to Base and resting. Then we would be stronger for a faster subsequent push to the top. But we had not put the question to ourselves in those terms. Instead, as if blindered, we were simply discussing the sequence of steps to the top. We had good weather and firm, stable snow, yet we were not ready—physically or mentally—to continue upward. We were in this predicament because we had arrived late in Nepal and, concerned that we would miss the best climbing weather before Christmas, had rushed onto Pumori. We had worn ourselves down before building ourselves up. It would have made good sense to descend, or at least rest the next day, then trust the weather to hold thereafter. We would then have a far better chance of succeeding in an early-rising, hard-driving push to the top. We had only to listen to our fatigue.

We failed, however, to act on what we sensed of our condition. The next day was December 23, and we felt we had no time to spare, that we were racing the winter storm season. Here in the dark, in the incubating warmth of our sleeping bags, it was easy to imagine the storms about to break over us like giant waves. We had difficulty viewing our situation dispassionately. We were exhausted, but skies were clear and we felt driven. We would try to dash to the summit the next day.

We agreed to set our alarms for five o'clock, since we had to start climbing early to make full use of the short daylight hours. We had already prepared our equipment—stoves were filled, hardware racked, backpacks loaded. I slept in my climbing suit and harness. The last words I heard were Jim's assurance that, "There's no need to set alarms. On a summit day, I always wake up early."

Full daylight—not alarms, not Jim—woke me the next morning. I lurched into a sitting position, the trajectory of my head neatly shaving ice crystals from the roof of the tent. I shivered as they shifted down inside my collar. I was agitated. It shouldn't be daylight. I looked at my watch: it was six-thirty. Like a tortoise extending, I looked out the tent door. The sky was clear, the wind moderate. "Jano. Up. It's late," I barked. "Jim, Steve." I wanted to turn the clock back.

Like an engine asked to perform instantaneously on a cold start, I ran badly after my initial flurry. A heavy, sickly sensation swept over me. I propped my head on my arm and looked east to Everest, Lhotse, and Nuptse. Their height still hid the sun, but orange rays, directed by the outlines of the peaks and highlighted by haze, shot up in a cone-shaped aurora. I looked up at Steve and Jim's tent tiered above, like a bunk bed fastened to a wall. All was quiet. Moments later an arm reached out of the upper berth as Steve absent-mindedly emptied his pee bottle in my direction. I retreated inside the tent to light the stove, but produced instead a sooty fusillade of flames. Jan, now awake, suggested I sign a nonagression pact with the mechanism, then neatly lit it.

JAN: Ned had slept with his clothes on, climbing harness and all. Or should I say he wrestled with them all night, and kept me awake? He complained that his one-piece climbing suit rolled up tightly in his crotch. I knew it would annoy him, but I couldn't suppress a laugh at the thought that being dressed for action in the morning could be worth a sleepless night.

I dressed quickly as Ned tried to fire-up the stove. I heard the harsh hissing of the stove's flame and low voices in the other tent. I knew that Steve and Jim, too, were up and performing the morning ritual of coaxing their stove and watching the water boil. Our light stoves had an ever-so-tiny hole to permit the gas to escape, keeping the cooking flame alive. Since we hadn't been able to bring our own white gas to these foreign parts, we had had to purchase some obscure, dirty fuel that clogged this hole. Combined with the problem of low oxygen at altitude, this meant that the stoves needed to be humored. With a little tender loving care, they would come around to your point of view, but they balked at any kind of brute force.

Ned was muttering under his breath because the stove had choked itself out. Looking down, intent on what I was doing so that my eyes wouldn't meet his, I filled the cooking pot with snow. After three years and two expeditions together, a glance could convey an entire conversation. Ned was cranky, and certainly wouldn't listen to any suggestions about lighting the stove. Ned slammed it down and rustled out of the tent, tugging at his twisted suit, still trying to settle his body comfortably inside it.

The tension seemed to blow out of the tent behind him. Relieved, I coaxed the stove to life. In a few moments, I heard Ned's heavy step returning. When he poked his head into the tent, I could see that he was grinning.

"Thanks, Babe," he whispered.

I stuck my head outside, saw Jim emerging from his tent, and called out, "'ello Ducko, noice dai for a cloimb." We'd gotten in the habit of chattin' like the Brits for absolutely no other reason than the fun of it. Jim gave me a "Yea," and flashed a grin like a boy caught with his hand in the cookie jar. I loved that smile because it was Jim, pure and simple. He was always getting away with something he probably shouldn't, whether it involved climbing or life in general.

Preceding: *Monk pinning up prayer flags*
Facing: *Hindu women sharing village news*
Top: *Kathmandu in early morning light*
Bottom: *Devout Buddhist at Bodnath temple, Kathmandu*

Top: *Whitewashed houses of Namche Bazaar, center of Sherpa trade and culture*
Bottom: *Sherpani granddaughter and grandmother, Tashigan, Arun Valley*

Sherpa boy with looking glass, Pangboche

Top, left to right: *Jim Bridwell, Steve McKinney, Craig Calonica*
Middle, left to right: *Jan Reynolds, Rick Barker, Ned Gillette*
Bottom: *Our faithful Sherpas, Pumori Base Camp*

Our yak caravan crossing the Khambu Glacier moraine en route to Pumori (background)

Top: *Wild lenticular clouds over Everest and Lhotse*
Bottom: *Steve climbing fixed ropes at 20,700 feet on ridge below Camp I*
Facing: *Jim (upper right) leading out of Camp I, in the "hole," as Jan (center) belays and Steve (left) waits his turn*

Facing: *Veranda view of Everest (and Ned) from Camp I*
Top: *Jim climbing near-vertical ice on the "Breadloaf," at 21,800 feet*
Bottom: *Jim on long, unprotected lead up the icy "staircase"*

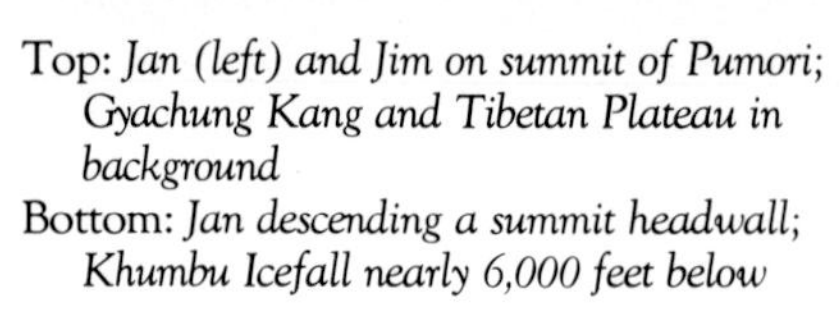

Top: *Jan (left) and Jim on summit of Pumori; Gyachung Kang and Tibetan Plateau in background*
Bottom: *Jan descending a summit headwall; Khumbu Icefall nearly 6,000 feet below*

Eerie evening at Base Camp, with Pumori under full moon (double-exposure photograph with Jan "painted" by flashlight)

Above: *Jan rappelling off Sherpani Col; Makalu in background*
Right: *Craig (left) and Jan on Mingbo Glacier, below the Mingbo La*

Top: *Jan and Craig cave-camping above Barun Khola*
Left: *Ned navigates the headwaters of the Barun Khola*
Right: *Jan's first food in days*

NED: In our tent, Jan finished filling water bottles with melted snow. Each of us would carry a quart bottle and a pint bottle—three pounds of liquid. We wouldn't stand a chance of reaching the summit without it, since the dry air at altitude would dehydrate us. Candy bars and raisins had already been shoved into our backpacks, along with down parkas and extra mitts. We carried one stove, one pot, one shovel—and no sleeping bags, since we planned to be back before nightfall and didn't want to be slowed by the extra weight.

We were all now in action, but nothing was as zippy as it ought to have been for a long summit push. When Jim finally left to climb, it was already nine o'clock. Clipping a single jumar to the length of rope left in place from the previous day's reconnaissance, he moved out from the protection of our hole, out of our sight. He dragged a second rope as a safeguard in case the anchors at the upper end of the fixed rope had loosened, or in case the rope itself had been sliced by falling rock. Steve gave him a loose belay.

Waiting for Jim to finish the traverse, my crampons long since fastened onto plastic double boots, I hiked up and out onto the far side of the camp hole. I wanted to photograph, in one frame, the camp, Jim climbing, and Steve belaying. The photograph seemed worth the risk of clambering about unroped, but it occurred to me that it would be a sorry epitaph if I should expire with a camera in hand instead of an ice axe.

I focused my 28-mm lens. But the composition was not what I expected—the belay man had vanished! More importantly, the rope to Jim snaked out unattended. Where, oh where, was Steve? He was squatting over the crevasse that sliced through the rear of the camp hole, contentedly relieving himself. His attention span on the belay had been short, no match for building intestinal pressure. Mercurial by nature, programmed for the steely 20-second span of concentration needed to ski-sprint at 125 miles an hour, Steve had belayed long enough, and now had simply wandered away. Somehow the gross distortion of priorities was funny. Jim, climbing on, never knew.

Jim finished the traverse and I, as second man across, readied myself. Steve grinned sheepishly. I laughed with him, then stepped around the crestline that defined the northern edge of our hole. I was temporarily alone. The traverse was 250 feet long, and wound horizontally under a bulge of ice before diagonaling upward. It ended at the base of a 1,000-foot snow slope we had named "the ramp." Jim was working there. My first step from the hole pushed out over 3,500 feet of exposure. It was electrifying. I concentrated on placing my hands and feet precisely.

With each step, I laid the front points of my crampons into the gray ice with an even pendulum motion of my lower leg. The surface of the ice was rippled, and I placed my spikes above each ripple, using it as a tiny platform to lessen the angle and ease my progress. A walloping kick would have fractured the ice, erasing much of the crampon's holding power. Chunk, chunk . . . slide my jumar with my right hand . . . chunk, chunk . . . slide. Maintaining rhythm lubricated my crablike dance on the steep slope. My ice axe and hammer hung in holsters at my waist. The perlon rope, strung across the face of the mountain and hitched by only four ice screws, was springy. It would have been better to use our polypropylene rope for this purpose, but when Jim led the pitch the day before, Steve and I were bringing it up from the old belay post. To progress we were often forced to improvise, using what was available rather than what was ideal.

The rope that I was on was a safeguard in the same way that an ejection seat in a jet fighter was: I wished not to test it. It would save me from falling to the bottom of the mountain, but it would not prevent a short fall. If I lost balance and toppled outward, I could not immediately correct my error. Anchored sparsely as it was, the perlon rope's dynamic properties allowed too much stretch. To compound the danger, the rope was horizontal. A fall would put a sharp, right-angled tug on my jumar, making the mechanism more prone to failure. As a back-up system I had clipped a carabiner on the rope, then tied it into my swami belt with nylon webbing. I felt like a lone performer on a high wire, yet I had the sense of allied support, connected by the rope to Jan and Steve below and Jim above.

When I reached the end of the traverse, I found only footprints in the snow: Jim had started up the ramp without a belay. I was discovering that this was his habit. The moderate climbing on this stretch was little match for a man of his ability. I took up his rope in a loose belay, then called up to him, chastising him. "It's beautiful going," he replied. "Easy. Fast. It's just getting out of breath that slows you down, Dad."

I had a few moments alone, standing comfortably on the belay platform. The air hardly stirred, yet the slightest zephyr brought a nip of winter. The sun had lifted high enough to soften the hard line of shadow that had defined the West Ridge of Everest earlier. Its North Face was still locked in half-night, but I could make out the Hornbein Couloir, the sliver of snow and ice that cut the rocks of the summit pyramid. In 1963 the Americans Tom Hornbein and Willi Unsoeld had climbed up the couloir during a bold traverse over the top of Everest. It was the single greatest achievement on the mountain since the first ascent.

Swinging my gaze to the southeast, I spied Ama Dablan and other lesser peaks. They lacked Everest's magnitude, but showed a more finely sculpted beauty. The landscape farther to the south was hidden by Pumori's shoulder.

I felt hidden, deliciously so. We had the place to ourselves—no other expeditions populated the head of the Khumbu. During the regular pre- and postmonsoon climbing and trekking seasons, the place would be alive with activity. Our precious solitude was a gift of the winter. It was as if the clock had been turned back to the 1950s and we were some of the first to visit the Khumbu.

Jan arrived, and clipped into the anchor. She, too, was happy to be moving. Romance here in the thin air was decidedly platonic, but I kissed her cheek. Bundled like mountaineering knights, armored with spikes and picks and axes, we had about as much sex appeal as armadillos. I started up in Jim's footsteps.

JAN: Jim clipped his jumar onto the rope that draped gracefully across the traverse of steep, lacy blue ice leading out of Camp I. His first couple of steps out were careful and deliberate, feeling the strength of the rope. Then his shoulders lowered, and I could almost see his muscles relaxing. His quiet, deft movements carried him steadily across the traverse. It was a joy to watch him display his strengths, to see him move with such confidence. I remember this image and hold onto it tightly whenever I'm disappointed in myself or in others, and it reminds me of the best in people—sometimes hidden, sometimes shining out.

Ned waited while Jim moved up to the belay 150 feet above. Given the nature of the traverse, it wasn't practical to have more than one person on the pitch at once, since a tug by one could send the other flying. I watched Ned make his way across and up.

I often live in my imagination when I attempt a physical endeavor. I had studied a bit of ballet as a child, and as I began the traverse I imagined that the front points of my crampons were the wooden blocks at the tip of my toeshoes. I forgot about the pack on my back and the layers of bulky clothing, and dreamed I was dancing ever so delicately across the stage for a terribly discriminating audience. Then I remembered I had put on toeshoes before I really deserved them. I hoped I had paid my dues for front points.

The ice had some fragile white lace on it, which shattered at a touch, but was mostly solid blue. A swift kick set my points, and the jumar hummed rhythmically in my right hand, sliding along the line. As I moved across, Ned belayed Jim heading up the next pitch. The wind was beginning to pick up as the day warmed. I looked down the sheer rock and ice gully below me, pleased that I felt more comfortable out there than I had expected. I wasted no time, knowing Ned would want to ascend as soon as Jim was settled, and that Steve was preparing for his traverse debut. But, most probably, I moved right along because I'll forever have this monkey on my back about keeping up with the boys. I finished the traverse, sighed slightly, then began moving up.

Ned and I had a quiet moment together on the belay stance before he continued on. Jim was anchoring the rope above, Steve moving slowly on the traverse below. We looked directly across at the Khumbu icefall, and the wind-shrouded crown of Everest, alongside Lhotse and Nuptse.

"Neddy, do you think we'll make it today?"

"Depends on what time we reach the "breadloaf" and how straightforward the summit pinnacle is." We had nicknamed the icefall on Pumori's crestline the "breadloaf."

I knew; I had just wanted to hear him say that he too thought the summit was within our limits. I held him for a moment, then he left. Feeling alone, I bent over and cupped my hands to yell to Steve.

"Come on up, nice views." I gave him a hearty welcome, wishing I could see his eyes underneath his glasses. Of the three men, Steve's moods were the most difficult to read. He always pushed an eager expression at you, leaving you guessing at his intimate thoughts.

"Feels good to be off the dread traverse, doesn't it?" I asked, in a tone that admitted I thought it was dicey, too."

"Yea. Ned's moving right along, isn't he?"

"M-m-m, we need to make some time today. I better get going."

I patted his back, clipped on, and began my steady step up. Both Steve and I are dreamers. I use my illusions to push myself, or to improve my performance. I felt as though Steve used his dream world to take himself away from where he was.

NED: The ramp was long and rose at a constant angle. We climbed upward on a slight diagonal line to the left. I hurried, knowing Jim could not move safely on the highly technical pitch that followed until I was in position to belay. I kept up a steady, head-down pace—chunk, chunk, chunk—my boots kicking into the steps. I could hear small avalanches—ice loosened from the upper wall by the sun—shooting down the couloir to my right. When I arrived at the first piece of protection buried in the snow, an aluminum plate called a "deadman," I knotted the rope to the carabiner. This anchored it so that Jan could start up. I continued moving, dreading the long monotony of this section, yet surprised at how soon Jim's red boots filled my field of vision.

I was soon at his stance at the base of the breadloaf, a nearly vertical wall of ice barring access to the Northeast Ridge. I began to chop a larger platform so we could both stand, first prying away a crust of old snow. It came off in small plates that fell straight down the slope. Our route angled off the fall line, so Jan and Steve weren't in any danger from it. Suddenly a plate a foot in diameter cracked off, stood itself on end, then cartwheeled downward. I watched it, but shouted no warning. There seemed no need. Then, like a guided missile suddenly gone astray, it veered—no, jumped—at Jan. She was climbing head down, and a warning cry now would only lift her head, exposing her face. With demented accuracy, it struck her on the head, driving her forward into the slope. Her stillness was sickening, alarming. But soon I saw her stand and investigate damage with an ungloved hand. She did not answer my calls, but soon started moving again. I knew her well enough to sense that her silence heralded some anger with me, not with the mountain.

JAN: From where Steve and I stood, the next pitch went up at a 45-degree angle for another thousand feet. Ned was busy above belaying Jim on the more difficult, upcoming pitch. I moved along in my rhythmical fashion, letting the low hum of the rope through my jumar lull me. I was very relaxed. Quite suddenly I heard a loud whizzing and felt a sharp pain. My teeth slammed together so hard that their impact made a big bang, and black spots in front of my eyes began to knit together into a black curtain. I made myself concentrate on watching each foot, as I focused on continuing to step up. I was deliberately forcing myself to move, because I was afraid that otherwise I might black out completely. I blinked hard several times and took a step. My tunnel vision expanded slowly as the black began to recede. I continued to move up.

Ned had seen this little episode from the beginning. I finally realized he'd been yelling "Jano, hey Jano, are you okay?"

I felt steady enough to stop, and reached for the top of my head. My hand was wet from the blood that had soaked through my hat and two silk balaclavas. My immediate thought was that heads bleed a lot, so it didn't mean much.

"Yeah, what was that anyway?" Before Ned could answer I remembered that Steve was below me. I glanced down to see if he'd been hit, but he was moving along fine, minding his own business.

"I knocked off a big dinner plate of ice."

Geez, I thought, dinner plate! That was more like a turkey platter with the whole bird on it. It was useless to try to carry on a conversation considering the distance between us. I just kept moving up, my head throbbing with every step. I kept all my headgear on, hoping it would help slow the bleeding. My hair already had a few weeks of grease on it, and I hoped that would help too. I was less concerned about the bleeding than about infection.

I told myself to be diplomatic as I climbed up, but I couldn't help myself. The first thing I said when I reached the stance was, "Hey, Neddy, why didn't you tell me that was coming?"

"Well, it looked like it wasn't going to cross your path and I didn't want to disturb you. Then it hit something and changed course. I was too late. If I yelled to you then, you might have looked up and gotten it smack in the face."

Relieved that that hadn't happened, I began to feel lucky.

"Boy, that was the closest I've ever come to blacking out."

"That thing fell about 200 feet before it homed in on you."

By now Steve had reached the stance, and we shifted around to make room for three. Jim was above us, still hacking away at a nearly vertical section of ice that looked like white Swiss cheese. I looked at Steve and said, "Maybe there's a big white mouse in there," hoping to get a laugh out of him. His reply was merely to look up, appearing to assess the difficulty of the pitch. I had the impression that he'd rather be almost anyplace else, but he wouldn't say so.

NED: Jim and I turned to the breadloaf. Our stance was at the base of a bulge of ice, and it felt as though we were at the mercy of a colossal wave that was frozen in place, curling off the Northeast Ridge. The ice wave hid any view of the summit and was of far greater magnitude than we had expected. It towered above and extended to the left and right along the entire ridgeline—a nearly perfect barrier. Directly above there was a single defect, a slot, as if this were the final break-over point of two waves joining. We felt a sense of urgency standing under the wall of frozen water. It seemed as if we had only glacialogical seconds to sneak through the passage before it closed. It also seemed we were in danger of losing our race to the top. The hand of the clock—our enemy more than the mountain—was moving into the afternoon hours.

Jim gazed at the faint diagonal scar that seemed our only hope of crossing the barrier. A great fin of ice seemed to have been peeled back from it, and hung out over the void. The slot rose less steeply than the wall, but even so it appeared to be just off vertical. Jim left his pack: he would be more efficient without it. Slipping his hands through the wriststraps of his ice tools, he unclipped from the anchor. I belayed him.

He moved right, out on the fin, then up its curved edge that bordered thin air. The placements of his tools were precise. Little explosions of ice bits sparkled in the sun as he worked smoothly upward, held delicately to the ice by an inch of crampon and axe steel touching only where needed. His instinctive grace, honed through hundreds of climbs, disguised muscle tension. There was no sign of struggle; his progress was more like a dance. Jim, a few feet away, and Everest, a few miles away but just visible beyond the fin, appeared the same size. The illusion was almost hallucinogenic.

Jim moved well, finishing off the fin and continuing up the slot; but it was a long pitch, exhausting at this altitude. I could hear the drafts of air he heaved in and out of his lungs, especially during the silence of his stops to place ice screws for protection. Eventually he disappeared around a corner in the slot. I monitored his progress by the rope running out through my hands. When it stopped, I barely heard his call: "It's okay to climb."

Hefting Jim's pack over mine, so that I carried them both, I followed, charged by the potential elevator-shaft drop out the bottom of the fin. I moved clumsily compared to Jim, but felt, by my standards, smooth and controlled. I was enthralled by the work, the place, the goal. I wondered if it was too late to be catching fire. Was the top still accessible to us? When I reached Jim, he said he was still tired from his effort. A cigarette hung from his lower lip, and his words came at me punctuated by little puffs of smoke. He asked me to lead the next pitch, which was far easier and appeared to roll over in a humpback onto the Northeast Ridge itself. I returned his pack and continued, exalting in the chance to be in front. As I progressed, the summit came into view. I stopped, looked left and up. Jim knew why I'd stopped. "How's it look?" he called.

JAN: I felt as though I were just a pack animal for this pitch: my function was to get the load up however possible. I used style when I needed it, but front-pointing at 22,000 feet, especially with a light load, made my calves feel like hot potatoes. At one point I stashed my feet in a hole chest-high, shoved my jumar as far up the rope as I could reach, and hauled myself up.

As I approached the relief in the slope, I spied Ned heading out and Jim at the stance. I slogged up to him. "Hey, Ned will reach the breadloaf and get a good look at the summit from there. You didn't want to lead?"

"My hands are freezing in these gloves," Jim said matter-of-factly.

"Here." I swung around and put my back to him, almost knocking him off balance with my pack. "Back left pocket."

He asked how I was feeling as he slipped the mitts on. Since I felt pretty good, Jim said, "Why don't you go on up?"

I was thrilled. I thought Jim was being quite gracious to allow Ned and me to be the first to reach the breadloaf, look into Tibet, and check out the route to the summit. I humped on up, looking back at Jim once. I smiled to myself to see Big Ol' Jim standing there with my little red mittens on that had JAN written over them in huge black letters. I'd grown quite fond of him.

NED: The summit pyramid rose above. Its East Face was heavily shadowed, accentuating its features. The shadows were notable, since they could have been caused only by the sun having moved into the western sky. That was of concern, but they also created a soft beauty that was bewitching. The ice on the lower slopes of the pyramid was criss-crossed with crevasses, which resulted in great blocks of ice. A route to the top would weave through the blocks, then climb to an open bergschrund that cut the entire face. A massive cornice curled off the top, product of the prevailing west wind, which was now dispatching a plume overhead.

"Will it go?" Jim was repeating his question. He must have thought my sudden petrification strange. Maybe it was the shimmer of the plume shadows, or the altitude, or my hopes for success, but I had difficulty assessing the situation. The summit was big, but I chose not to perceive it as such. Like a mirage, it seemed graspable. "Yes, it'll go," I answered. "It's just a short push to the top. It's easy terrain. We've got it."

Immediately, my own words bolstered my confidence. Like a lost desert rat thinking of palmed oases, I ran toward the ridgetop. In 10 steps I loped, in five more I walked; I was at 22,000 feet. The little sprint cleared my perception. I stole more glances upward. The mirage was quickly dissipating. In its place was an increasingly realistic assessment of distance, vertical rise, difficulty, and time.

When the slope leveled, I anchored the rope. Tibet was hidden behind a barrier of ice blocks standing on top of the ridge. Impatient for my first look, I untied, heaved myself onto the nearest block, jumped a small crevasse, and eased to the edge of a second block. Like a deep-sea diver emerging at the surface, I suddenly burst upon another world.

Tibet spread at my feet. The Pumori Glacier, young and snowy, flowed into the huge West Rongbuk Glacier, which appeared rumpled and creased, like an aged face. The great, glaciated peaks of the main Himalayan crest extended to my left and right. Beyond the shoulder of Pumori, Gyachung Kang, a white giant, dominated the western horizon. The ridgeline on which I stood seemed like a wave that appeared to be breaking to the north—the colossal push of the entire Himalaya about to tumble over the dry sands of Tibet. Northward, beyond the Rongbuk, all was brown. Barren hills of 20,000 feet extended to the horizon.

I stood on the edge of forbidden territory, *terra incognita*. From the crest of the main Himalayan chain I looked into a land that is a treasure trove of mountains. Hundreds of untouched peaks begged for attention, hundreds of untouched valleys hid rich culture. I could imagine Lhasa, the Forbidden City, the real-life Shangri-La, just beyond some lost horizon. Except for British attempts on Everest in the 1920s and 1930s and Chinese sieges during the past 30 years, there had been precious little opportunity to test such a mountain inventory. From a climber's point of view, the land lay fallow. But there was a difference now. I did not feel the total frustrations of my predecessors at being so close to a tantalizing lodestone. Tibet had finally opened—in a guarded way, but enough to allow controlled expeditions. I knew that I would soon be walking in Tibet on the second half of our circle.

I was not so sure that I would be visiting the summit of Pumori. It loomed above, cloaked in increasing shadow, displaying its true proportions. Standing still, I felt the bite of the west wind eddying off the upper slopes. There was no longer anything mirage-like about Pumori. I looked at my watch: it was past one o'clock. I walked back into Nepal. Jan was waiting. She had climbed strongly, and was obviously pleased with herself. She had put in a no-nonsense day, sticking to the job of getting herself up the mountain in an efficient manner, and she was happy to be here. I was not so pleased.

My thoughts were farther up the mountain. Although I hadn't yet voiced or admitted it, we were unlikely to catch up to those thoughts. Instead, I announced that I had just been over in Tibet for a short visit. Would she care to join me? Yes, but let's wait for the others.

Within minutes Jim was with us. Before he could catch his breath, I took the offensive. I wanted to revise my initial report of the proximity of the summit. That first assessment now seemed of another time, another place, another mind. Jim just chuckled in reply. Somehow we hadn't been able to shake the holiday mood of the expedition. Still breathing hard, lighting another cigarette, he burbled, "Yuh. I was thinking the same thing. This thing is bigger than any of us thought." It was a generous reply that immediately defused any tension.

It was two o'clock in the afternoon, and little more than three hours of daylight remained. Our perch was now in the shadow, and the temperature was plummeting. Severe lenticular clouds capped Everest and Pumori's plume had lengthened since I first arrived. We had no proper bivouac gear. Huddling in conference, we turned our backs to the wind. Even so, it ripped our words and distorted them. The cold penetrated, and with it the growing realization that we were not going to make the summit.

The mood became somber. We would live with the decision to retreat or not for all our years ahead. Hold on! Here was Steve breaking over onto the easier ground near us. Was he crawling? Mirages seemed epidemic. He was crawling! One of the strongest men I had ever met was on his hands and knees! Even in his time of trial on Pumori, Steve had never lost his ready humor. Creeping toward us, he looked like a disheveled pilgrim doing penance. Coils of rope hung from his shoulders and waist in looping festoons. He had stepped through several of the coils, which now tangled his legs. As last man up, he had collected all available residue, like a bag lady in New York. Jim was mildly chastising. "I told you there was no need to heft all that rope beyond the breadloaf."

Steve's refugeelike appearance confirmed this as our high point. The summit, lying 1,500 feet above, was out of reach. Continuing would entail an all-night bivouac without food, water, sleeping bags, or shelter—insanity in the killer cold of winter. We had reached the border, if not the summit. We had miles to go to finish the entire Grand Circle of Everest, and must get on with them. We had tried to dash from Camp I, but had ended crawling. With a shuffling gait, we men, ambitions dissolved, turned to the descent. Jan, returning from her visit over the ridge to Tibet, leapt toward us in a graceful bound, landed, stretched her arms skyward, and, bowed. She alone had reached an inner goal. She was satisfied for the moment to have climbed well in the winter time, and pleased to have established our circle by touching the border. Moments later, as I began the first rappel, Pumori's summit began to grow as my consuming goal. The calling was faint, but it was no longer a mirage. Our failure would become the catalyst that would soon harden our determination to reach the top.

JAN: We had worked hard and we had worked together. This was the best blend of personalities I'd seen on any climb. We enjoyed each other's company, as opposed to merely tolerating each other. We knew we had failed at our first common objective, but we each tried to shelve our personal disappointments for the sake of the others and the expedition.

I said, "Well, you guys, this is the border running along this ridge to the summit. We can legitimately begin the circle. I suppose our climb isn't a failure in that sense."

We actually were standing on the border between Nepal and Tibet. The

Everest Grand Circle could go on to its other objectives. Still, it was odd. We all sort of milled around on the ridge looking at Everest, the summit of Pumori, and over at the Lho La in Tibet where we were planning to ski during the second half of the circle. Nobody wanted to start down, but we all knew that was the only real choice.

Slowly a feeling of elation rose in me. From this vantage point, our imaginative approach to Everest was unfolding before my eyes. This was one of the joys of circumnavigating Everest rather than climbing it: there was always a new adventure around the corner. We hadn't failed, we had just begun.

These thoughts warmed and cheered me, and I turned my attention to the others to see how they were adjusting. Steve gave off slight scents of relief, and an indication of being anxious to descend. I'd heard him say jokingly once that Ned was Captain Ahab; and Pumori the great white whale, and I didn't feel that his own disappointment cut too deeply.

Ned and Jim, I could see, would be drowning in dissatisfaction—they hadn't fulfilled their expectations of themselves. They made a good climbing duo: Ned is as strong a workhorse as you could ask for at altitude, so he'll lug the extra load while Jim, unencumbered, moves quickly over ice and rock to run up the rope securely. They wanted success together. I knew they'd never consider reaching the ridge a success. They were trying to cover their moods, but I could see the disappointment working inside both of them.

Rappelling back to camp went along routinely. Jim hacked some sturdy bollards for anchors, and footing was good. When we reached the Swiss-cheese pitch, Ned had me dangle around awhile for some descent shots. I noticed that I felt irritated at being interrupted in my descent, and began to wonder if my disappointment ran deeper than I knew.

Recrossing what we had nicknamed the "dread traverse" back to our camp in the hole seemed more difficult under the strain of the long day. Thoughts of hot tea and warm sleeping bags on the other side coaxed me along. On an expedition it is seldom possible to choose an activity to suit one's mood—the key is responding to the situation at hand. My legs were soft with fatigue and my mind somewhat vacant from the hard work at altitude without proper acclimatization, but I forced myself to concentrate on my foot placements.

I was looking right into the hole of Camp I during my journey across the traverse. It looked to me now like an open blue mouth with large white teeth, and I was tiptoeing right into it.

We all rustled into our respective tents, anxious to get the stoves going. The din of voices in the other tent quickly began rising in decibels. We heard "hey-watch-it" and roaring curses. Then suddenly a burst of flame catapulted out of the front of the tent, burning the delicate nylon in its course, and landed in the snow with a metallic clank. Jim had handled the stove with the old theory, if you can't deal with it, destroy it. We had replacement stoves below, and that was where we were ultimately heading, so I saw humor in the event. Laughter, however, wasn't appropriate.

Ned had been hovering and fussing over our stove for some time now, and I could see the pressure gauge rising on his face. I knew we all needed to get this stove to light properly, so that we could melt some snow for drinking water.

"Ned, let me light it. It worked for me this morning."

No response. I really dislike being ignored.

"Ned, don't be dumb. You're making it worse. Give it to me." I knew I was badgering. My concern for water overwhelmed my more diplomatic self. Ned turned his black tangle of hair and beard toward me. His eyes had that look of rapidly eroding self-control, and he lashed out. "Someday someone is going to smash your nose in." Ned's threat was like a bucket with a hole for a bottom. He didn't say *he* was going to smash my nose in, so I ignored him and lit the stove anyway.

Later, Ned's hollow threat became a great classic between us. When either of us is treading on thin ice, the other just smiles sweetly and repeats it. It defuses the situation and makes us cool down with laughter. But it was no laughing matter that night on Pumori.

We drank a great deal of tea and water that night, but there was very little to eat. With our fuel supply all but depleted, and with no edible food remaining, we didn't have the option of resting there to make another summit bid in the next day or so. Besides, all our bodies had been drained by the cold, wind, lack of food, and high altitude. On top of that, our minds were out of sorts.

At last, after the final cup of tea, I sank gratefully into my sleeping bag. To my chagrin, two great tears rolled down my cheeks. The silence in the tent since the stove incident hadn't been golden. Ned rolled on to his side, looked at me and his eyes began to soften. "Why are you upset now, after all the trying times during the day?"

I stared at the top of the tent. I hadn't meant to say anything. I try to be strong, cheerful, and easygoing on an expedition to guard against unnecessary tension, and to defuse uncomfortable situations. I feel I have to tread carefully around Ned's moods, so I often keep intimate thoughts to myself.

"Sometimes I'm afraid to speak my mind to you, because I know you'll write about it," I answered slowly, turning my gaze from the top of the tent to his eyes. I explained that sometimes there were things I wanted to express, but that I held back because he was always furiously recording in his notebooks. I didn't ever want to appear apprehensive or frivolous in his journals. I suppose I was suffering from the fear of being exposed, analyzed, criticized. But, as the night drew around us, and we were warm and comfortable for the first time during this long, physically demanding day, it made me weep quietly that I was afraid, almost ashamed to whisper to Ned about my true thoughts and feelings about the day gone by.

"I'm sorry," Ned breathed out slowly. He rolled over, and it wasn't long before I could tell by his heavy, rhythmical breathing that he was asleep.

My head was throbbing where I'd been smacked by the ice earlier. I'd cleaned it up a bit, but it had never stopped hurting. Besides that, I felt as though a hurricane was raging in my digestive system. I had to rouse myself up out of my soft, warm bag to relieve myself several times during the cold of the night. Ned woke and lent comforting words when he realized that I was under the weather. We laughed about how he had kept me up the night before, wrestling with the gear he slept in, and now I was keeping him up with all my tossing and turning. But I had eased him into the day, just as he was easing me into the night. Soon we both slept.

8

CHRISTMAS

"We've completed a major portion of the circle. We should be celebrating!"

Jan Reynolds

JAN:  There was no joy in packing our goods before the long descent all the way back to Base Camp. We worked quietly and monotonously. I was trudging up and out, toward the beginning of our fixed rope at the top of the ridge, when an awkward step caused my knee to buckle. I fell and caught myself. I had already known that I was physically weak from our hard work at high altitude with little food, but now I was aware that I wasn't mentally acute, either. A lapse in concentration caused my slip. I could see myself falling prey to one of the most familiar truisms of climbing: because the descent is anticlimactic, attention drifts, and climbers are more vulnerable. Most climbing accidents occur on the way down.

I reached for the fixed rope, and as soon as I gripped it the world seemed to be a better place. My pack was heavy and swung my body around under it as I rappelled. Our loads in this final descent were the largest so far, since we were leaving the mountain and needed to take everything down with us at once.

I rappelled last. The descent was painfully tedious and wearing, especially when I broke through the crust of a snow hole on the ridge. Because the hole was deeper than the length of my legs, and because I had extra weight on my back, I had to claw with my hands to drag myself out, crawling on my belly as I floundered around. I swore like my father did when the milking machinery used to break down in the barn. When I had successfully extricated myself, I had to laugh at the things children learn from their parents and then keep with them forever.

After we had negotiated the lattice work of ice on the ridge, Jim decided we should hack a bollard out of the snow to anchor our rappel ropes, which we could pull down behind us for use again on the next rappel. The bollards were oblong lumps carved out of ice and snow. About two feet in diameter, they looked like giant doorknobs.

Before we descended we had a discussion to determine the pecking order. Should the heaviest go first to test the bollard for our maximum load? Or should the lightest go first, followed by the rest in graduated succession? We all agreed it probably didn't matter either way about Ned, Jim, and Steve because their loads were of similar weight. But it was decided that I should have the dubious distinction of rappelling last. The others rationalized that the lightest should be last because that person would be the least likely to tip the rope over the top of the bollard. After Jim and Steve had gone down, I held the rope down on the bollard for Ned.

"Whatever happened to ladies first?" I asked with mock indignation. He laughed, told me to be careful, and began working his way down.

The lower we descended, the lower my heart sank. Leaving the mountain unclimbed was like opening a gorgeously wrapped package only to find nothing inside.

Yet, I felt warmed to see Anu's eager face waiting for us at the Advance Base Camp. "Congratulations. You make the top." Oh, no, I thought, the upper portion of the route wasn't visible to them from Base Camp, so when we made our push from our high camp in the hole, our Sherpas had assumed that with all that good weather we'd surely reached the summit. I replied simply and softly, "No, Anu, we just weren't prepared." It hadn't dawned on me until now how deeply disappointed and almost embarrassed I was to admit to someone else that we had failed. Anu just shrugged and hugged me again.

Since we had no supplies here, we still had to make the long walk over the moraine before we could indulge in the comforts of Base Camp. The moon was rising and cast a gray glow on the rocky glacier's tongue. Ned kept looking back at me, calling for me to join him, but I wanted to be alone. It was Christmas Eve and the night was beautiful. I wanted to wrap myself in the stars, and saw absolutely no need for hurry. We had been all together on our umbilical cord up the mountain for several days. I had forgotten the delicious feel of independent decision and freedom to move, and I was savoring it now.

In a couple of hours, when we all finally gathered together in our big dining tent at Base, the mood had shifted 180 degrees from that of the morning. The Sherpas served us hot french fries and catsup, along with gallons of sweet tea. We had eaten meagerly for the past five days, so the fries were not only palatable, they were a feast. We laughed at each other. We laughed at ourselves. In the cozy glow of the lantern light and with full bellies, our past perils became a source of levity. In retrospect, the first night in the hole with all four of us in one two-person tent, Ned's threat to punch my nose in, and Jim's daring dash out on the traverse were all very humorous. We had already begun to forget how awful our ill-prepared summit attempt had been, and could view the recent events through different eyes. As we got sillier and sillier that evening, Jim announced, "Royal Robbins once said my problem was that I wasn't serious enough. You know, I had to keep myself from just singing that little kids' song, 'Row, row, row your boat, gently down the stream, merrily, merrily, merrily, merrily, life is but a dream.' " Jim had us giggling so hard, hearing his rough voice singing a nursery rhyme, that our tightly stuffed stomachs hurt and we begged him to stop. I went to sleep that Christmas Eve satisfied that we'd all shaken our failure from our minds.

NED: "Fools and energy are easily parted," Jim muttered in Christmas greeting to Jan and me. Steve was still sleeping.

"So are fools and summits," I added. I needed little encouragement from Jim to lapse into a grinch grump. It was Christmas morning, and we sat in sunshine at Base Camp, sipping tea. Phutashi served omelets, fried potatoes, and pancakes with apricot jam from a tray decorated with a brightly colored cloth.

Jan sang the first stanza of "Deck the Halls," and tried to cajole us into joining her. I mumbled something about not needing any morning caroling calisthenics.

I had awakened early that morning, while Jan was still asleep. I crooked my neck, peered out. The camp lay in a cold shadow that seemed to coat the sand and rocks like steel-blue varnish. I felt sulky, like a child who knew he wasn't getting what he wanted for Christmas.

I sat looking up at Pumori. It was a balanced structure—half rock, half snow and ice; half black, half white. It was not as high as many peaks, nor as remote. But, even as Everest's subaltern, the mountain had an exquisite dignity and presence that held the eye. Its beauty was simple and innocent, like that of an unsophisticated little sister seen in the shadow of her famous elder. If you asked a child to draw a mountain, the result would be Pumori's triangular pyramid, symmetrical and pointed.

For the past day and a half we had been on the defensive, the hours filled with a series of repetitive rappels down the mountain. There is no fatigue like the fatigue of defeat, which is psychological as well as physical. Yet at first I experienced a certain relief when we had turned back at our high point. But as every hour had passed and each foot downward had been lost, our failure had become increasingly unacceptable. That preoccupation during the retreat had eroded our confidence so much that we had to force ourselves to concentrate and avoid mistakes.

As the four of us sat together eating breakfast, I was plagued by the feeling that we had bungled our attempt. First, we had established Base Camp two weeks later than originally planned. Second, we had worried too much about the weather—allowed it to dictate and hurry our actions. By failing to take into account our partial acclimatization and our different levels of expertise, we had overestimated how fast we would be able to climb. Our strategy had failure built into it: we should either have gone slowly enough to stock more camps and get strong on the climb, or have acclimated fully and then gone as rapidly as possible. Finally, we had run out of food at Camp I after the one summit attempt. We had discussed these problems and possibilities before the climb, but reality was a tougher teacher than theory.

I had to remember that we had enjoyed at least a measure of success: we had touched the border between Nepal and Tibet at nearly 22,000 feet. Within the narrow, self-defined concept of the circle, our failure on Pumori was a success. Was that good enough? It was in our gloomy mood of that morning, a depression somehow heightened by the fact that it was Christmas. We had a whole circle ahead of us. That was what we had come to do, and that was what seemed most important. When Anu joined us after breakfast, I told him to send Angpura out to fetch the porters and yaks. We'd break camp and get on with the circle.

As Phutashi was gathering up our breakfast plates, a messenger arrived carrying a note from our outfitter in Kathmandu. He was relaying word from Kim Schmitz informing us that he would be unable to join us for the next leg of the circle as planned, and that Craig Calonica would replace him. Jan and I were somewhat concerned, since we had never met Calonica and knew nothing about him. The new note said he would be arriving the next day.

"If Calonica is coming in," Steve blurted out, "I'm leaving."

Steve's sudden announcement caught me by surprise. The night before he had still been planning to cross the high passes with us, and Craig Calonica was an old friend of his. But I didn't argue. He had never felt at ease on the expedition. His mind was made up; his focus lay elsewhere.

"Impetuous youth," Jim said.

The messenger also delivered a plastic quart bottle of yellow liquid with Jim's name written on the side. He roared with laughter—it was the nighttime pee bottle that he had left at Anu's house in Namche! Not realizing the nature of its contents, the Sherpas had been careful to return it to its owner.

JAN: I woke Christmas morning with childlike anticipation. Just what I expected, I'm not sure, but holidays in my family had always been something very special. Years ago, Christmas was a fantastic free-for-all among the seven children in my family. Ned, on the other hand, referred to Christmas as "just another obligation." But to me it felt like a very special day. "Ned, we can't let ourselves think the cup is half-empty. It's Christmas! Besides, we've completed a major portion of the circle. We should be celebrating!" My remarks immediately sent Ned into a tailspin. He took off on a lecture about Christmas being just a public rip-off—buy, buy, buy. And it also settled the fact that Ned wasn't going to enjoy this Christmas, in particular. It didn't look as if Jim or Steve was either, given the looks on their tired faces.

During the trek in, I had told Anu about Christmas, its historic roots, and the traditional celebration we have at home. He seemed very taken with the idea of Christmas, and was my right-hand man in creating the festivities at Base Camp, in the sand pit of the Himalaya. Indeed, Anu quite outdid me. He had his mother contract with some local weavers to make us each small carpets with the peak Pumori woven in. I danced with surprise and delight when I saw them, and hugged Anu for his thoughtfulness. He also relayed my request to Angpura and Phutashi to cook up a special Christmas dinner. It couldn't be the usual turkey and cranberries, but yak meat in thick sauce would do nicely.

As evening began to draw around us, I checked on the cooks to see how dinner was progressing. Then I slipped into the dining tent, lit several candles I had brought in especially for the occasion, and laid out several small presents for the others. In Kathmandu, I had purchased such items as Himalayan snuff and Tiger Balm, then carried them with me to Base Camp. I wrapped the packages carefully and decorated them with strings and bows. I tried to push the excitement out of my voice when I called Ned, Jim, and Steve to dinner.

As I sat there waiting like one of Santa's little elves, I imagined the surprise on their faces when they saw the delicious dinner, lovely candles, and Christmas presents. I was just beginning to get that warm, snug feeling of holiday cheer that you get when you light the Christmas tree for the first time.

The three of them crawled in simultaneously. "What is this?" one of them asked.

I hadn't realized, as I was wrapping packages and humming Christmas carols all day, that they had ignored the holiday. To them, Christmas was something that happened in other parts of the world, but it didn't travel. To them Christmas was a place, not a feeling, and the place was home and we were here, so there was nothing to celebrate.

Ned, Jim, and Steve opened their presents out of a sense of duty, and almost died when I asked if we could sing some Christmas carols. That may have been my worst Christmas ever. They made Scrooge and the grinch look like nice guys.

NED: After a delicious dinner, Jan played Santa. She had presents for all, including the Sherpas: little cans of snuff and of hot balm, all tied with colorful ribbons. Anu was also in the spirit. He gave each of us small rugs of Tibetan wool. They had been designed especially for us, with letters spelling "Pumori" woven over an image of the mountain. Mama Anu had sent white scarves of fine linen that symbolized good fortune.

The next day, Craig Calonica walked into camp. He had spent only eight days in transit from San Francisco to Pumori Base Camp, but except for a bronchial cough, he seemed to be handling the altitude well. Although I was irked that an unknown was joining the expedition, I took an almost immediate liking to him.

◆ ◆ ◆

The winter before, 1980-81—the first "fully booked" winter climbing season in Nepal—there were seven expeditions in the field; only one was successful. After-Christmas conditions had proved ferocious, with heavy snowfall, low temperatures and high winds. January of 1981 had been stormy for all but two days, with winds clocked at 140 kilometers per hour at the relatively low elevation of 21,000 feet. We knew that if we made a second attempt on Pumori, the usual winter storms might also exhaust our resources and thereby jeopardize completion of the circle. On the other hand, Jim and I both maintained that, on expeditions, we were lucky with weather. We were tempted by ambition to let go of our weather worries. Had we descended to give up or descended to regroup? Until we met unclimbable conditions, how could we not climb?

These were still but half-digested thoughts when I retreated to the tent early that evening. Jan soon joined me, and dropped off to sleep. Camp quieted quickly, but I lay awake, thinking. Only the Polish team on Everest and one other expedition had been successful in the Himalayan winter. Climbing Pumori, even though it was far smaller than Everest, would be a solid second-stage pioneering effort. Given the horrendous experiences of the previous winter, and the failure of six of seven expeditions, only two other expeditions beside ours operated this winter. We had the place and the opportunity to ourselves.

At 2:00 A.M. I started from a restless sleep. Propping myself on an elbow, I looked out of the tent. The cold, soft air floated a half-moon that draped Pumori in a splendid blue light. Our rationalization about the importance of completing the circle could not set right our failure. Pumori was too beautiful to leave undone. Suddenly, I decided on a second attempt. I had no immediate script for Act II, but I was absolutely certain of success. My gloom and frustration fell away instantly—my Christmas had come a day late.

JAN: Craig Calonica made it to camp in time for dinner that evening. I was curious to meet the person who would be an indispensable part of our team on the next portion of our journey around Everest.

My first impression was of a heavy, barrel-chested man with a cherubic face. His hair, wound in tight, dark, frizzy ringlets, framed glowing cheeks. He wore several wild scarves knotted around his neck and his fleece mountaineering clothing was embroidered with deep colors. His speech was slow and filled with the latest slang. He was a good-time California boy, footloose and sniffing for adventure.

Craig was also strong and experienced: he had climbed with Jim in Yosemite and raced the speed-skiing circuit with Steve. Craig could hold his own and more.

Early the next morning, before the light of day, Ned woke me and asked if I would try to climb Pumori again. I had known this was coming, I just hadn't known when. I mumbled a "yeah," rolled over, and dipped back into dreamland. When we rose the next morning, Jim was already packing. Perhaps Craig's fresh blood had encouraged him to try again. Jim and Ned had had trouble settling themselves since the failure, and a second attempt seemed to be the only way to do that. My main concern was the weather. It had been so good for so long, how much longer could it hold?

NED: On December 28, Steve left. Craig, Jan, Jim, and I packed to move back up to Advance Base Camp. Before we departed, the Sherpas again conducted a short ceremony to bring us good fortune, burning in a little stone altar branches of "holy juniper" that had been gathered from a special place far from any traveled path. As the fragrant smoke swirled around us, I asked Anu why juniper was holy.

"It has always been so," he replied. "From old times mothers always burned juniper when men left home."

On December 29, Jim, Craig, and I worked on the lower part of the route, replacing the ropes we had pulled down during our retreat. Craig was strong and competent, and I liked his fresh spirit. That night we went to sleep at 5:30 and slept 13 hours. The only disturbances were a loud rockfall that sounded as though it were coming through the tents, a strong wind that rocked the tents, and everybody's dry-throat coughing and hacking. The next day we all carried food and gear to the top of the staircase and cached it there.

During the last day of 1981 and the first day of 1982, we forgot about the weather, the mountain, and the circle and took a good, long rest. It was just as well, since Jim had a light touch of the flu. I read the first pages of the book I had brought, *The Right Stuff*. Jan and I talked about summer in Vermont, fixing up the house and planting a garden, auctions, and learning to ride horseback.

9

PUMORI: SUCCESS

"The only thing worse than failing is reaching your goal."

Someone

JAN: 

We had first reached Base Camp at 17,500 feet on the evening of December 11. By the beginning of our second attempt, more than two weeks later, we were all much better acclimatized.

For me, most of the mystery that surrounded the climb had evaporated, and now it would just be work. I already knew how each pitch would unfold, the riddle was so nearly solved. I hadn't yet forgotten all the hardship we had endured on the first try, but if the others were going back up, so was I. I'm not one for watching the nest while the others fly.

Craig had come in to climb the passes with Ned and me but felt strong enough to try Pumori as well. He had been taking a drug called Diamox during his trek into Base, in hopes that it would aid acclimatization, and he seemed to be doing very well. He might have done just as well without it, but there was no way to know. He indicated that he was feeling fine and was ready and eager to climb high.

Ned continued to take charge, making demands, setting our sights, and constantly pushing us and himself even harder. His enormous drive sufficed for us all. He was geared up to climb Pumori less out of desire than out of a sense of unfulfilled obligation, but his determination infected us all with the desire to succeed.

Jim, in his boyish way, seemed genuinely excited rather than nagged by duty. As we trudged up to Advance Base again, he puffed out a song, "What a difference a thousand feet makes," to the tune of "What a Difference a Day Makes."

On the following day, as we all crossed the solo traverse, a few rocks came whizzing down, humming past Craig's head. He didn't know whether to move backward or forward, but had little chance for an effective decision anyway, since his climbing harness slipped down around his legs. He simply ducked and hoped for the best, and the rocks all flew by him. I couldn't help feeling that this was an inauspicious greeting from the mountain. Looking back at Craig after his near disaster, I saw that even his climbing attire exhibited a certain flair. His jumars were bright yellow, hung with purple nylon webbing that attached them to his climbing harness. He wore black sunglasses and his electric black hair was tied back with a maroon and white woven scarf. None of this classic goggle-and-balaclava business for Craig. I sensed that he had always been a bit of a renegade.

Craig was as silly as Jim was funny, and had a wonderful deep chuckle. Craig and I went up close together, laughing over bits and pieces of nonsense under our heavy loads, while Jim and Ned, climbing ahead of us, were more intense and moved with a sense of urgency. When I began singing a song I had

Pumori climbing route.

made up, called the "Himalayan Hack," Craig paused, peered at me from under his corkscrew locks, and asked between his heavy breaths, "How can you *sing* up here?" I had to laugh. I had been unaware that I was this excited to be climbing again.

All four of us gathered on the perch, like satisfied hens on their roost, and clucked and cackled together over a snack. This was a favorite place of mine on the route because we could all sit so comfortably together on this island of rock surrounded by an ocean of ice, with a view spreading before us that few in the world would ever see.

A little higher up, on the staircase pitch, I was sandwiched between Ned and Jim. Those two set a mean pace, but the hard work felt good. I remembered how cold and fragile I'd felt on this pitch during our first attempt, when I bullied the haul-bag up. I had climbed with good speed then, but the additional strength I had now convinced me that nothing would keep us off the summit this time.

"Hold up for a second," Jim called back to Ned behind me. "I was just going to leave it, but why don't you check it, Ned—the ice screw by your hand."

I paused between Ned and Jim, balancing delicately on my front points while Ned, secure on a stance below, took out the ice screw. This left the line slack all the way from Jim down to Craig, but Craig wasn't aware of what was going on above and was tugging on the line. Jim saw me teeter-tottering below, trying to keep my feet in contact with the ice as the rope through my jumar swayed back and forth because of Craig's movements.

"Craig," Jim bellowed down. "Will you stop climbing and pulling on the rope! You're going to pop Jan off."

I hadn't been going to say anything, since I thought I could hang on until Ned got the screw in again. But Jim often seemed to have less patience with Craig than he had had with Steve, even though Craig was the more competent climber. I knew that Jim and Craig had been climbing partners in Yosemite, and wondered if that closeness made them harder on each other, as brothers often are.

I imagined that Steve was probably all the way back to Lukla by now. When he was leaving, he said, "I know I'm going to have to live with my decision if you guys make it." Yet somehow his delivery lacked conviction. I could see him weighing Pumori on the one hand and speed-skiing and his girlfriend on the other: The latter interests simply weighed heavier.

I realized that my mind had drifted, and I pulled myself back to where I stood, moving up so I wouldn't slow down our train. When my father caught me drifting off like this as a child, he would say, "Janet's traveling with the fairies again." But my mind's ability to travel has enabled me to sort out and cope with a variety of situations. Daydreaming is a natural protective instinct for me, as well as a positive force. I often imagine myself having completed the task I'm in the middle of performing. When I tentatively explained this to Jim once, he just looked at me and said, offhandedly, "That's how I direct the outcome of situations."

We reached the bottom of the ridge leading to the hole at one o'clock that afternoon. It had taken us only four hours to get the ropes up and secured in place—half as long as it took us to cover this ground on our first attempt. We rappelled back down to Advance Base Camp and curled up in the tents with steaming mugs of tea. We felt smug. It all seemed so easy this time. The next step was to carry everything up to the hole and make camp exactly where we'd had it before. Then we'd tote our gear up to the breadloaf, our previous high point, and set up a second camp. From the breadloaf, we figured we could make the summit round trip in a day.

The following day, December 31, was declared a rest day. We spent much of it discussing our subsequent climb over the three 20,000-foot passes that would complete our half-circle in Nepal. Thinking of more strenuous work before we'd even washed our hands of Pumori oppressed me. High-altitude mountaineering is, in fact, just a grueling, long-distance event—one that deals with time in terms of months, not hours. It's an event where mental fatigue may play a more debilitating role than physical stress. The real high points on an expedition are about as rare as natural pearls found in a bed of oysters. But with the perseverance of a strong mind and the willing ability to continue, these high points can be strung together like pearls on a necklace.

The next morning Jim announced that he wasn't feeling well, and wasn't up to climbing, so we spent New Year's Day in camp, waiting.

On January 2 we pushed hard up to the ridge where the gear had been tied in. Ned and Jim clipped their jumars onto the polypropylene rope left behind from the first attempt and made their way on up. Craig and I clipped on behind them, and again became a talkative duo climbing near each other.

This ridge was a narrow spine of rock partially covered with snow that had become a brittle crust. The sun, wind, and dry air at this altitude continually wore down the snow surface, making it ever thinner and more fragile. Consequently, foot placement was precarious at best. Occasionally, a rock might roll out from under my foot or the frozen, lacy ice would give way. Climbing this pitch a second time around gave me a deeper appreciation for the line Jim had artfully crocheted up through the intricate ridge on that dusky evening of our first attempt.

Our assault tents were too much trouble to assemble, considering that speed and efficiency meant so much this high in the mountains, so we brought up a larger two-person dome tent. This tent had been bombproof on our other expeditions, so we decided to use it again on Pumori. Ned, Jim, and I shared the larger dome tent, and Craig had one of the newly designed mountain tents to himself. The sleeping arrangements suited me—I eagerly accepted the warmth of the middle position between Ned and Jim. My concern was for Craig. Since he was the team's most recent acquisition, I didn't want this to make him feel like the odd man out. When I asked him if he felt cold and lonely in a tent by himself, he just chuckled and assured me he was fine.

The next day Ned and Craig descended to pull up some ropes and extra gear while Jim and I worked fixing the traverse out of the hole. We had planned to move camp up to the breadloaf the following day, but when we woke in the early morning the weather was ugly. When Craig unzipped our tent and crawled in, he revealed the whiteout outside. We were engulfed in a thick cloud.

"Doesn't look like today, does it?" he mumbled.

"I wouldn't want to take the chance of being caught out if this storm takes hold," Jim answered. He was anxious to get the climb over with, and I could feel our morale sinking. The climb had seemed so much easier and the organization so much smoother that I had never stopped to think we might not make it this second time around. But there are certain things about an expedition that can't be controlled, starting with the weather.

I knew at least one day had to be spent here at 21,000 feet in a two-man tent with three antsy teammates, surrounded by a storm, but the last thing I wanted was to listen to everyone's complaints and misgivings, so I scanned my mental files for entertainment. As it turned out, I had no trouble getting the rest of them to join me in a medley of rousing word games.

We ate eagerly the next morning: the weather had lifted, the sky was clear, and we were ready to go. Craig had been exceptionally quiet at breakfast, and his announcement explained why. "I don't feel too well, and I've got a headache that's getting worse. It might be the kerosene fumes in the tent, but it could be the altitude." Craig had never been this high before and didn't know if what he was feeling was normal or not. It was impossible for the rest of us to determine which condition Craig was suffering from.

The course of action that Craig chose left a lasting impression on me. I only hope that someday I can be so gracious. Although feeling good enough to climb, Craig was unsure if his condition would deteriorate, so he chose to rappel down and let the remaining three of us go up alone. His decision had nothing to do with fear for himself. He was just concerned he might jeopardize our summit success if he held us back. Craig was unselfishly thinking of the rest of us.

It took Ned, Jim, and me four hours to reach the breadloaf. Jim had lead the whole route with his own pack on this time, even up the exhausting 70-degree Swiss-cheese pitch. We nestled into our Camp II in tight to the icefall, protecting ourselves to the south and west and exposing ourselves to a gaping crevasse on the other side. I was absolutely elated to be here, despite my raw throat and hoarse cough. The "Himalayan hack" affected all three of us, especially when we had been working hard and breathing heavily. Ned and Jim were pleased to be here, too. Warm friendship and positive energy surrounded the three of us who had persevered to this point. If the next day dawned clear, we were on our way to the elusive summit at last.

The next day, January 6, the weather looked very stable. We left Camp II for the summit about nine, expecting to reach the summit in three hours. Now that we were climbing above where we had been before, my excitement returned.

The mood was upbeat and alive with energy; I was gleeful and Ned and Jim were playful. The first portion of the day was spent winding through the maze of the icefall, hopping a few crevasses, and scouting for the line of least resistance. The route steepened up a gully that looked as if a giant ice cream scoop had dredged down the mountain and peeled it out. More gradual snow slopes followed, with occasional steep pitches. After a morning of straightforward hard work, we paused for lunch, gazing at Everest and watching the soft clouds chase each other around its peak. We left our packs here, expecting to reach the summit in about an hour. Soon it became apparent that our estimate had been inaccurate. Jim began to hurry, and admitted that his feet were freezing and that he couldn't feel his toes. I was relieved that my thin cross-country inner boots left enough room in my boots for proper circulation. I had two overboots on as well, and Jim had on only one. Since our thermometers didn't go below minus 20 degrees Fahrenheit, we didn't know exactly how cold it was, but the wind was gusting up to about 40 miles per hour. The relaxed day had drawn a sense of urgency around itself.

Jim began to push himself with an intensity I hadn't seen. I was tied in behind him, hoofing as fast as I could manage. The rope became taut between Ned and me, and Ned assured me later that he wouldn't have wished for any faster pace. The last 500 feet were dotted with sastrugi snow cones two to three feet high created by the continuous high winds. Jim continued to charge ahead, even after it had become obvious that we would reach the summit. He was also winding in and out of these horns of snow and ice, so that I had to keep stopping to unwrap the rope from the horns. By the time I got the rope straightened out, I had to scramble straight up the steepest portions of the slope to avoid having the rope snap taut between us. It was exhausting. My breathing was coarse and uneven as I sucked in the air that was so cold and dry my throat felt like it was burning.

The wind was howling so fiercely we had no audible communication. Jim finally realized what he'd been putting his second through when he dashed up a ramp to the north side and continued across the summit plateau. The rope tightened between us and I faced an overhanging climb to reach the summit. When I stood my ground, Jim came to an abrupt halt. He retraced his steps over the elliptical plateau, realizing he'd have to leave me some slack to reach the ramp. I walked up slowly, still puffing, and stood at last on the summit. Only a few feet below, I had been protected, but on the small plateau the wind pushed me around and stung my face. I had no time to savor reaching the top, since I had to belay Ned, giving him plenty of length to negotiate the ramp. As Ned moved up, Jim began jumping and stomping around. I wondered if Jim had gone crazy, then remembered his feet. Meanwhile Ned began circling us, snapping what seemed at the time hundreds of photographs. It was probably about 30 below zero Fahrenheit, and the wind was blowing at least 60 miles an hour. It was a slicing, noisy cold. The roar of the wind killed all other sound, so I was observing Ned and Jim as if I were watching a movie. Then I was suddenly pulled into the scene as Jim began to howl like an animal. He wanted off. He looked at me and I threw my arm in the direction of the ramp, indicating as best I could, "Let's get the hell out of here." Ned, oblivious, was pulling on the rope in the opposite direction, furiously recording the event. While Jim and Ned had been moving about the summit, I had been stationary, gazing at the 360-degree view. Situated between the two of them, I was subject to the maypole effect: they had wrapped the rope around me and I was working frantically to untangle the mess.

I tugged on the rope to Ned, urging him to come along as I tumbled after Jim down the ramp. Once under the overhang of the summit, we could hear one another as we shouted.

Jim was frantic about his feet and was worried about whether Ned and I could keep up with his rate of descent. I told Jim to go ahead and untie if he felt comfortable alone, and he was off like a desperate rabbit. Ned looked up from the tangled mess of rope he was trying to unravel and glared at me as he saw Jim disappear. I grabbed the rope from Ned, coiled it, and we tied in closer together. Ned was angry not because I'd made an erroneous decision, but because I'd taken charge without consulting him.

NED: I was last on the rope, and so last up to the top. I had imagined a pinpoint summit; I found a dance floor. This was the summit! We'd done it! My first feeling was of exuberant celebration. I clenched both fists and threw up my arms into the wind. "Yeah!" I shouted, triumphant. Jan and Jim were standing in the center of the summit area, their bodies cocked toward the west, leaning into the wind. They looked like frozen mannequins, their arms blowing about. In my fatigue, it was funny in an odd way. For a moment, the fight had gone out of us. A remark I had once heard popped into my head: "The only thing worse than failing is reaching your goal." Then another bullying gust shoved us, and we snapped back into the professional efficiency that had brought success on the second attempt.

Jim stamped about on the snow, roaring like a bull, maniacally anxious about his freezing feet. On the other end of our 600-foot polypropylene rope, I backed up, preoccupied with photography. It was awkward to manipulate a tiny 35-mm camera while wearing bulky mittens. Although I snapped only 15 photos, the others were impatient with my request to pose. Between us, tied into the center of the rope, Jan tried to keep all the loose rope lying about in some order.

I fixed my eyes on Everest even as the wind slammed me back and forth. From this distance, in the clear air of winter, the big mountain looked beautifully groomed and perfectly formed. I felt a lingering pride for the three of us having made it to the top of Pumori. When I turned toward the north, I could see at least 100 miles across the brown landscape of Tibet. There was a certain unburdened timelessness to the minutes we spent on Pumori. Then we retreated down under the cornice, escaping the wind.

"My feet are gone!" Jim cried, throwing off the rope. "I'll see you at camp." He turned and ran down the mountain like an escaping desperado. His moonlike bounds seemed to defy gravity.

Jan and I, roped together, started down the summit headwall at a much slower rate. At first we had far too much rope between us, so loops snagged again and again on the sastrugi formations. Usually we yanked it free, but the release tipped us dangerously off balance. When the loops cut deeply into the hard snow lumps, we were forced to retrace our steps to free the rope. It was slow and exasperating progress. At the bottom of the headwall I again coiled all but 60 feet of the offensive tether we used to tie ourselves together. I slung it over one shoulder, but the coil was so big that it dragged on the ground and threatened to trip me. Once I snared a crampon in a loop and sprawled on the snow slope. I cursed the coil again and again. Jan thought I was angry at her, but it was the awkwardness of traveling with the coil of rope that made me impatient.

I kept close track of the time. Here on the East Face the shadows intensified early, and their deep blue hue seemed to make the cold penetrate deeper. Even though our position on the eastern side of the mountain provided a lee, the west wind eddied around the mountain, hitting us in small, pulsating cyclones.

Our progress was slow, but steady. Occasionally we exchanged a few words of information or encouragement, but mostly we down-climbed silently, concentrating on each step. The snow was so hard that our uphill footprints had left scant impression, and we temporarily lost sight of them. We found our old tracks again near the bottom of the summit pyramid. They led us through the seracs that tilted crazily against each other, then down a steep couloir where one slip could have sent us tumbling onto the lower part of the mountain. Traversing to more moderate ground, we zigzagged around a group of crevasses and walked along the ridge with one foot in Nepal and the other in Tibet. I finally caught a glimpse of our tent snugged under a little cornice. We hailed Jim, who stuck his head out to greet us. Jan and I flopped down on the snow in front of the tent and asked Jim about his feet. "They're fine but prickly," he said.

Jim had prepared cups of steaming tea. Jan and I sat on the snow, sipping and basking in the glow of success. We didn't bother to remove our crampons and overboots for several minutes. Laughing, I chided Jim about his prediction earlier that day that the summit was "a half-hour away." From that point we had moved upward for two-and-a-half hours. Jim just chuckled good-naturedly.

Later, inside the darkening tent, we kept the stove fired up and churned out cup after cup of hot tea and orange drink. I felt an immense, smooth satisfaction. We had made the top, but there was more. We had finally consolidated into an efficient team during our second assault. Once we were acclimatized, we had been energetic and decisive, always moving along at a steady clip. Our efficiency made the climbing far easier than it had been during the first attempt, and we had learned to read the weather more accurately. We had become the first Americans to climb successfully in the Himalaya in the winter, and Jan was the first woman to do so. Yet that in no way overshadowed the spontaneous enjoyment we felt from simply being here with good friends. I admired Craig's decision to descend from Camp I in order not to jeopardize our chances. Now that we had been successful, we all had a sense of humor about the whole climb, and spent much of the evening chuckling about what we now saw as minor mishaps.

Clear skies and light winds greeted us the next morning. When we descended to Camp I, it looked like a messy hobo encampment, littered with clumps of discarded food and yellow pee-holes. Once the Camp I gear had been loaded into our packs, they each weighed about 45 pounds, which we knew would make the rappels awkward. We decided to push on, though it was already afternoon.

Getting the 600-foot rope down was a problem, since nobody wanted to carry it down the first series of fixed-rope rappels. Jim suggested, since he was first down, that he tie it to his waist and "pull" it down as he descended. The plan was for me to pay it out until he got to the next major stance, which was exactly 600 feet down. There he would pull the rope through all the pieces of protection, and so have it available to rig below, where there was no fixed rope.

This was the most intricate part of the mountain: the route wove back and forth on both sides of the rock and snow ridge, along traverses, down couloirs. Jim quickly descended out of sight, pulling the rope. Soon I paid out enough that it was impossible to distinguish by feel between its own weight and Jim's progress.

"Jim seems to be rappelling amazingly fast," I remarked to Jan.

When all the rope was out, I dropped the end, as planned. It snaked down out of sight, and I started my rappel. When I got to the big couloir, I was amazed to discover nearly the entire length there in a great, horrid, tangled wad. Jim, out of sight farther down, was yelling furiously. The rope was so entangled that it had arrested his rappel, and of course he assumed that I was still holding the end. From his expletives, I gathered that he had been hung up for a long time.

I tried to shout and explain the situation to him, but we were too far apart for him to understand much. I now faced the unpleasant and dangerous job of climbing down the couloir unbelayed and gathering 400 feet of unruly rope. I plucked the maverick loops off the ice and hung them in disarray on myself, all the while standing on the front points of my crampons. I climbed back up, ludicrously hampered, cursing and cursing and cursing. Jan, descending, was appalled by the sight and sound. She waited while I took 20 minutes more to sort out the mess and release poor Jim.

When we joined Jim, he hurriedly cast the long rope off for the next rappel. The anchor was an ice bollard that now measured six inches across. At the beginning of the climb, when we had first used it, it had been two feet across. The sun, even in winter, had reduced it. Jim started sliding down the rope, but once again it had hung up, and lay tangled on the stairway. At this point Jim lost his cool, fuming and cursing when he had to stop every few feet to tug the rope free. Finally we all descended to the lower ropes, and rappelled them. Then, for the last time, we traversed toward Advance Base Camp in gathering dusk.

Anu, Angpura, and Craig were waiting on the ledges above Advance Base Camp to take our packs. By the light of a full moon that poked over the North Ridge of Everest, we followed them back to Base Camp.

JAN: Ned and I eased our way back down to camp, talking and looking. Jim had dashed down over an hour faster, and had tea ready and his toes protected by the time we arrived. Dusk began drifting in around our tent as I lay down, coughing after all the hard work. Jim kept badgering me affectionately, calling me a pinhead because I wouldn't eat some chocolate he had out for me. I knew I would throw it up, but he persisted, so I pushed it down, then promptly deposited it outside. This time I knew I could safely say, "I told you so." When I laughed, Jim just looked at me quizzically, unsure why I saw humor in the situation. He kept looking at me and said, "I have never seen a face as determined as yours was today."

"I didn't think you turned around long enough to focus on anything. You were wild. I had to dredge up any grit I had to stay on your trail." The day had been long and arduous, and now the paramount emotion was relief.

Our descent off the mountain was quick, and so were our tempers. Ned screamed when the slack rope between him and Jim caught in a gully; Jim swore all the way down the staircase over a tangle in the rope; and I tripped on the bergschrund, fell flat on the ice, and cursed myself for getting cut. We were letting out what we'd been holding in during the ascent.

Two days later I was sitting on a box in the cook tent at Base Camp, swinging my legs absentmindedly, surrounded by warming steam, bubbling pots, and good smells. The heat felt wonderful, and the level ground gave me such a feeling of freedom. I didn't have to be conscious of every foot and hand placement, as I had been on steeper territory. Down here I could walk where I wished when I wished.

I peered out of the tent and saw Saile floating into camp carrying a load of wood. Even when encumbered, she moved with a shy grace. When I stepped out of the tent to greet her, she flashed a big grin, pointed up at Pumori, and nodded her head up and down vigorously. I reflected her smile and slowly nodded "yes." At that moment, the initial emotion of relief was replaced by a growing deep, smooth satisfaction. For me, successfully climbing a peak doesn't bring about elation, just a strong, satisfied feeling that I accomplished what I set out to do. I was pleased to tell Saile that I had made it.

NED: My muscles twitched with fatigue, as if I were plugged into a faint electrical current. Kukari rum stung my mouth, slowed my brain. The celebratory dinner that the Sherpas had served bulged my stomach.

It was the evening of January 8. Two days before we had stood on top of Pumori. Now, lying belly up at Base Camp in a happy, light alcoholic haze, we laughed and remembered the highlights of the climb.

Then the mountain came apart.

There was no warning. The night was still; then it was filled with a roar that lunged upon us like a fast freight train bursting from a tunnel. Strangely hypnotized by the mountain's bellow, no one moved for a moment. Then the four of us spurted through the tent doorway and into the moon-flooded night.

"Avalanche!" Jim gasped.

Ice cliffs high on the East Face had collapsed. Falling, they had toppled other blocks and towers. An entire quarter of the mountain in our view was exploding. On the leading edge, a vast snow cloud reared into the air. We stood distant—safe, yet tense. We were more than detached spectators. The avalanche swept over the lower part of our climbing route, where we had been little more than 24 hours before. We could have been under that avalanche.

The rumble subsided, then rose again, echoing off the walls of Everest as the snow cloud settled. Then we were wrapped once again in quiet moonlight.

10

HIGH PASSES

"Skip it! If I'm going to die, I should do it alone."

Jan Reynolds

JAN: 

The morning after the avalanche, the yaks and porters arrived. We left Base Camp for Namche, where Ned, Craig, and I rested for two days. Jim, his job done, headed home.

"Can't wait to watch 'Sesame Street' with Layton," he called back over his shoulder as he started walking south, toward Kathmandu and home.

The three of us who remained settled into a relaxed pattern of eating and lounging in the sunshine outside Anu's house. Now and then we'd stir enough to sort through a portion of our gear, repair a piece of broken equipment, or talk of the upcoming trek.

Early one morning in Namche, Ned woke me to solicit my opinion.

"We could actually hike the local trails all the way around to Makalu and then just a bit beyond the peak to the border. We'd simply be swinging a wider circle around Everest, instead of the tight one going over the high passes," he told me. I made the mistake of taking Ned's suppositions seriously. I liked the idea of immersing ourselves in the local culture, of weaving ourselves into the lives of the people who lived here as we trekked the trails. I was satisfied with my climb on Pumori. The Nepalese people had captured my interest now, and I was more than willing to trade the hard grunt work of climbing isolated passes for fascinating social enrichment in local villages along the trails.

I didn't realize immediately that Ned was merely toying with options, that he never really considered changing our original plan. I wished I'd known that earlier before I began feeling there were several good reasons for swinging wide around Everest: better photographic possibilities, more cultural information for a book, on and on. Perhaps I was a pest, but not a fool. When it became obvious that I wasn't making any headway, I hardened myself for more high, exposed, cold-weather travel.

NED: Jan and I had different routes in mind by which to accomplish the next leg of the circle, but we agreed on the final goal: swing south around Everest to try to reach the border on the east side, near Makalu—at 27,790 feet, the fifth highest mountain in the world. There were two choices. We could climb over three 20,000-foot passes—each nearly as high as Mount McKinley, North America's tallest peak; or we could swing farther south along forested trekking paths at considerable distance from Everest.

The morning after Jim left, Jan and I sat talking on a stone wall, each pleading our case. She summed up her argument by saying of mine: "It's silly.

Why risk the mountains again? Sometimes I think you ask too much. Too much from luck, too much from the Sherpas, too much from me."

We talked on, searching for a solution with which we would both be satisfied. I wanted to go over the three high passes; that was the original plan and had style and adventure. It was mountaineering, not trekking. It also kept us close in under Everest, and my sense of the Grand Circle was that we should be able to see the mountain from any point on our route. The weather was still good, the snow was still perfect for traveling, and we were still reasonably strong.

Since the latter part of our climb of Pumori, Jan had been gently lobbying for amending the itinerary. Why?

"Maybe it's woman's intuition," she said. "I'm superstitious that something bad is going to hit us. It's not my head, but my heart that I'm listening to. And the fact that we'd have more time in the villages, which I like."

Intuition is important; but I didn't want to make such a major change in plans unless it was backed up by fact. As far as I could see, there was no solid reason to shift the course of the expedition. A few days earlier Jim had said to me jokingly: "Ned, as leader, never let the democratic process take over!" But Jan and I were fifty-fifty partners in this venture, and I didn't want any irreparable division at this point. Craig and I could do the passes alone, but I wouldn't have felt right about leaving Jan behind.

"Tea is ready," Anu called from the upper window of his house. We were saved from an immediate decision. Jan and I put on sweaters and went inside. As usual, it was cold and dark, but the sweet milk tea offset our instant chill.

"I have asked again our boss to let us carry for you over the passes," Anu said. "He says no Sherpas must go there in winter time. Too dangerous. We must fly to Kathmandu, then fly to Tumlingtar, then trek in on the lowland route and meet you on other side. Bad news also. Phutashi must not go. His mother asked high lama. Lama says very bad luck to go Makalu."

"Just bad luck for Phutashi?" Jan asked, not looking up from her tea.

"Yes, yes," Anu answered quickly. "Okay for you. Okay for Angpura and me. We walk in from other side. Meet you at Makalu Base Camp. Now we decide when we meet you."

Craig, Jan, and I spread out the map. "It'll take about a week to traverse the high passes," Jan announced, as if there had never been a question in her mind. I grinned. Apparently she had made a decision.

Now it was my turn to worry. I had heard many horror stories of parties getting stranded on long treks, especially in Alaska, while depending on hired help to bring in food caches. But we had no choice. If we went unsupported without porters, we couldn't carry enough supplies to make it to Makalu, then to the border, and then out to the nearest village. We worked out a precise time schedule and precise meeting location with Anu. It would be absolutely critical not to miss connections, especially in the winter, when the high country was deserted. There would be little chance of aid or rescue if things went wrong.

The next day Anu and Angpura headed south to Kathmandu. They took with them all the excess gear that we would not need on the passes, including our skis. My instructions to Anu were to bring them into Makalu Base Camp so we could use them to ski up the Barun Glacier to the border.

JAN: We bid farewell to Anu and Angpura. They would not be climbing the passes with us, but would fly back to Kathmandu and on to Tumlingtar, and then trek in to meet us when our half-circle was completed. It would be a chancy rendezvous, since Anu wasn't familiar with the area where we had planned to meet. We simply trusted our luck and Anu's good sense to see that we would both reach the same vicinity at the agreed upon time.

NED: We left Namche and headed up the Khumbu once again. Phutashi, his brother Pudashi, who helped carry loads in this section, accompanied us.

I had grown to like Craig very much during the three weeks since he had arrived out of the blue at Base Camp. He was a jolly, tall, square-built man with a shock of unruly hair, a rock-steady gaze, and a resolute decisiveness. He worked hard and appreciated the chance to come to the Himalaya. There was a lot of Italian in him, "Mafia blood," as he put it. But the Latin fire burned serenely inside, tempered by California living. A shrug and a laugh were enough to answer any question. "Mañana" was good enough, he said; but by tomorrow a lot had always been done.

He was a carpenter in the summer (usually in Alaska) and chained-up autos heading over Donner Pass in the winter. He was not famous. He held life so easily that he was always where he wanted to be, like an eternally satisfied gypsy. His only tie that bound was a post office box.

The next morning Craig and I walked together as we set out for Mingbo. He told me that he had been a very good speed skier—fifth in the world at one time—but never top dog, and that seemed to bother him.

"I've got the talent. I know that. One good run and I can get the record. One good run. I ain't finished yet."

Yet he was here on an expedition during speed-skiing season.

"I once had the world's record fall," he continued. "In 1978 at the Kilometro Lanciato. Stalled in the compression and hit the snow face-first at 193 kilometers per hour. It didn't hurt, 'cause I got knocked unconscious.' I don't remember a thing. They say the helicopter crew that flew me to the hospital flipped out when they stripped off my vinyl stretch suit—I didn't have a thing on underneath!"

His laugh punctuated each sentence. He liked the story, and told it in his particular kind of self-deprecating slang.

"In those days I had a plaited ponytail. I was naked except for my dark glasses when they wheeled me into the hospital. They slapped me in the mental ward! When I woke up it was impossible to get released. So I snuck out. McKinney found me wandering around Cervinia in slippers and a bathrobe!"

Miraculously, the weather still held. Although there were thin, scalloped clouds high in the sky, we walked in sunshine and mild temperatures. For some reason, I was confident that we would make it over the passes before the long overdue winter storms caught us.

We had made two critical decisions. First, we had left our skis behind. The original plan had been to ski over the passes, and without skis, we ran the risk of getting snowed in on the glacier plateaus. But no significant snow had fallen during the previous two months. The ground was bare and the glacier surfaces were bullet-proof hard. The short stretches of snow we might find to ski did not warrant toting the extra weight of skis. Using climbing boots and crampons on the icy sections, we would walk the 30 miles from the Khumbu to Makalu. What had started as a ski trek around Everest had, unexpectedly, turned into a climbing jaunt.

Second, we would carry food for only six days—enough for minimal travel time to Makalu. Like skis, emergency food would be too weighty. There was no surplus to wait out a long storm comfortably, or to cover a trek out from Makalu if we missed the meeting with Anu.

A couple of miles north of Pangboche we turned east, left the main trail to Everest, and descended to cross the Imja Khola on a narrow bridge built of two logs. We climbed out of the gorge, then continued steadily upward along yak trails that meandered through stubbly pastures. As we headed up ancient moraines into the Mingbo Valley, only a few miles away from the "freeway" Khumbu trail, the country was untraveled.

At noon we came to the summer herders' village of Mingbo. "Best stop here," announced Phutashi. "Short day. Long day tomorrow to glacier."

The elevation was 15,000 feet. Ama Dablam, "mother's charm box," dominated the northern horizon. A bleak, jagged mountain flank closed us in from the south. Low stone walls had been built to form corrals, and two stone huts roofed with large slabs of rock bulged out of the narrow lines. The sun was warm in the still air. We lounged about all afternoon on the brown grass, and put the next day's trials out of our minds.

I woke from a nap to the giggle of girls. Two Sherpanis had arrived to fetch hay stored in the stone huts. They flirted shyly with Phutashi and Pudashi; then, as the cold afternoon shadow crept over camp, they departed under huge haystacks perched on their backs. When Phutashi resumed cooking, smoke squirted out of every hole of the hut. It looked as though the rocks were on fire.

Craig walked out to the edge of the pasture, and stood silhouetted against a gun-metal sky. Billowing clouds rolled up the Khumbu, filling the valley to within 500 feet of our campsite. The fortresslike bulk of Taweche rose out of the western sky. From my vantage point I could see Pumori peeking around Ama Dablam's shoulder. As the first star winked, Jan played "Wayfaring Stranger" on her recorder.

JAN: We calculated that the three 20,000-foot passes—Mingbo La, West Col, and Sherpani Col—would take us about a week. We packed accordingly, carrying our homes on our backs like turtles. There was no opportunity to cache supplies anywhere along the way, so we were forced to carry absolutely everything we thought we'd need, as well as a limited supply of food. I felt like a feminine Atlas bearing up under my load.

January 15 found us leaning lazily against a stone barn in the high country pastures below the billowing skirts of Ama Dablam. The sun on the stone was warm and comforting as I pressed my tired back against it. With my eyes closed, my mind wandered freely. I heard Craig, lying in the grass beside me, begin to snore lightly. We were camping here for the night, intending to position ourselves strategically below the Mingbo La the next day.

I had lost between 10 and 15 pounds this far into the circle, and our packs were the heaviest yet. Starting up again today made me feel like an unambitious kid being sent to summer camp by her parents against her own will. Even Ned, the strong man, said that he felt as if he were "walking under water." The engines were reluctant to turn over. Craig had the best solution—to doze in the sun—because from here on it was ice and snow again.

I had neatly tucked away my wishes for an easier cruise around Everest. That wasn't what bothered me. What did was wrestling with the change in attitude since Jim had left us for his home in the States. His good humor had balanced Ned's frequent gloominess, and had added snap and color to our conversations. He had also shown a certain respect for my attitude and suggestions. Suddenly I felt as if I had been demoted to the class of draft horses and yaks. It was easier to excuse Craig, who had been thrown in with two strangers. Since Ned seemed to be *le grand fromage,* Craig stuck close to him, seconding his decisions. It irked me when Ned and Craig ignored my comments as they discussed our route over the open map, or folded the map up before I got my two cents in. I was disturbed that Ned had not heeded my calculations concerning money and the number of porters we needed. We ended up, just as I suspected, short of cash and asking our Sherpas to carry more than they should have. Several times I had to remind myself to cool off, that regardless of minor muck-ups we would ultimately get where we were going, that that's what mattered. I tried to relax and enjoy letting Ned and Craig run the show.

NED: The next day's excursion took us up seven miles to the end of the Mingbo Valley as we skirted the base of Ama Dablam. The narrow, precipitous gorge broadened as it rose, ending in a glacial amphitheater, where a dozen glaciers converged like spokes on a wheel. There was no trail. We each followed our own direction, clambering among boulders that once rode the backs of glaciers and now waited for the next flood of frozen tide. We pitched our tents on a prong of tiered granite separating two tongues of ice. Waiting for dinner, I poked about on the beautiful rock.

As I looked under the eaves of a big rock, I saw shrouded human legs sticking out from under a crude stone wall. I started back with a prickly chill. But instead of turning, I bent to look closer. Seeing the outline of a body, I finally realized that I was looking into a grave. I told Jan of my discovery, but she didn't share my interest and didn't want to go look.

The sinking sun smeared a yellowish-red tint over our rocky home and an inferno of fiery clouds moved up the valley toward us. We were living near a dead man. I thought about black magic and white magic. The power of Buddhism is that there are specific methods for dealing with obstacles on the path to enlightenment, and thus with the demonic. There are many fierce deities that are malignant unless they are befriended.

Walking over to Phutashi, I said, "There is a dead man under that rock."

"He was expedition porter. Very sick. No doctor. No *jangris.* Not get better. I know him."

Three decades ago two dozen jangris, or shamans, lived in the Khumbu. They were medicine men, or healers. Unlike priests, who dealt with gods, shamans wrestled with demons, which were thought to bring on sickness. At one time, the shamans were greatly feared by villagers: the most effective healers were the most feared. Today there are only four or five shamans in the Khumbu. I asked Phutashi why.

"Hospitals," he replied. Doctors using modern medical techniques have for the most part replaced shamans as treaters of the sick.

"How does a man become a jangris?" I asked.

"Sometimes choose people that very sick, then get better. When sick, they very close to demons, so know them. Maybe they don't want to be jangris; they have other plans for life. But they must."

White, or right-handed, magic was always supposed to be directed toward the light. It became black when a shaman took it for his own; when he succumbed to temptation. But Tibetan Buddhism, which influenced the Sherpas, still didn't see the good and bad of a shaman in absolute terms, as we in the West would. The magic was more like obstacles on the way to enlightenment. The dark side sometimes grew out of what was inherently good: Shamans with black magic sometimes made people sick.

"The Sherpa under the rock," Phutashi concluded, "died in the night. At night, jangris can work backward. Magic not good. Work with left hand, making magic go backward. Make people sick. Can heal in morning, but sometimes too late."

Far above our campsite, whitish clouds that had lost the last fiery light of the sunset moved among peaks tattooed with glistening, white flutings. It seemed like a physical manifestation of white magic, an umbrella of good luck.

The next morning, January 17, we got ready to leave Phutashi, Pudashi, and our four porters. Craig and Jan hoisted their packs onto their shoulders, hugged everyone, and started off. Phutashi tugged at my arm, pulling me aside. He slid a silver ring with a knob of imitation coral and jade off his finger. Lowering his head shyly, he pressed it into my hand. "This from my aunt in Tibet. Don't sell it. For you."

I accepted it silently and put it on my finger. I hugged him, said "namaste," then turned and followed Craig and Jan, my movements stiff in the early chill. My double boots padded over the rock, crunched through the ice that filled little depressions. The ski poles I used as walking sticks tapped the rock. I turned a bulge of rock and passed out of sight of the Sherpas. We were on our own, a tiny group heading into remote, wild country. I felt no apprehension, didn't think there was any black magic clouding our travels. But I was expectant in a low-key way, as if psyching up for a demanding sporting event still hours away.

JAN: I took my pulse as I heaved up to the height of the Mingbo La, 500 feet on a 50-degree snow slope. It was 100 beats per minute and pumping harder as I approached 19,000 feet under about 60 pounds. I had a negative mantra going, whispering over and over to myself as my breath hissed out, "I hate this so much." Ever-cheerful Jan had an attitude problem, but somehow my angry energy fueled me up and over the pass. And my grumpiness dissolved altogether when I viewed the new terrain from the crest of the pass. The valley was austere, serene, beautiful. A gradual gradient on the backside of the pass met with a frozen stream that curled into a lake. I was soothed by the scene's desolate calm.

To get off the glacier at the bottom of the pass and onto the stream, we had to negotiate some irregular ice that looked like crystallized froth. It supported my weight, but I had to step lightly, picking the most solid looking route through the maze. I reached a spot where I would have to jump down three feet to the next level—I could just see myself shattering through the intricate icy lace on impact. Instead I sat down, rolled onto my belly, and lowered myself to the next level. Ned laughed so hard when he saw this unorthodox move that I started giggling too.

"You might be low on style points with that technique, Jano, but it looks like it works to me," he yelled over, checking to make sure I was laughing and not offended. The tables had turned. Now Ned had to watch out for someone else's grumps.

We settled camp on a frozen sandy shore of the lake. There was little snow, and I laughed to myself, remembering that this was supposed to have been a ski trip.

Something out there somewhere figured that if Jan was slipping into a crotchety mood, maybe she needed something to really be crotchety about. That evening as Craig, Ned, and I settled into the two-man dome tent together, something smiled on me with a diabolical grin.

First my inflatable mat went flat. I had carried this heavier mat instead of a closed-cell foam pad because I thought the comfort and the extra insulation from the cold ground would be worth it. I had compensated for its extra weight by taking my lightest down bag. Now my deflated pad was close to useless for anything.

Ned lit the stove to brew some tea before dinner, hoping to dispel my melancholy. But then he accidentally dumped the pot of water on my thin sleeping bag, matting down the precious feathers. I thought nothing else could happen to make my night more cold and miserable, but I was wrong. The tent zipper broke on my side and the breeze came surging over me.

I had tried to play down the fact that my mat was destroyed, I had rebuffed Ned's and Craig's teasing, I had excused Ned for spilling the pot. But when the zipper broke, I couldn't help it—I burst out laughing. Ned and Craig joined in, and my ill humor faded into the night.

NED: We started up the glacier that led to Mingbo La, a pass over 19,000 feet high. The bare ice had been rumpled by past sun melt and water erosion, and lacy hoarfrost decorated the surface of a frozen meltwater lake nestling in a pocket. On the other side of the lake the ice steepened. We sat down to put on crampons, then continued up into a small ice canyon that turned out to be a cul-de-sac. We roped up and Craig led a pitch on 65-degree ice out of the canyon. The wall was a giant pincushion of ice spears, and debris showered down as he knocked his way upward. Jan and I followed, then I led up the final steps to the top and through a crisscross of crevasses.

We found ourselves on a smooth snowfield leading to the foot of the pass. We were close to the location of the "Silver Hut" study of the effects of high altitude, which was conducted in 1960. The prefabricated building that housed it, with its aluminum foil skin, was temporarily the highest dwelling in the world, at 18,765 feet. The investigators found that after a period of deterioration, the bodies of those working at high altitude showed physiological adaptations to the environment, including new capillaries and increased hemoglobin.

At the foot of Mingbo La, we unslung our packs and rested, nibbling dried fruit and chocolate. The slope above us rose at a moderately steep angle and was unusually symmetrical. Like a necklace, the crest draped evenly between peaks on either side. A series of perfectly matched runnels of hard snow ran parallel from the top of the pass to the bottom.

"Take your pick," Craig said after eyeing each line. "Any of the grooves will get us up and over. It's just a matter of being in the prettiest one."

We chose the centermost runnel. Trailing our single 9-mm rope, I led over a small bergschrund, then climbed up and diagonally left across the 60-foot-wide couloir. The snow was hard—perfect for secure cramponing. I balanced by using my ice axe like a cane in my uphill hand, and moved quickly to a stance on a clump of rocks. The others joined me. Below, over a mile away, we could see the Sherpas retreating in a line toward home.

Craig took the next two pitches, tackling the midsection straight up the center. He hoisted himself with methodical front-pointing—chunk, chunk, chunk. But with three of us tied into the same rope, he was limited to leading out only half-lengths before he was forced to stop and belay Jan and me up to him. We did two short pitches in this style, then at the end of the third pitch, the solid snow suddenly turned into ice. It was so hard Craig couldn't get an ice screw in. He anchored himself by draping a sling around a small rock that stuck out of the ice no more than six inches. Jan, then I, climbed up to him. He had chopped out a tiny platform and we huddled precariously, our bulky packs awkward, shifting carefully to keep from knocking each other off.

"Don't pull outward on the sling," Craig advised. "It'll slip off."

The half-rope leads were slow. It looked like about 150 feet to the top—one full rope length. To speed progress, I decided to tie in a dozen feet behind Craig so that he and I could climb together and run out the rope. Jan belayed us.

Craig and I started up moving in synchronized fashion. We were so close together that one miscue by either would probably have pulled the other off. If that happened, it was doubtful that Jan would be able to stop the fall; all three of us would tumble to the bottom. But the slope reared upward at a constant angle and we moved onto hard, chalk-like snow again. The conditions were perfect for choreographed climbing. Strangely, it did not seem dangerous, such was our relaxed concentration.

Then, 40 feet from the top, the snow ended. Hard ice ran to the crest, which was guarded by a small cornice. We each had only one ice axe. On hard ice, climbers usually use two tools, one in each hand. But we were committed. Wordlessly, we inched up to the cornice. We swung our axes into each new placement with careful precision. Our front points penetrated only half their length into the ice, and the wind rocked us to and fro as we clung to the slope.

We made it to the cornice, but as Craig made his last move, his ski poles—which were strapped to his pack and sticking up over his head—jammed into the underside of the bulge. The sharp arrest nearly tipped him over backward, but he regained his balance. Coolly, he surveyed the problem. The cornice was too steep and unpredictable to haul himself up and over using a single tool. So Craig chopped through it, swinging his axe overhead to clear a passage. All the while he stood balanced on the points of his nonrigid crampons, which flexed slightly under his boot sole. From my stance a few feet below, I watched the operation apprehensively. I could imagine his calves starting to burn from the long, intense stance on his front points. I looked down the length of the rope to Jan, far below. The rope ran cleanly. We had put in no protection during the entire lead, since the footing had been secure on the hard névé snow.

His hacking finished, Craig moved up into the shallow slot. But once again his ski poles stuck into the cornice. He tried to wrench them free with brute force—I could hear him grunting. But they were solidly jammed. Finally he chipped them out with his ice axe, then, with a huge effort, hauled himself to safety onto the snowy ridgeline. I climbed to the top. Craig sat on the snow, done in. I congratulated him, then turned and shouted to Jan to come up, belaying her progress.

As soon as Jan arrived we scurried off the ridge to escape the wind. We jumped a couple of small crevasses, then emerged onto a gentle slope that led downward toward the valley floor. It was three o'clock in the afternoon. We stopped briefly to rest and view our new surroundings. This was an exciting moment, for we looked into an area that, for us, was unknown country. To the east spread a vast, bowl-like valley crowned all around by large peaks. This was the valley of the Hongu Khola. With the map, we identified Baruntse, 23,688 feet, and Chamlang, 24,012 feet. Glaciers spilled down from all sides of the circular valley. Great moraines had been piled higher than the glaciers themselves, a sign that larger glaciers had been at work in the past. Nowhere did there seem to be a sign of life amid this rawness. Beyond the mountains of the Hongu a granite pyramid broke the top line of the valley and dominated even the closer peaks. That was Makalu.

Once over the pass, we walked into a world far removed from the relative luxuries of the Khumbu and the Sherpa culture. Here we faced a different risk than we had dealt with on Pumori's technical flanks. We carried no radio, since we wouldn't be within communication range of anyone, so if there were problems or injuries we would have no swift way to summon assistance.

The risks of a small party moving over great expanses of uninhabited and untraveled wilderness terrain, more than gymnastic climbing, had been my specialty during past ski mountaineering expeditions. I referred to those expeditions on light cross-country skis in the great ranges of the world as "adventure skiing." Risk is subjective: it depends on the individual's level of experience and skill, as well as his or her disposition and physical fitness. Familiarity minimizes risk. I was familiar and at ease with the kind of risk we now assumed on Nepal's high passes in midwinter.

I had not been as familiar as Jim was with the risk on Pumori. Over the years I had developed a moderate degree of climbing expertise—enough to haul myself up Yosemite's El Capitan, but not enough to do the most demanding free climbs. After 10 years devoted to cross-country ski racing, I was interested in something less specialized that would draw on a variety of skills: the ability to move safely, quickly, shrewdly over mountainous terrain, and the proficiency to climb ice and rock where skiing gave out. I saw climbing not as an end in itself, but as a means to an end: traveling over vast areas of peaks and glaciers, traversing on skis where it was possible, climbing where it was necessary. I owed a great deal to my self-imposed limitations as a climber, because they enabled me to keep my focus on skiing and develop my expertise as an ex-Olympic skier. The combination encouraged me to carve out my own niche and follow my own direction as an adventure skier at a time when little ski mountaineering was being done by Americans. I determined to lay claim to being one of the more imaginative expeditioneers of the day.

As we continued downward from Mingbo La, the glacier was deep in shadow. We walked two miles on glacial snow that lay as smooth as a carpet. It would have been perfect for skiing, but ahead we could see a vast expanse of bare ground. But the footing was solid and we made good time. Our immersion in pristine country compensated for our lack of skis and growing fatigue.

To the north, beyond an intermediary ridge, Everest appeared. A plume boiled from the top, and the west wind flung it toward us, veiling the East Face as if half the mountain were a steaming volcano.

It was getting dark as we neared the end of the glacier. To avoid the crevasses guarding the snout, we moved to our right and followed a frozen stream that snaked along the boundary between rock and ice. It fell in little waterfalls, and we cramponed down each one.

Craig quickened his pace, saying, "I want to be off this slippery roller coaster before the light goes and it gets any colder. I'm headed for a campsite on dry ground."

I speeded up to stay with him. It was a merry pace, but not a race—simply a good feeling of charged-up activity that would put a punch into the end of the day.

"Hold on," Jan shouted. "No way can I move that fast in this light."

"Just stay on the stream," I yelled back. "If we head off it, I'll wait." I took a couple of steps forward. Craig was moving on rapidly.

"Okay, big man. Go with Craig."

I stopped, frozen in place by Jan's desperately disappointed tone. She came closer, and I could see that her face was set and pale. These were more than words of complaint: they were words that asked for simple consideration and companionship. I shut down my adrenalin pump and walked beside her.

Jan was tired. Worse, she still hadn't shaken her feeling that trouble awaited us on the high passes, and that put her on edge. But there was something more. She'd been sharp with me yesterday, too.

Jan would never ask outright for assistance or reassurance or a change of attitude. I had to listen between her words, sense her direction, observe her body language. I remembered that she had needed me to stay with her during the final hour of climbing on Muztagata while Galen went on ahead. She hadn't asked with a question. She'd asked by voicing one statement of determination: "If you're going, so am I." In the end we had made it to the top together, and the experience had been far richer because of our mutual concern.

"You neglect me, go to Craig on decisions, and race off with him," she charged. "That's a change from the way we started. There's an easier way to do this section, but I agreed to your way. Yet you keep pushing me away. We started this thing together, and we should finish it together."

We walked on silently before coming to the brink of a frozen waterfall that was too steep to climb down. We headed left onto the glacier, then helped each other down dark cascades of ice that formed the snout of the glacier. At the bottom we hugged each other—our arms too short to wrap around our backpacks. I was glad I was with her. Craig's whistle beamed us to a campsite on sandy outwash.

We slept for 12 hours that night, and didn't leave our nylon "beach bungalow" until after eleven o'clock in the morning. We walked out onto a large, frozen lake. The ice was turquoise, then as it thickened, navy blue. We called it "Dalmatian Lake," after the white polka dots of trapped air etched under the glassy surface. We scooted along, swinging our arms and legs as if we were ice skaters, laughing and falling. A loud rumble stopped us. An ice tower at the end of the Mingbo Glacier had keeled over into the lake. The water surged and gurgled under the ice, and I felt a weird, elastic undulation underfoot. For a moment I thought the ice might break up, and we all hurried toward shore.

Once off the lake we trekked downhill over snowless, boulder-strewn terrain, then followed a little meandering river. I imagined how it would look in summertime, sporting green shoulders decorated with colorful alpine flowers. We worked our way upstream to Hongu Pokhari, a milky-blue lake that was only half-frozen. It lay cupped in the lowest point of the immense amphitheater. Even though it was only two o'clock in the afternoon, we set up the tent on the "beach." Ice chunks had been pushed up onto the shore, and from inside the tent it looked like frozen surf about to wash over us. Overhead, the sky was quiet and clear. There was only one sound—the lake water under the ice pulsated like the beat of a huge heart.

Mountains ringed us on all sides. We spent a lazy afternoon. There seemed little reason to hurry; Anu would be meeting us in four days and we'd already covered a good percentage of the distance.

JAN: There was a special magic to this section of the circle because of its remote isolation and tranquil stillness. Little did we know that this was literally the calm before the storm. Late in the afternoon the day after we climbed Mingbo La, as I began to tire and lag a bit behind, we came upon a higher winding moraine that looked as if it might dead-end, blocking the easiest route to the base of West Col. I suggested camping there at the edge of the moraine for the night and exploring for another route to the col in the morning.

"I'm just going a little way up onto the moraine to see if I can get a look at the col or find a way up onto the glacier to camp for the night," Ned explained. Then Craig and Ned disappeared. I waited for awhile, and when they hadn't returned, I hefted my pack and wandered on up and through the moraine, which placed me easily on the glacier before the pass. I spied Ned's and Craig's packs lying up ahead and dumped mine with theirs. Then a wave of curiosity swept over me, and I lifted Craig's pack to compare its weight to mine. Mine was slightly heavier, but I felt ashamed at thinking that the extra weight had slowed me down. I left the packs, following footprints to the site Craig and Ned had selected for our camp. As I walked I chided myself for wanting to turn around and lift Ned's pack as well.

NED: Our goal, like that of the first explorers who had probed unknown mountain regions years ago, was to thread our way across the rugged countryside. We had the advantage of maps, but the game was the same—locating and crossing passes that gave access to further regions. Passes have a lure of their own, and have often been strategically important. Until the end of the nineteenth century, for example, the British in India were interested not in conquering the highest peaks, but in discovering and controlling the passes through which Russia might sweep into India.

Francis Younghusband, a tough, ambitious British officer who possessed uncanny powers of negotiation, journeyed overland from Manchuria to India in 1887, crossing the Gobi Desert and the Himalaya en route. He wove his way through the Karakoram Himalaya by a daring traverse of the Mustagh, a pass of 19,000 feet near K2, the second highest mountain in the world. It was the most difficult crossing of a pass ever done, and marked the end of an era of climbing passes with one notable exception. In 1899, another Englishman, Douglas Freshfield, led a high-level tour around 28,146-foot Kangchenjunga on the Nepal-Sikkim border, the third-highest peak in the world. The expedition circled the massif, an accomplishment I found to be inspirational for our own Grand Circle.

◆ ◆ ◆

When I woke early on January 19, Jan and Craig were still asleep. It was crowded with three of us in our two-person dome tent. The air was foul with freeze-dried food, flatulence, and stinky bodies.

I crawled out of the tent, stood groggily, and relieved myself. My stream seemed to go on forever. It splattered on the frozen earth, and I danced to escape the rebound. Reduced to basics, the essence of an expedition is peeing clearly and copiously, which means you're not dehydrated. Dehydration inhibits acclimatization and endurance.

The sun beamed its first light onto Everest and Lhotse. Both peaks were reflected perfectly in a small lake. I stood motionless, no longer muddle-headed. A familiar, special sensation crept through my mind and body—the tranquility of solitude.

Craig let go a colossal fart, and suddenly my morning was humanized. Jan, aroused, frantic for fresh air but still ensconced in her sleeping bag, bucked her way out of the tent, rocking on elbows and knees like a beached seal.

After eating and packing, we once again headed east, starting a gradual climb up and eventually out of the Hongu amphitheater. A series of miniature valleys wound through glacial rubble, and tiny, dessicated plants shuddered in the westerly wind. We broke out onto an old lake bed, where we left footprints in the light brown clay, then skated on our boots up a frozen streambed.

We walked upward over stony terrain toward a great chunk of rock that separated two arms of the Hongu Glacier. Skirting the right side, we found ourselves under the eaves of the glacial ice that rose cleanly and vertically above. It was a strange formation to see on a temperate glacier, the edges of which are usually chaotically crevassed. I was reminded of the polished, cliff-like termini of the polar glaciers I had skied past in 1977, during a 500-mile trip to 83 degrees north latitude on Canada's Ellesmere Island.

As we walked on I mulled over the number of things that could prevent

Anu from meeting us at Makalu on time. Although we had looked at the map together, Anu might have misunderstood. Air flights might have been cancelled. He might have difficulty hiring porters in the Arun area. Worse, the winter storms might hit and dump deep snow on the trail into Makalu, delaying or even turning him back.

Then my thoughts turned to yet another concern—Jan. She seemed bothered and had borrowed all the furrows I sometimes wear and pasted them on her own forehead. Perhaps she was as concerned as I was about our upcoming meeting with the Sherpas.

We rested, and when we stood to continue I offered to help Jan heft her backpack to her shoulders. "It's easier if I do it myself," she insisted. Her pack was as heavy as Craig's and mine at the moment because she carried the rope. We had thought we were distributing the weight fairly by giving Jan the rope as her share of community gear, but we had found more snowless terrain than we expected. Soon we'd be back on the glaciers, and using the rope, and so lightening her load.

We continued up to the prow of the big rock that split the glacier, and pitched camp at 18,700 feet. The shadows enveloped us immediately, and the cold was intensified by a blustery wind. We hurried into our tent, and prepared to cook in the dim light. Jan sneezed, mopped her mouth, and laughed. "Maybe I'm allergic to the night, to the cold, or lugging this pack around."

I knew Jan would dig deep and pull through. I was more immediately concerned about the little tidal wave sweeping over the floor of the tent toward me. Craig, now nicknamed "Boy Blunder," had, for the second night in a row, with uncanny timing, kicked over the stove and pot just as the melting ice had filled the pot with water.

We started a new pot of ice melting, and Craig hauled a package of biscuits out of his pack. Their crisp texture was a wonderful relief from the slurry we ate at breakfast and dinner. Between munches, he entertained us with a story of escaping an avalanche that wiped out a speed-skiing chute in Portillo, Chile, during the trials. When the warning of the slide was shouted, everyone else shoved off downhill in a tuck to outrun it. Not Craig. He climbed up a few steps onto a rock outcrop—skis and all—and watched it run past.

After dinner, we lay in our bags and listened to the wind blast through West Col, 1,500 feet above. The pass divided Baruntse, 23,688 feet, from Pyramid peak, 22,430 feet.

In the morning the air was quiet and cold when we started up toward West Col. I had slept poorly, and had difficulty gathering my energy and enthusiasm for traveling. We wove through a series of crevasses, then moved up a gentle glacial slope toward the start of the climbing. The snow crust was unevenly consolidated: after a few steps on top, we'd break through and posthole for several yards, zigzagging from one firm, crusty section to the next.

West Col was a broad pass running north and south; we approached it from the southwest. Directly above us a series of jagged fractures cut across a steep snow and ice slope. It looked formidable, so we continued north along the base, searching for a route. Five rock buttresses split the part of the pass under which we now moved, with ice and snow couloirs between them. The first two did not extend to the top, but ended in a rock tier. The third cut through to the crest, so we veered toward that one.

A 20-foot-wide bergschrund extended along the bottom of the slope. We teetered along the lower edge of the deep hole, searching for a place to cross. We examined a flimsy snow bridge, but proceeded on in hopes of finding a stouter crossing point. There was none. Retracing our steps, I set up a belay around an ice block to safeguard Craig as he inched across the bridge. It looked to be constructed only of sagging, powdery snow, but there must have been hidden reinforcement, because it held. A few moves up a series of ice pedestals brought him onto a snowy area. Jan and I joined him there, and we set up a boot-axe belay.

Craig, still peppy, started up out of the powder snow. After 30 feet he hit hard snow and diagonaled up and left. A hundred feet beyond, a small ice face demanded front-pointing to a rock belay on the opposite side of the couloir. Jan and I climbed together. Above the belay stance was steep, solid ice; so, following the line of least resistance, we diagonaled back to the right on hard snow and intermittent ice patches to the opposite rock ridge. We finished the pitch up broken rock to a sling belay. The wind velocity increased as we climbed higher, and, in spite of the hard work, we needed windproof jackets and pants.

A four-inch-wide fracture that cut the icy face above in a lopsided Z pattern led directly to the top of the pass. The lower edge of the fracture was offset just enough to accept the inner side-points of our crampons. We climbed it by balancing on the little ice edge, and checking ourselves with our ice axes whenever a gust of wind hit.

The crest was an unpleasant surprise—a serrated rock edge that dropped vertically to the east. We had two choices for escape: rappel straight off, or down-climb and traverse 100 yards to the north along the sharply pointed ridge. Having only one rope, we went north.

Sharp reddish blocks the size of automobiles formed the top of the ridge, and nothing seemed to be connected to anything else. We unroped, more afraid of such a tether pulling off rocks than of one of us actually falling, and removed our crampons. Fighting our way down the ridge was nerve-wracking business: precipices dropped to either side, and when the wind batted us, we were forced to crab along the razor crest on all fours. When we bent that far over, our packs seemed to double in weight. Twice, to move around gendarmes, we had to step out on the west face, inching sideways in precarious balance.

Finally we emerged onto snow, and were safe on a section that turned out to be the lowest point of the col. An old rope left fixed by some earlier party dangled down the west face. We walked off to the east, onto the north fork of the Plateau Glacier—a vast expanse of ice and snow. Underfoot, the snow crunched in the deepening cold, and we followed our own shadows that lengthened as the sun sank in the west. Jan was feeling energetic, but Craig and I were starting to tire, so we pitched camp in the middle of the icefield. There was absolutely no protection from the wind, so we built a token snow wall on the west side of the tent and crawled in for the night.

I was happy to lie on my sleeping bag as Jan heated water for soup. We were camped at an elevation of 20,300 feet, approximately the height of Mount McKinley. The sky was blue-black, but fast losing its blueness. I gazed out the tent door at a polar scene of enormous proportions. We speculated on the whereabouts of Anu. Only two full days of rations remained. If a storm moved in, it might be impossible to move; we were on a flat glacier and there was not a rock feature within two miles by which to navigate in a whiteout.

We had endured storms on previous expeditions. In 1979, during a traverse of the heart of New Zealand's Southern Alps, our four-person team had been pinned down for seven days in a two-person tent by a ferocious sleet gale. Rationing two days' food supply, we had lain shivering in wet sleeping bags. It had been Jan's first expedition. Here, in Nepal, we laughed at the memory.

Now Jan was bubbling in unison with the stove, and began to sing golden oldies with Craig. I grinned to myself. She was regaining her old vivaciousness.

JAN: Because Craig and Ned were exhausted when we reached the bottom of West Col, they started sniffing around for a campsite. But I felt good and saw no reason for ending our day so soon. The hours of daylight remaining enticed me to move closer to Sherpani Col. It would be possible to negotiate the pass the next day if we situated ourselves close enough to it. Yesterday at this time I had been ready to settle in for the night, but Ned and Craig had coaxed me on. Today I was urging them to go about the same distance farther before calling it a day. These were the beginnings of the extreme physical and mental swings we were all starting to feel and would experience much more dramatically in the coming week.

Sherpani Col was deceptive. From our morning point of view, it was a walk-up. We labored through a couple of hours of postholing, punching our legs through the crust and sinking thigh-deep in the snow. At first the wind was licking our faces, but as we neared the blunt edge of the col the gusts threatened to knock me off my feet. The wind pushing up the glacier on the opposite side hit the col furiously and tumbled over the top to where we stood.

I looked over my shoulder and noticed that Ned, our passionate scout, had already left our protected shelter and was fighting the vicious, wintry blasts, looking for the line of least resistance down the rocky side of the col to the glacier. I thought to myself that Ned's intensity might well affect his moods, but that it also drives him to unhesitatingly risk his comfort for the rest of us. Whenever we suffered misfortune, Ned was a pillar of strength and a man of action. As I watched him struggling along the ridge, searching, I felt repentant for thinking of Ned's shortcomings and allowing myself to forget that regardless of his harsh words, he was always someone I could count on.

To get to the most logical rappel route, we needed to traverse the entire length of Sherpani Col. I thrust my ski poles deep into the snow to act as anchors as I moved across. We bumped and banged down the awkward, irregular rappel. Craig went first, then I did. I slipped down the ropes over a great bulge, then had to hold fast and swing off the huge bump to funnel the rope down a more practical line. Craig was climbing down while I freed the rope for Ned. "Do you want a belay?" Ned asked when he reached me.

"I wouldn't turn one down." Ned huffed and puffed, and I could see that he had only offered to be polite, and didn't think that one was necessary.

"Skip it," I said. "If I'm going to die I should do it alone." Ned misunderstood me. He thought I was being sarcastic, but I had had second thoughts about being roped together, and meant what I had said. I knew Ned intended to continue climbing down, roped or not. If one of us took a spill while we were roped together, that one would take the other along. But Ned had heard my comment as a wisecrack. He threw the rope at me with a curt swing. I was dismayed when I realized there'd been an important misunderstanding in a touchy situation. Rather than trying to resolve it then and there, I just tied in and continued down cautiously.

When we reached Craig near the bottom of the col, he said he was concerned about hidden crevasses lurking beneath a shallow snow cover, and asked to tie in with us. His request settled this to-rope-or-not-to-rope question, and I relaxed.

We camped that evening below the col on an expanse of glacier, surrounded by sharp, peaked seracs that looked like giant shark fins cutting through an icy sea. I lay back in the tent, satisfied that we had made the passes in the time we had calculated. Everything had gone well. During the week Craig had become more than an equal partner, and now was like a well-worn shoe, fitting comfortably without any binding or chafing. The three of us had grown to be an effective team, able to cover long distances in difficult conditions and enjoy it.

NED: I propped my head on my arms and looked eastward. Makalu reared over Sherpani Col, the pass we would try to cross the next day. The French first climbed Makalu in 1955, and perhaps because all eight men on the team made the summit, the mountain had acquired a reputation for offering successful expeditions. I had always wanted to climb an 8,000-meter (26,260-foot) peak, of which there are only 14, all in the Himalayan chain. That evening I decided that my 8,000-meter peak would be Makalu. (Later, in Kathmandu, I discovered that the next permit available was for spring of 1986; I applied, and eventually received one.)

In the morning our small expedition set off across the polar landscape. An authoritative wind pushed us from behind toward Makalu, which was crowned by an ominous lenticular cloud.

We passed East Col on our way to Sherpani Col. In June 1952, after their abortive attempt on Cho Oyu, Shipton, Hillary, Charles Evans, and George Lowe had crossed this same ice plateau, then descended via East Col into the Barun Valley. There, they had turned north and followed the Barun Glacier to the Tibetan border. In all likelihood, this was the same point on the border to which the 1921 British Reconnaissance to Everest had climbed from the opposite side. The importance of the 1952 trek lay in the fact that this was the last link around the base of Everest to be explored. It had taken 31 years, many expeditions, and hundreds of thousands of footsteps by numerous individuals, but the mountain had finally been circumnavigated.

We continued on to the southeast, moving up an easy slope to Sherpani Col. As we neared the col, the wind velocity increased as it funneled into the narrow opening. The ferocious air current sped us upward as if we were defying gravity. I was first to the top, and inched toward the edge. Without warning a hurricane blast chopped me from behind, almost lifting me off my feet. I quickly fell onto my axe, driving it into the hard snow, and aborted my impending launch directly into the Barun. Chastised, I crawled behind a boulder, then beckoned the others to my haven as they approached the crest.

We were at the low point of the col. Below the boulder behind which we hid lay a short snow slope, and we assumed we were in the right spot for the descent. Moving downward, we soon discovered that, at the end of the snow, the col plunged away in a long vertical drop. We climbed back to the boulder, prepared to search elsewhere.

To do so we had to move out of our alcove and into the gale. Craig went first, trailing the rope, and battled his way against the wind with jerky, straddling steps. He worked his way along a buttress of rocky teeth that blocked the pass for the next 100 feet, then Jan and I followed him to the far side of the buttress. Beyond, a white edge of snow formed the crest. Jan belayed Craig as he crawled along the crest on all fours, a few feet to windward, his windproofs flapping and buzzing. Twice he dropped onto his belly and slithered to the edge to see whether the ridge was corniced. My head was filled with the roar of the wind gone wild.

On the far side of the white edge, Craig nestled among some rocks and belayed us over to him. We continued along the rocks for 50 feet, then climbed over the rocks and crouched down behind them. The wind screamed a few feet over our heads, but the air was serenely quiet where we were. A descent from here looked possible. Craig slung webbing over a horn of rock, threaded the rope through, and rappelled down a steep, smooth wall crisscrossed with fractures. Jan went second, then I followed. We ended on a small, snow-covered ledge. Below us the slope was less steep, but the rock was decomposed and sometimes covered with powdery snow. Craig was already climbing down—by the time I had pulled the rope, he had pioneered a route halfway down to the bottom. Jan and I roped up and moved off in his footsteps. Farther down the slope, we unroped.

We soon joined Craig, who was waiting at the edge of Sherpani Glacier, basking in the sun and its warmth beyond the shadow cast by the col. We threw our arms around each other in congratulations.

"The Sherpas can't be far away now," Jan beamed, bursting into laughter that rocketed through a high-range octave. Her merriment was once again on a hair trigger.

"Cakewalk comin' up," Craig assured her.

We roped up as a safeguard against crevasses and started down Sherpani Glacier toward the base of Makalu. That night we camped on the glacier, our tent nestled among turquoise seracs.

Because we were a small party, decision-making—even though Jan thought it painful of late—was quick and clean and involved us all. We were far more mobile than a large expedition would have been. In our self-sufficient circumstances, additional members would only have increased the possibility and probability of error or injury without increasing the odds of success. We were a cohesive, single-minded unit: we were all headed in the same direction at the same time, and we would all share the same rewards.

Shipton had known the recipe: "The strongest mountaineering party," he wrote, "is one in which each member has implicit confidence in all his companions, recognizes their vital importance to the common effort, and feels himself to have an indispensable part to play . . . . To my mind it can only be achieved with a relatively small, closely knit party . . . . Remove, then, the impression that one is engaged in a vast enterprise upon which the eyes of the world are focused, realize that one is setting out to climb a mountain . . . and one will add greatly to one's chances of success, and, more important still, enjoyment" (Rowell, 1980).

11

ESCAPE

"When I go out for a hike, I don't take a trail. I make my own."

Craig Calonica

NED:  On the morning of January 22 we broke camp, worked our way off the glacier, and then hiked two miles down to the Barun Glacier. The valley floor was littered with large, light gray granite boulders. The going was painstakingly slow, and we didn't arrive at the Barun until early afternoon.

We had traveled as far east as we could, and were now up against the wall—the West Face of Makalu, whose yellowish gray granite towered 10,000 feet overhead. From our position at the junction of the Sherpani and Barun glaciers, Makalu looked youthful and muscular, a sudden igneous intrusion burst from the earth. In contrast, Everest had seemed far more aged—a colossal, metamorphosed, sedimentary mass built up slowly over the eons, tier by tier. At the top of Everest the horizontal limestone strata were stacked at a cockeyed angle, as if the foundation of the mountain had slowly settled under the northern end.

I looked north, up the Barun Glacier, and could see Everest beyond the crestline of peaks that marked the border between Nepal and Tibet. Our plan had been to meet the Sherpas here, resupply, then make our way up to the frontier via the Barun Glacier. Not only were the Sherpas bringing in food, but also skis, to speed our ascent of the glacier. My goal was to put one foot in Tibet, in that way truly finishing the first half of the circle.

Anu and our new supplies were nowhere in sight. That was a disappointment, and a critical turn of events that left us in a quandary. Should we wait here for Anu? If so, how long should we wait? We had expected him to be here when we arrived. Had we allowed too little time for him to get into Makalu? Had he run into unforeseen difficulties that delayed him? To compound the problem, nothing within sight looked to be a likely spot for Makalu Base Camp—our agreed upon place to meet—even though Anu had said it would be obvious. We needed to consider our alternatives.

"I had counted on Anu," Jan said, her disappointment clear as she put her pack onto the ground and sat to rub her sore knees. It was sunny and warm in the lee of a huge boulder. We mulled things over.

"Knowing Anu," I offered encouragingly, "he's doing everything he can to get to us."

"I wouldn't count on anybody," Craig said. "Never do."

"I wonder how many days it would take to trek up to the top of the Barun?" I wondered aloud.

"Enough so you'll be very hungry," Jan asserted.

Going back the way we had come to resupply ourselves with food would take six days; we had no idea how far we were from food if we kept on the way we were headed. Jan was right. I would be hungry; we all would be. We were virtually out of food: only one freeze-dried dinner remained uneaten, as well as assorted lunch leftovers. Via the Barun—its lower surface strewn with rubble and carved by seracs, its upper reaches a vast snowfield—the border was almost 10 miles distant. They would be very hard miles on empty stomachs, and when we came back—another 10 miles—we would still have no food, unless Anu had arrived in our absence.

I looked at the sky. A high scud layer of clouds was slowly gathering. Were the winter storms finally at hand? Would we soon be wallowing in snow so deep that travel would be exhausting? And of course snow would slow Anu's progress as well as our own.

But we *had* counted on Anu, *had* taken a calculated chance that we would meet. We had all been leery of the plan, but it had been the best choice of several poor alternatives. Now our next move must be the right one. We were in remote country during winter, so we could count on no other expeditions being in the vicinity for aid, food, or rescue. We were at the point of no return: we assumed it was farther to retreat to civilization the way we had come than to go forward to it. We searched the immediate area for two hours, but failed to find Anu and the new provisions. It was time to make a decision.

I looked north up the Barun once again. I had never failed to complete the entire itinerary of an expedition. Or, if I had failed the first time, as Galen Rowell and I had on our first attempt to climb Mount McKinley in one day in 1978, I had returned to do it on the second try. Were we here strictly for the accomplishment, at any risk? Or were we here out of a love of being in the mountains? I thought of Shipton and his philosophy of expeditioning: ". . . it is my belief," he wrote, "that to take unreasonable risks deliberately is usually a sign of irresponsibility and arrogance, while to do so unawares shows lack of experience and judgment; and that a narrow escape should be deemed a failure of competence and not a matter of pride" (Shipton, 1969).

I was acutely aware that we were a small expedition in an uninhabited area: a small mishap could have extremely serious consequences. Under the circumstances, it seemed foolhardy to tackle the upper Barun or to wait here for resupply and possibly be locked in by winter snows. The Sherpas might never make it. If we started down the valley, we might bump into Anu soon enough to allow us to retrace our footsteps back here and then continue to the border.

"Let's move forward," I said, finding the words surprisingly easy. After all, it would be only a temporary regrouping.

We started walking south, down the new terrain of the lower Barun Valley, clambering over the boulders that lined the edge of the glacier. Many were precariously balanced and shifted under our weight. We used ski poles in each hand as walking sticks.

JAN: We decided that the most likely place to find Anu would be in the area where many expeditions had set up Base Camp for Makalu. The site is southwest of the mountain, near the terminus of the Barun Glacier. A trail would surely lead into the camp from the lowlands, and if there were a trail, Anu would take it.

We headed down the valley, picking our way along the moraine that ran next to the glacier. The boulders varied from the size of my fist to that of a small car. The rock felt cold and hard, and much of it was unstable, sliding or rolling as I stepped or hopped from place to place. The unwieldy pack threatened to throw me off balance with the slightest wrong move. I thought about how easy it would be to slip between a couple of rocks and break a bone, and the incredible ordeal it would be to get someone with a broken leg out of here. Ned, Craig, and I each selected our own routes through the rocky maze, keeping a watchful eye out for each other as we moved ahead. Even with a map, I had trouble keeping the landscape in perspective. I became extremely aware of just how insignificant we were and imagined the three of us as little sand fleas crawling among pebbles and sand on a beach.

NED: As Jan and I pushed along behind Craig—adding ever more distance between ourselves and the border—I rehashed our decision. If we never had the chance to return, the aesthetic purity of the trip would be compromised: we would not have quite closed the circle. But our joy at being in the mountains would remain intact.

We walked down the boulder field for an hour, as ill-tempered clouds washed overhead. The valley narrowed, and divided into a series of shelves and steep gravel slopes above the broken glacier. We caught up with Craig, who had lost the faint trail expeditions use to the start of Makalu's climbing routes.

"Don't know where the trail went," Craig annouced. "But come on, let's move onto the glacier. My friends say that my way is always faster than following a direct line, but seldom easier!"

We wove our way among small ice towers created by sun melt and scrambled over sharp rocks frozen into the glacier surface. A narrow gully led off the glacier and into an alcove between the ice and earthen banks. It was paved with striated bedrock and decorated with black, white, and yellow stones. Fan-shaped patterns of sand suggested water flow during warmer times. Farther on, the stream that had been gurgling deep under the boulders presented itself, but still it ran unseen, now under a sheath of ice. As we descended, we dropped into purple mist that blanketed the moonscape, and snowflakes tingled on my cheeks. The valley walls closed further in on us, and presently we entered a rocky glen.

JAN: With almost no food, there really was no need for a lunch stop, but we took a midday break anyway to pool ideas. Now that we had negotiated the moraine shoulder of the Barun Glacier, we encountered a small frozen lake with a stream emptying from it and winding down valley. This stream was the headwaters of the Barun River, which eventually would feed into the great Arun River. We figured that at the very least we could always follow the Arun until we reached civilization in the lowlands. Speed had become essential, given our lack of food and fuel.

"The only thing to do is to follow the lake's outlet and keep an eye out for any signs of a camp," Ned offered. Neither Craig nor I had any other solutions, so we quickly agreed. We knew from Liz Hawley in Kathmandu that a Frenchman whom she had found "intriguing" was trying to solo Makalu in winter on the difficult West Pillar route. The weather had been so kind to us while we were climbing Pumori and crossing the passes that we assumed he had taken advantage of the cold calm and would be off the mountain and gone by now. But we hoped to find remnants of his camp, and perhaps our Sherpas, somewhere in the vicinity.

We decided to leave the stream in search of a comfortable campsite for the night. The clouds had been building ominously, and looked heavy with snow. It was dark and cold—time to call it a day. We had been on the move for seven hours and hadn't seen a trace of a Base Camp or a sign of our Sherpas anywhere.

NED: We had each eaten only a single candy bar during the day, but the tiredness we had felt earlier was now held at bay by the mystical beauty of our surroundings. We wandered through a primeval serenity that, temporarily, distracted us from our worries about our probable predicament.

The ice-covered river spilled into an evil-looking cleft. We left the glen by hiking up a bank of loose gravel and emerged onto a grass-covered shelf. The shroud of fog parted for a few moments and Makalu loomed above, yellowish red. Even after it disappeared, we could still hear the wind booming against its walls.

We turned south on a faint crease cutting the ground—the trail into Makalu. Daisylike flowers, dried and stiff, stood in scattered clumps. We followed the path down a small U-shaped valley that ran parallel to the glacier. When we couldn't see any longer in the thickening darkness, we pitched our tent on a pebbly outwash just beyond the terminus of the Barun Glacier.

While cooking our last freeze-dried dinner by the light of our headlamps, I inventoried our rations. It didn't take long: I counted three small bags of tropical fruit mix, one plastic bag of chocolate drink mix, one bag of dried milk, six tea bags, and a handful of bouillon cubes. One fuel canister remained.

"Precise planning on the food," I said to Jan, with a congratulatory note in my voice. "Perfect if Anu had been here."

"You know, Anu didn't really want to come into here," Jan answered as a way of weighing our chances of meeting him. "His mother was afraid of bandits down in the Arun. She made him leave his necklace at home, so that it wouldn't be stolen."

We were tired, but somehow blindly optimistic about the immediate future. I decided this would be an appropriate time to announce a little problem that was about to arise. "Tomorrow, if we continue out, we walk off our map. I don't have the next one. I sent both copies around with Anu by mistake."

The tent was very quiet for several moments. I was glad it was dark. Craig rose to his knees, switched on his headlamp, and fixed me under its accusing eye. "Guilty!" he bellowed, then laughed. As he rolled back onto his buttocks, Boy Blunder grazed the pot with his elbow, knocking it off the stove. I welcomed the flood this time, because it took the heat off me.

Shaking off the worst of the wetness, we settled into our bags for the night. The wind roared over the peaks, and it began to snow lightly. The winter storms had finally arrived. I wasn't deeply worried yet, but lay awake wondering how all this would end. My thoughts were rudely interrupted by my noisy stomach gurgling its request for food.

JAN: From our vantage point high in the side canyon at the terminus of the Barun Glacier, the valley looked grand and barren. We could see large rock walls and uneven moraine. Despite our circumstances, I was overwhelmed by the landscape that unfolded before us. The Arun Valley is a 20,000-foot chasm, the deepest in the world. The scale is appropriate, since the valley descends from Everest, the world's highest peak, on one side, and from Kangchenjunga, the third-highest, on the other. The Arun River itself, which we could eventually come to if we continued to follow the Barun River, is actually older than the Himalaya.

NED: The next morning, January 23, we breakfasted on powdered chocolate drink mixed with dried milk. Each of us got one cup. As we lay in the tent quietly savoring the hot liquid, we heard a bird chirp. We emerged into a somber, gray dawn and stretched the night's stiffness away, then set out over a landscape of hummocks mottled with snow. As soon as we had left the glacier the day before, we had removed our stiff mountain boots for easier walking. Now small shrubs caught the shoelaces of our lightweight hiking shoes.

We chugged on for two hours, toward the Lower Barun Glacier and a spot on the far edge of our map labeled "Shershon," dropping below 16,000 feet. The air seemed heavy. Rounding a hillock, we stumbled upon three tents. Anu? An animated figure dressed in red from head to foot shot out of one tent. He ran toward us, arms waving, shouting, "Bonjour! Bonjour!" A sparkling man with wild eyes and tousled hair hugged us. "Mes amis. Mes amis. Qui êtes-vous? Ahh, oui, oui. You must be the American skiers. Liz Hawley told me about you before I left Kathmandu. Where are your skis?"

We were briefly taken aback by our new acquaintance's exuberance, but we quickly recovered and shook hands all around. "Have you seen a Sherpa named Anu wandering around here?" Jan asked.

"Non, non, non. Nobody. Just me. But come in. I have tea."

We entered his mess tent and sat down. He threw sticks on a smoldering fire, and we introduced ourselves.

"I am Ivan Chiraradini," he said. "Chamonix guide. Twenty-eight years old. I am climbing Makalu this winter. Solo. It is better that way. Pure, with only the wind and the ice and the rock. But the mountain, she has not been friendly. Non! at 7,000 meters on the West Pillar, I am blown off. Voilà. Tea. Sugar?"

"They say winter is not winter in the Himalaya until you get above 7,000 meters," I observed.

"Such bad wind. Mon dieu!" Ivan spat. "I cannot throw my ropes down to rappel. No one can live in such wind. She is a hard mistress." I was only half-listening to what he said as I eyed the carton of sweet biscuits behind him. I could hardly keep from drooling as he went on. "I climb only alpine style. Everything I need is in a small rucksack. Ten kilograms. I do not used fixed rope. I eat almost nothing. I cannot believe mountaineers. They eat what you call gorp. They eat meat. Incredible! The spirit—that is what is important. It is like iron. Would you like peanuts, raisins?"

"Thank you. Do you get lonely?" Jan asked.

"Lonely? What is that?"

"Lonesome."

"Ohh, oui. Non, non, non. Never. I have the mountains. No books, no radio. Only the mountains."

"No Sherpas?"

"Three. One here, two away. And one liaison officer. Always the liaison officer, non? He has gone out to ask the Ministry for permission so I can try again on Makalu—the regular route. Sherpas will bring word. I am waiting." He laughed. "My wife, she at first comes in with me. To Base Camp. But," he shrugged, "she is not so happy here. Good-bye to me. I am staying." He laughed again, but sadly. "I am crazy—un peu."

He held up his thumb and forefinger, positioned them an inch apart in front of one eye, closed the other, and sighted through the gap at us to indicate the degree of craziness.

"Do you . . . ah . . . do you have an extra map?" I ventured.

"Oui, oui, oui. It is not so good." He unfolded the map and spread it across his knees, then pointed to a spot far down the Barun Khola. "There. The trail makes sharp turn. Be careful to see it. Attention! Up the frozen river. Very bad. Very steep. You will need the crampons."

"Frozen river?" I was puzzled.

"The stream has run over the trail up the pass. Maybe a mile. Very steep. Do you have a map of Everest?"

"Yes," I answered. "Here. You keep it. If we need it again, we'll be in deep yogurt."

"Pardon?"

"Nothing. American expression. Tell us, how far is it to the nearest village?"

"Two days to Tashigan," Ivan said, "if you are fast. Mon dieu! The snow, it is deep below this camp." He positioned a hand at his knee to indicate the depth.

"The snow gets deeper as we lose elevation?" Craig asked, incredulous.

"Oui, oui. Ahh, a map of Everest. Magnifique! It will be good reading to pass the time. Très bon. I am waiting."

"Maybe you've brought in too much food?" I asked nonchalantly.

"Comme ci, comme ça," he answered, fluttering his hand from side to side.

"We have little food left," I muttered.

"Ohh, oui, oui, oui. Here. Porridge." Ivan slapped a plastic bag into my hand. It was filled with something that resembled sawdust.

"Thank you."

It was tempting to set up camp here with Ivan and wait for Anu. We were still close to the Barun Glacier and therefore to the border. But to do so would mean depleting Ivan's resources. And, if there was deep snow and difficult traveling between here and the nearest village, as Ivan predicted, Anu might be delayed a good many days—or might never make it.

There was little choice but to continue. We left the tent and started down. Ivan danced along beside us, skipping on top of the rocks that lined the trail, singing and gesturing in his red suit like one of Santa's elves. Together, we walked along a series of moats and shelves that ran parallel to a large glacier. Our new map showed big peaks rising above the glacier, but they were invisible in the lowering whiteout. At the terminus the ground angled down sharply. It was now snowing heavily, big flakes that were likely to accumulate rapidly.

Ivan hugged each of us in farewell, but hung onto Jan an instant longer, muttering, "Mon dieu." He pranced off into the swirling snowstorm, but an instant later he was back. "There is a little cabin at Na." Then he was gone.

Craig chuckled, addressing the snowflakes: "And how far is Na?"

JAN: The man who welcomed us into his tent was handsome and effusive. He spoke some English and I spoke some French, enough to communicate where we'd come from and where he was going. High winds had kept him off his route, and he had only days left to complete an official winter climb. His supplies were limited because he'd been in the area longer than he had planned, and his wife and some of his staff had already left. Still he intended to do a route in the short time remaining. He offered us some tea, cookies, and a small bowl of peanuts which Craig, Ned, and I fell upon, struggling to maintain a polite veneer over our urges to grab and hoard. Ivan, assessing our predicament, gave us a bag of raw oatmeal to tide us over until we reached civilization.

We tore ourselves away from the relatively luxurious comforts to make our way out to Tashigan, the place Ivan had named as the nearest village. He hiked down the trail with us for a mile or so, which I thought was a gallant gesture. He sped over the terrain with such strength and agility that I felt embarrassed about my skinny, weak limbs and careful movements.

When Ivan hugged us all as he said good-bye, I realized how lonely he had been. He was an emotional, flamboyant man with the grin of a child. I could understand why he had made such an impression on Liz Hawley.

The clouds folded over us, wrapping us in cold moisture, and it began to spit snow. Minutes after Ivan left, any signs of the trail vanished. The false sense of security we'd gotten from our meeting with a fellow climber fell away, and we faced the fact that if it kept snowing, we could be aimlessly trekking in the Arun Valley for a long time.

NED: We turned, tilted our heads, narrowed our eyes under the hoods of our anoraks, and continued following a snowy path down into the storm. It was now a total whiteout. We assumed it was the start of the winter storm season—a full month later than usual. (Later we learned it snowed steadily for the next 30 days.) We had escaped from the high country in the nick of time, grabbing the last of the good weather. We were isolated from our surroundings, and, for awhile, from each other as we pushed along deep in our own thoughts. I had no choice but to focus all my attention on the task at hand—navigating the hundred or so feet visible ahead. The environment was wildly agitated, air and snow churning all around. Although a savage wind belted the unseen peaks above, a far gentler wind washed us. In the valley, it was the kind of snowstorm you wished for at Christmas.

It was about 30 degrees Fahrenheit. The snow mounted fast, making it difficult to decipher the path in the scrub land. One opening through the bushes looked as likely as the next. According to Ivan's map, which was little more than a rough sketch on a scale of 1:250,000, the lay of the land was complicated. In the whiteout, it would be easy to go astray. Except for the Everest and Annapurna regions, the mountains of Nepal are still poorly charted. In the old days of national xenophobia, map making was discouraged as a means of excluding visitors, and what maps are available have not been updated.

"I wouldn't trust that thing," Craig concluded, folding up the map. "I trust my instincts, and my instincts say follow the river down." He grinned. "Even though we can't see it or hear it!"

We descended onto a flattish shelf where three stone huts awaited the occupation of shepherds in spring. Their sagging roofs made us wonder if the shepherds still came. At least they told us that we were probably still on the trail. Sheltering in the lee of one, we finished off two packets of tropical fruit mix.

"That's it on lunches," Craig announced. "No need to ration. We'll be in Tashigan tomorrow night."

Once we had passed the huts, we couldn't find the trail. Impatient, we cast off from the shelf, slipping and sliding down steep, muddy, unfrozen ground which underlay the snow. Our ski poles helped to control the descent. At the bottom, we worked along a side hill, then broke out onto another shelf covered with unyielding bushes. At this lower elevation they grew higher, and grabbed at our clothes, not just our shoes.

Since we couldn't see the mountains, it didn't seem as if we were even in Nepal. The immediate scrub land reminded me of cattle country in the western United States, but that impression soon shifted as we moved into an area of rhododendron bushes that grew to shoulder height. These dumped their loads of snow on us as we passed between them. Dozens of rivulets flowed diagonally across our line of progress and we zigzagged along, following each tiny watercourse a short distance and then branching over into the next.

Soon everybody's shoes were soaked. Snow lathered them after we sloshed through each stream, and we seemed to be padding along in oversized cotton balls. Our feet grew cold and painful. We stopped to put old plastic lunch bags on our feet to act as vapor barriers. They soon tore. We continued, the movement of walking diluting the pain in our frigid toes. As long as we could still feel them we were not worried about permanent frostbite. We just kept moving. There was no reason to stop—we had no more food for snacking.

We wandered through the snowy maze all afternoon. Since paths are first laid out from lowland to mountain, their shape and logic are usually clear to travelers following them that direction. But the route may not be apparent to the traveler who first follows it in reverse, from highland to lowland. This is especially true when clues are submerged in deep snow, calling for clever sleuthing. We simply followed our instincts and pressed on into the storm.

A dark shape that loomed out of the murk turned out to be a gigantic boulder, with one side overhanging enough to form a dry sanctuary. Rocks had been piled in front as a windbreak, and the roof was blackened with smoke. It was tempting to stop under the sheltering eaves for the night. My feet felt like blocks of wood, and I would have loved to build a fire and revive them. But a couple of hours of daylight remained, and we decided to use them.

The valley narrowed and we plunged into a forest of pine trees 100 feet tall. The trees gave us a sense of perspective, and the whiteout became less threatening.

The snow cover was thinner under the trees, and we soon found the trail. There were no footprints, so Anu had not been here. At five o'clock, in deep dusk, we crossed a cantilevered log bridge that spanned the Barun Khola. It swayed and sagged under our weight. On the other side we found a tumble-down shack built of hand-hewn boards.

"Home," Jan said. "Must be Na."

JAN: Toward the end of the day, we dragged ourselves across the Barun River to the remains of an old wooden shed that we could just make out through the parting clouds. Intuition and common sense had kept us near the logical route to the lowlands. We gathered bits and pieces of dry twigs and branches to burn, so that we could save our precious stove fuel and dry our soaking clothes. Then it dawned on me: we were low enough to be among living, growing plants and trees. We were probably as low as 14,000 feet now.

Over my shoulder, I heard Craig exclaim in a slow, breathy drawl, "Look at those walls. There's routes all over the place. This is as good as Yosemite. Maybe better." The clouds had cleared themselves away and exposed steep, solid-looking cliffs thousands of feet high.

I started a fire in the shed and we put on some water for oatmeal, wrung out our socks, and hung our clothes by the warm flames. The snow had drenched us, and the heat felt wonderful. My insulating body fat was virtually all gone by now. Besides that, we'd had so little food to eat that I wasn't getting enough calories to maintain body heat. No wonder I'd been so cold lately. Even in my bag at night I sometimes felt too cold to sleep. During the day, regardless of how hard I was working under my heavy pack, I never seemed to warm up. Thinking of all this, I put my bare feet even closer to the fire.

Craig was effervescent that night. This was his first expedition, and he had adapted well. I laughed as I listened to Craig in the firelight. "I just love bush crashing. Whenever we had to hike to a climb, I'd leave the trail and bushwhack. I've got good sense of direction. Everyone else would stay on the trail and call me a fool, but I loved it. When I go out for a hike I don't take a trail, I make my own."

NED: The muffled sound of footsteps outside came to me slowly: swish, swish. I looked at Jan, then Craig. They had heard them—their heads were cocked and motionless, listening. Guttural grunts punctuated the footsteps. The sounds came nearer—crunch, crunch. A foot banged itself clean against the corner post, then a figure stooped through the door and came inside. A dark brown face, haggard but smiling, peered out of snow-encrusted clothing.

"Namaste," the face said. We nodded.

A second man entered. He wore an open-necked shirt under an ancient dress-suit jacket. His cotton pants were black with grease and dirt, almost hiding the checkered pattern of the material, and his shoes were basketball sneakers.

"Namaste," we responded. "Hello. Do you speak English?"

"A little. You come from Makalu?" the face asked. "You see Frenchman?"

"Yes," I answered.

"He still there?"

"Yes."

"I mail runner for him. Sherpa. Bring message."

During the exchange, Jan, Craig, and I had gotten to our feet and made space at the fire. The two men sat down and held their hands open to the warmth.

"Very difficult to see to walk," I said.

"We walk 12 hours today. Important hurry. Frenchman is waiting for message to climb."

"Yes or no to climb?" Craig asked.

"No message. We wait many days. No message comes." He shrugged. Snow fell off his shoulder into the fire. "Maybe he must stop."

(Later, in Biratnagar, we happened across Ivan's liaison officer. Unlike ours, he was conscientious and hard-working. He had been able to secure permission from the Ministry for Ivan to make a second attempt on the regular route, but apparently the message had not gotten to the mail runner before he left. It didn't matter—Ivan tried the mountain again anyway, but was beaten back by the storms of late winter.)

"Would you like tea?" Jan offered.

"No, no. We must go on tonight." The Sherpa stood. The man in the suit jacket did not.

"Please stay," I said. "There is plenty of room for all of us."

"Okay." The Sherpa immediately sat down with a big grin and began unlacing his shoes. Craig hung them from the roof beams to dry.

Jan gave them hot tea in our cups, and poured in the last of the dried milk. The Sherpa offered us something that looked like dried corn nuts from a small sack. He also fished a hunk of dried meat from his jacket pocket and sliced off a small piece for each of us. It was succulent.

"The snow is deep for walking," Jan said.

"Okay for here," the Sherpa responded. "Different from Khumbu. Always winter snow here. This house good. People from Sedewa build it for trekking to Makalu in spring and autumn. Nobody comes here in winter."

"Have you seen a Sherpa named Anu?" I asked.

"No other Sherpas near."

Later we arranged boards on the floor so nobody would have to sleep on dirt, then rolled out our sleeping bags and slept. One of our guests snored abominably.

I woke to the sounds of the man in the suit jacket beating his shoes and socks against the wall. His rapid-fire action looked like some bizarre form of morning calisthenics. Apparently his shoes and socks had frozen during the night, and this was his way of working them into submission.

It was January 24 and very cold. Inspired by the energetic performance I had just seen, I got up and ducked out of the hut into sunshine. The snow had stopped, but clouds still hung ominously at the top of the peaks. What peaks they were! Gigantic rock walls soared above, streaked with frozen waterfalls.

Inside, Craig had rekindled the previous night's coals. He too was having a battle getting into his shoes, which were burnt and shrunken from having been too close to the fire. Our white socks were yellowish brown and stiff, and stank of smoke and sweat.

The Sherpa spoke. "There is food cache at Monbuc. Behind big stone. Above frozen river." The two men waved and started north. We unfolded the map while brewing a cup of chocolate drink. The taste and warmth of the hot liquid were delicious, but did little to allay our growing hunger.

"I don't see Monbuc," Craig observed. "Where do you suppose Monbuc is?" We shrugged. After our hot drink, we headed south.

Although it had snowed throughout the night, the footsteps made by the Sherpa and his companion were visible, and we followed them. They became less distinct as we progressed easily down a wide, flat-bottomed valley through meadows and an occasional stand of trees. The Barun Khola meandered lazily, as if enjoying a respite from the cataracts upstream, and readied itself for the rough passage ahead. We were in good spirits, almost peppy. Like the river, we meandered serenely along this wilderness boulevard under the sheer rock walls. Walking in sunshine, we felt at home in this beautiful place. It reminded us all of Yosemite.

JAN: The day seemed long. We were following the Barun River, traveling on its steep banks. I felt slow in the morning, but kept pushing myself. As I began to pick up, Ned began lagging back. We were prey to the ups and downs again. Craig was doing well, keeping a steady pace. In some places the snow had piled up thigh-deep, making tedious work for us and hiding the undulating terrain beneath. I was beginning to find it hard to remain alert. I was tired of watching every step for so long. An expedition isn't like an athletic performance, where you can go home afterwards and have a beer on the couch. Constant attention is required, but I was gradually letting myself lose the sharpness our travel demanded. On a very steep section of the bank covered with deceptive snow, my foot broke through and I began to slide uncontrollably down towards the river 60 feet below. Fortunately my reactions were still intact, and I grabbed an unsuspecting rhododendron bush, jerking myself to a halt. I still don't know how I gripped the thing with one hand bundled up in a mitten, but when adrenalin is flowing, your limits are extended.

NED: After four miles the valley narrowed and angled downward. We walked out onto a wedge of meadowland that simply ended at a point where the mountain wall dropped in an unbroken line into the river. The water was suddenly wild and frothy as it crashed into enormous boulders 30 feet below. We had come to the end of our boulevard as surely as if an auto roadbed had been cut by a flash flood. The way ahead looked tough and, mentally, we shifted gears. We moved out onto the gravel bank and sidled across it, facing inward while using our hands above our heads for balance. Some rocks that stuck out of the bank looked solid, and we trusted our weight to them; otherwise we created our own steps by working our feet back and forth and digging into the gravel.

Two hundred feet along the bank the mountain wall bulged more steeply and we were forced down to the water's edge. Luckily a series of boulders provided passage—we jumped from one to the next while the river churned a few feet below us. Our backpacks were unwieldy, and we had to compensate for their weight at each leap. Balance was precarious on the wet rocks and a ski pole in each hand gave us a four-point stance. It was delicate, dangerous progress, and I was glad we had happened upon it early enough in the day to be at relatively full strength and concentration. If one of us slipped into the river, there would be little chance of survival. The boulder-hopping was one of those small, grotesque near-disasters that are most interesting when they're behind you.

After a quarter-mile the valley wall tilted back enough so we could scramble up from the river. I was glad to be away from it, since the incessant roar had suddenly become almost unbearably irritating. I had felt strong and alert 10 minutes before, but now I was utterly exhausted. It was all I could do to drag myself up the slope. Jan and Craig seemed not to share my exhaustion, so I said nothing.

We found ourselves on a series of narrow, flatish shelves covered with birch, juniper, and rhododendron. It was early afternoon, and the energy I had felt in the morning seemed light-years away. I plodded along behind the others, head down, numbly determined. The shelves were not continuous, and in the steep places we used the small trees as handholds to swing across channels that ran down into the river. I finally asked for a rest stop, and we sat on some rocks and drank water from a nearby rivulet for lunch. The clouds had moved in again, and an even gray light settled into the valley. It matched my mood.

"You'd think we'd see at least a hint of the Sherpa's footprints along here," Jan observed. "But nothing. The last print I saw was way back before we left the wide part of the valley."

"I've been looking at the other side of the river," Craig replied. "There is no way the terrain we just came over is a major route. I'll bet there was a bridge across the river a mile or two back that we missed. And look ahead. The river makes a big bend from south to east. That means the banks on our side will be scoured and steep because we're on the outside of the bend, and the other side will have more shelves. It also means the other side will soon have a southern exposure and much less snow. But there's no way I'm retracing our steps. I say push on and hope for the best, even though the terrain looks tough."

We stood and slung on our packs. Craig led off, strong and boisterous. I was amazed to discover that I had regained my strength, and paced along energetically. Before long I noticed Jan falling back. She was experiencing a low period like the one I had just shaken.

We worked our way toward the bend, which was a mile away. The shelves petered out, as we had expected they would, and we were confronted with a relatively continuous snow-covered slope that wasn't too steep. It looked straightforward and encouraging; but, since it fell away directly into the river, we took the extra precaution of unlashing our ice axes from our packs and carrying them in our hands. Craig marched onto the slope through 10 inches of snow. Twenty yards out his feet shot from under him, but he expertly arrested his fall with his axe. The furrow he left from his short slide told the story: blue ice lay under the snow!

The slope continued for several hundred yards, and we debated whether or not to put on crampons. "I say we can do it in our light hiking shoes," Craig said. "Now that we realize what's under here, we can shuffle along and test each step." It made sense. In retrospect, I think that as we grew more fatigued we were probably loath to expend more immediate energy—either physical or mental—on any kind of change. We tended to travel more and more on automatic pilot instead of making those little adaptations that, in the long run, ensure speed and safety.

Jan pulled herself together and started out, and I followed her. It took us an hour to cross the slope. Fortunately, it turned out to be mostly snow lying on dirt or gravel, but there were numerous patches of ice. Each patch demanded careful attention to balance and to placement of feet on the frozen ripples that modified the ice. We fell several times, but all avoided any major misstep that might have sent us skidding into the river. I felt good enough to lead across much of the slope, and enjoyed the exercise in judgment and technical skill. But at the end both Jan and I were exhausted, and even Craig looked beat.

Nevertheless, he started right off around the big bend. Our side of the valley was a broad scree field of large rocks that had tumbled down from the cliffs above. Initially, the line of least resistance led us along the river's shore. Then it started to snow, and I felt myself plunging into another low period. In an effort to stave it off, I knelt beside the river and scooped water into my mouth. The cold water gave me a temporary headache, and I sat on a rock to clear my senses, cradling my head in my hands. Then I looked up and saw Craig far ahead, scrambling over the slope of scree. I lowered my eyes, deciding I didn't want to look that far ahead. All the while Jan was waiting nearby for me. She was concerned, and her thoughtfulness was comforting. I smiled wanly at her in thanks. Hoisting myself to my feet, I decided to cure my blahs by looking at my tiredness as strictly a matter of attitude. So revived, I trekked on.

Before too many more steps, we angled up into the scree. The rocks were covered with snow here on the dark side of the river—treacherously slippery—and the holes between them waited to gobble a leg that slipped into them. Regardless of my resolution, I hobbled along behind Jan on legs that felt not quite attached. My whole body seemed made of wood. My feet were as cold and painful as they had been the day before, yet I didn't seriously consider changing into my stiff double climbing boots. I proceeded through a pervasive dullness, buried in fatigue. The roar of the river echoed in my head, and irritated me even more than it had earlier in the day. I paused and looked down at the source of the hateful sound. Below was a bridge made of two logs: now it was obvious that we should have been on the other side over the course of the last few miles. This and the upriver bridge we assumed we'd missed earlier gave access to and from easier terrain on the other side of the river.

A thousand foot placements later I perked up. The entire day was turning into cycles of drastic ups and downs. It was as if I were hooked into alternating electrical current—now positive, now negative.

By the time we reached the end of the boulder slope it had started to snow more heavily. Craig was waiting 150 feet above the river, which seemed strange. We plodded up to his stance, Jan struggling more than I now. It was easy to monitor each other's fluctuations.

"I saw some of the Sherpa's footprints heading up," Craig said in greeting. "Almost missed 'em under the new snow. I wouldn't have thought the trail climbed this high off the river."

We had been lucky. Logically, the trail should simply have paralleled the course of the river. But here it jutted off uphill. The trail led into a rhododendron forest. I went first, figuring the stimulation would keep me going strong for awhile. We passed into a delicate fairyland of huge plants with yellow bark. The trail was crisscrossed with roots, and gradually led upward even farther away from the river. I was glad to get away from the sound of it.

An hour before dusk we found a large cave. The floor was carpeted with dry leaves and the roof was blackened with the creosote of past fires. Birch trees grew out from the rim of the opening like eyebrows. It was inviting, and Jan and I voiced our opinions that it would be a fine home for the night. Craig wanted to press on, and tried to convince us.

"I've got a feeling that Monbuc is just beyond. Remember the Sherpa said there was a food cache. Maybe even another cabin. Let's walk at least until dark."

We had been traveling for seven hours; that was enough. In answer to Craig's suggestion, Jan and I simply sat still. We had had it, even though we were far short of the destination we had chosen when we looked at the map in the early morning. We were going to have to measure distance on this leg not in miles, but in vertical feet climbed, whiteouts navigated, and empty stomachs neglected.

I put my hand on my stomach. It was sadly concave from our unintentional fast, and excruciatingly empty. In a strange way it felt good, as if I were somehow more in tune with it empty than full. But we were fueling our travels from our muscle and what little fat remained—eating ourselves up, as it were. Craig was determined to prove himself right about Monbuc. Leaving his pack, he set off to explore further.

Sitting in the cave, I felt dazed, like an undertrained marathon runner who had just gone the distance. We didn't dare sit too long for fear our muscles would stiffen. After a brief rest we went out to the steep, forested slope and wrenched dead stalks from wiry rhododendrons and obstinate birches. The directed action revived me, and once we had accumulated a big stockpile I climbed into a cleft next to the cave to gather the icicles I could see there. I carried them back in my arms like silver cordwood—they would be our water supply, eliminating a long hike down to the river. Since we were without food, we took special care to bolster our water intake whenever we could. Waiting with Jan in the cave, I felt like a Neanderthal camper.

Forty-five minutes later Craig returned, huffing and puffing. "No sign of Monbuc, but the trail is awfully steep and slippery above here. It goes straight up the mountainside. Must be Ivan's 'ice river.' "

We all started to build the fire. A stick laid by one hand was realigned by another. Jan warned us to back off, saying, "This is a one man—ah, woman—job!" We all laughed. While she worked, Craig and I rigged a drying line over the prospective fire.

Soon Jan's blaze made us snug. We hung our fetid socks to dry, then thawed our toes near the flames. When the water boiled we made two cups apiece of flavorful but not nutritional bouillon for dinner, and followed it up with a dessert of multiple cups of hot water. I was immensely satisfied. The day had been trying, but was ending with relative creature comforts and happy camaraderie. Already I had forgotten the dangers and depressions. There was no doubt in any of our minds that we would make it out—the question was: when? Ivan had predicted the trip out would take two days; the next day would be the fourth.

We roasted our shoes by propping them close to the fire, and the steam and stench that rose from them effectively curbed our appetites. We dozed off—until Jan woke to discover her shoe insoles in flames. Pulling our shoes away from the fire, we discovered that each had been customized into a quirky shape that little resembled the original footwear.

Once in our bags, we fell asleep instantly. In the morning, the fog that had rolled in during the night locked us into a claustrophobic world. We were so hung over with fatigue that Craig started the fire without getting out of his sleeping bag.

Jan spoke from her bag. "Ned, remember the chocolate rum cake at Hapleton's Restaurant in Stowe?"

Craig served us breakfast—a tea bag apiece. "Help yourself to as many cups from the same bag as you like," he offered graciously.

As we packed to leave, Jan quipped, "I hope there will be no more perils today."

"Voilà," Craig announced, imitating a French accent, "it ees time to go very, very steep up the ice river. Non?"

A hundred feet beyond the cave the trail made a right angle turn and, at a relentlessly steep pitch, headed straight up the canyon wall. This new direction of the trail was a surprise, since we had assumed all along that we'd follow the river *down* to civilization. We had been lucky to find the point where the trail left the river. Strung out as we were, not finding this point might have led us into terrain that would have exhausted our little remaining strength.

Craig displayed his usual fitness, and I felt strong as I had the morning before. Jan, on the other hand, felt weak. She'd lost so much weight that her cheekbones stood out sharply. She didn't complain, but I could tell that she was struggling with each step. I tried to encourage her, as she had me when I was low.

Digging the sides of our hiking boots into the ground under the snow, and using the roots of trees as steps, we gained elevation through heavy vegetation. Patches of ice lay hidden under the snow, and we resorted to hauling ourselves hand over hand upward by gripping rhododendron branches. The pace seemed slow, and I was restless to be up and over what I imagined to be a short incline. I reminded myself how exhausted I'd felt the afternoon before, and that a moderate pace now might well pay off later. It was just as well. We climbed up and up for four hours—seemingly forever.

At the halfway point the trail veered to the right into a shallow gully. It must have been a streambed in the summer, because hard ice underlay the entire snowy area. This was Ivan's "ice river." We struggled upward, slipping and falling. Again we contemplated switching to climbing boots and crampons, but didn't because we thought the ice must end soon. We were so tired that such a switch seemed like a major undertaking. It went on for a half-mile, with no one saying much, except to offer advice about foot placement or offer a helping hand on a particularly steep section.

To lighten the mood, Craig chanted, "Where the hell is Monbuc?" every so often as we climbed.

Shortly before noon, the incline eased, and we continued up through a mature pine forest. There was little undergrowth, and we could see far to each side through the trees. It reminded us of the Sierra, and the familiarity was heartening. We stopped to drink from each stream running across the path.

"Where the hell is Monbuc?" Craig intoned.

We broke out of the forest, weaving through shrubs toward a big amphitheater formed by bald, rocky knobs. We were back in the high mountains, and the snow was deeper. Then the sun appeared, and we wilted under its enervating blast.

When Craig stopped to adjust his socks inside his shoes, I pressed on, with Jan right behind me. I had already experienced one of my familiar low cycles, but now I felt good and I was determined to make time while the motivation and energy lasted. I put my head down and charged, just as I had in my cross-country ski races years before. I was overextending myself, and knew it, but it felt good. Suddenly I heard snorting wheezes behind. When I stopped and turned, I saw that Jan was hyperventilating and couldn't catch her breath. Her mouth worked open and shut as she gasped for air. Her pale face and wild eyes frightened me. I flung off my pack and sat her on it, and before long she was breathing normally. Craig joined us and we all rested, agreeing that this was no time or place to run races.

Pacing ourselves, we marched above tree line to the crest of a pass. We estimated that, since that morning, we had climbed over 4,000 vertical feet. But the pass was no place for self-congratulation or resting: a stiff wind poured over it and we were soon shivering. We put on windproofs and scurried down the south side of the pass on a wide path free of snow. It ended in a colossal bowl that cradled two turquoise lakes. It was half past two when we stopped beside the first of them.

"Maybe this is Monbuc," Craig said.

"Whatever it is, it's home for the night," Jan said.

Leaving Jan with the packs, Craig and I split up to scout the area. We found a few stone hovels tucked into sheltered alcoves, so this was obviously a summer pasturing area. But there was no sign of a food cache. Maybe this wasn't Monbuc. Maybe we'd passed it, or maybe there was no such place.

We returned to Jan. It was time to decide whether to stay put or push on. Looking south, we could see the Sherpa's footprints leading up through deep snow over another pass. Again we were lucky to be guided by the prints—the logical move would have been to the west, following the stream that drained the lakes out through a break in the amphitheater. We looked at the map and tried to approximate our position and that of what we thought might be the nearest town. But the scale of the map was so small it was difficult to be very accurate. The question was whether a small village not marked on the map was closer. We were looking for food, after all, not a metropolis.

"We've got to get out of here," Craig said, forcibly. "Now. Let's move on while we can. We're above tree line. If another storm moves in, along with a whiteout, we could be pinned down. I still feel strong. I'll break trail."

Jan voted to stay put, saying, "You're right, Craig, but I'm out of gas; running on empty. I'd be dangerous on the next pass. I've spent the last two months looking at my feet, putting one in front of the other, and one more day won't matter."

For once, I kept my mouth shut.

Craig grinned. He unzipped the lower compartment of his pack, exhibited the last tropical fruit mix which he had preserved for just such an occasion, and offered it to Jan. She hesitated for a moment—too proud to take the extra rations, then silently dipped her hand into the packet and ate.

Craig and Jan were both right. We were terribly tired, and had not eaten a square meal in five days. But if we could muster a last spurt of energy, it would be to our advantage to climb over the next pass and get down below tree line.

After she had eaten the snack Craig provided, Jan simply said, "Okay, let's try it." Our feet were once again painfully cold, so we put on our double climbing boots for the long snowy slog ahead. To lessen the weight on Jan's pack, Craig took her ice axe and I took her crampons. It was more a psychological than a physical aid, but for once she didn't offer any argument at discriminatory treatment. At a quarter past three we started up the snow slope to the south, out of the bowl. Craig led, plodding rhythmically in the Sherpa's half-buried steps. Jan matched him step for step, doggedly determined—so close behind that he once turned and snapped at her for breathing down his neck. I followed along as the caboose.

We didn't stop to rest for the hour and a half it took to climb the slope. A rock shrine had been built on top, and a few tattered prayer flags flew from it. We descended steeply on the south side, which was free of snow. Four hundred vertical feet down, the Sherpa's footprints veered off into heavy snow and traversed under a stony ridge. We followed them across—mired in thigh-deep snow that had drifted in—and wallowed up over a third pass. On the far side we escaped the snow once and for all, and sat down briefly to enjoy the feeling of freedom. Below us, beyond hazy blue foothills that dropped lower in regular tiers, stretched the lowlands of Nepal. We knew we couldn't be far from some sort of village.

We teetered along a pointed ridge, then followed it sharply downhill. The sky turned red in the west as the sun set; then the night caught us. We had hiked for 11 hours, and it was time to stop. After setting up the tent, we started the stove outside and melted snow from a nearby patch. As the snow turned to water, Boy Blunder elbowed the pot, dumping all the contents. By the time a second brew was ready, Craig and Jan were asleep. I drank the warm water in thoughtful solitude—too satisfied to let the day go quite yet.

JAN: Early the following morning, Ned found a mashed bouillon cube in his coat pocket. We used the last of our gas to melt snow into lukewarm water and then divided the cube among the three of us. As we were toasting Craig's capable bushwhacking with our anemic drinks, I heard a sharp, quick "Hey" outside. I unzipped the tent enough to poke my head out—and there was Anu, with his troops behind him. I flew out of the tent and wrapped my arms around Anu and Angpura so tightly that I nearly choked them.

The Sherpas began crashing through the bushes, snapping off dry branches and twigs. I'd never seen such a large fire built so quickly. Anu had brought up fresh eggs from a settlement below and began cooking them and explaining what had happened at the same time. Apparently none of the locals had been willing to hire out as porters because of the nasty weather and the tough traveling it created. They also thought it was bad luck to go beyond the snow line, and they weren't equipped or prepared for the mountains in winter. Alas, Anu had known we would have been out of food for days. He was so worried he finally persuaded some locals to show him the way in to Makalu at least as far as the snow line, which was where we had just spent the night.

The eggs were an incredible delight. After most of two months eating freeze-dried food, then no food at all, real sustenance was overwhelming. We poured ketchup on top of the eggs, and the spicy sauce went off like fireworks in my mouth.

We trekked downhill together for miles and miles. My knees hurt, and so did Craig's toes—I had to laugh when he cut the ends of his shoes off to relieve the pressure on them. We reached Tashigan, a small settlement of thatched bamboo houses on a stream high in the jungle, in the late afternoon. The villagers were curious about us, to say the least. Since we hadn't trekked through their village on the way into the mountains, they had trouble figuring out where we had come from.

The people belonged to hill tribes that had originally come from Tibet and were often the poorest of six or seven major ethnic strains in the Arun Valley. Most were barefoot—only the rich wear shoes. Most of these hill settlements are isolated, being up to two weeks' walk away from any large bazaar town, and are self-sufficient: the wildlife and the barley, wheat, and potatoes they grow can sustain them. Some people never leave their villages during their entire lives, and intermarriage with other groups is uncommon. The outside world supplies only a few essentials—salt, jewelry and metal for knives.

I was anxious to clean up a bit, and wandered down to their glacial stream for a bath. Despite the temperature, it felt wonderful. When I returned, sleek as an otter, the locals looked at my wet hair with amazement because they very seldom bathe, and never in these temperatures. The most they would do would be to splash some water on their hands and faces. I stood by the open fire our Sherpas had built and were cooking dinner on. The warm, moving air billowed my clothes and reminded me of standing over a heat register in our farmhouse when I was a child, letting the warmth fill my nightgown. I was content.

It took us a few days to trek down to Tumlingtar, where we could catch a flight to Kathmandu. As we passed through the lower villages I noticed the sprawling farmlands and the devastating erosion. It is the yearly monsoon that eats away at the steep hillsides in the valley—20 percent of the arable land in the Arun Valley has been washed away. Anything above 7,000 feet in Nepal is unsuitable for farming because the thick monsoon clouds block the sun, so only 14 percent of Nepal's land can support farming. But the population is increasing rapidly: in the past 25 years, the total has gone from 9 million to 12 million people. The increase in the number of mouths to feed has led to overuse and abuse of the land: hillsides that have been terraced for more productive land sometimes slide into the river. Although the Arun Valley was lush, beautiful and mysterious, it showed signs of going the route of the depleted Khumbu. I had come to look at all of Nepal as an incredible land with an uncertain future.

◆ ◆ ◆

I looked over at Craig, then squeezed Ned's hand as we were lifted into the air on the plane out of Tumlingtar. It was January 29, 1982. All the pain, cold, and hunger, as well as the deep satisfaction, achievement, and supporting camaraderie that we'd shared seemed like a dream, as if they had happened to someone else. My imagination had already begun to shape the adventure by polishing the good points and erasing the bad. It was strange to see the land speeding away below us and remember the effort it had taken to travel a mere mile. Now, as we flew home, I was being swept away to another time and place. I was reluctant to leave the spectacular scenery, warm people, and intriguing culture. But I was grateful to have been to the top of the world once, to have traveled through the region step by step, and to have met and befriended the people who live there.

12

LHASA

"But you know the Tibetans are peasants. They are ignorant and dirty."

Tsao

JAN: 

Jim Bridwell had consented to join Ned and me on our "Tibet Ski Trek," as the Chinese called our northern half of the Everest Grand Circle. "This might be my one and only chance to see Tibet," he said. "Besides, it'll give me a chance to orchestrate a movie." I was happy that Jim was in. Steve McKinney wouldn't be along, since he would be defending his title as the fastest man on skis. Craig Calonica wouldn't be with us either, because he'd be challenging Steve's world record on the speed skiing circuit. Ned decided to invite Rick Barker, an easygoing expert skier and avalanche forecaster from Sun Valley, Idaho, to be the fourth team member. Ned and I had taught skiing with Rick in Vermont a few years earlier.

The four of us landed in Beijing in mid-April 1982, and although we were anxious to laugh and drink with our Chinese friends once more, we braced ourselves for endless negotiations. In 1980, before Ned and I skied off Muztagata, negotiations with the Chinese Mountaineering Association had taken nine days in three separate cities. But we were pleasantly surprised to find that the Chinese had become adept at handling expeditions: 30 teams from 14 countries would climb in their mountains in 1982. Still, Ned was worried about exposing our secret or being denied permission to ski near the Nepal-Tibet border while working out the specific route of our ski trek during negotiations. The Chinese were still unaware that we had a grand plan of encircling Everest and that we'd already completed half of the circle to the south in Nepal. Although we had the general expedition permission in hand, the Chinese had held out until we'd arrived in person before giving permission for our specific route, just as Mr. Sharma of the Ministry of Tourism had in Nepal. If the Chinese refused to let us near the border, the circle would never be completed.

The Chinese couldn't understand why we wanted to ski in Tibet. They had even sent us a telex in the States, before we'd even begun the circle, which read, "According to material we get, the ice-skating or skiing cannot be conducted at the Rongbuk Glacier. Please consider your itinerary." But Ned handled negotiations beautifully. It took only an hour and a half, and in the end the Chinese gave us carte blanche for roaming the area around Everest on skis, calling us "pioneers of skiing in Tibet." Ned quickly responded by complimenting the C.M.A. officials for being "pioneers of free enterprise." A couple of days later Ned, Jim, Rick, our interpreter, Chang Chong Min, and I were on the plane flying to Lhasa, Tibet.

NED: We flew by jet from Beijing to Chengdu, then on to Lhasa in a turbo-prop Ilyushin. Before take-off a female voice, amplified by the plane's loudspeaker, instructed us in careful English to "Please fasten your seatbelts." We looked, then dug under our seat cushions in vain. Later I asked the stewardess about the lack of seatbelts. "Oh," she replied, "we do not wish to upset our passengers. Seatbelts are for trouble."

Below our flight path I counted many of the great rivers of Asia, which radiate from the eastern portion of the Tibetan Plateau: first, the upper reaches of the Yalong and the Yangtze; then, in succession, the Mekong, the Salween, and the eastern branches of the Tsang Po. Here, in highlands only sparsely inhabited, the waters were clear and fast. They flowed through deep gorges that twisted under ridges of dark sandstones and basalts and pale limestones. The ridgetops of the Daxue Shan and Hengduan Shan lay under wraps of snow, so remote their separate peaks were unnamed. Beyond rose the Great Himalaya.

Later the rivers would emerge at a drowsy pace onto the lowlands to the east and south, sustaining nearly half the world's population in China, Southeast Asia, and India.

Although we spent much of the flight with our faces pressed against the oval windows, looking down on the exotic landscape, we also talked enthusiastically about our expectations of Tibet and traveling around the north side of Everest.

Jim had turned into a good friend, so I was delighted to have him with us for this half of the circle. I was also a little worried that the trip might turn out to be a letdown for him. The Tibet leg promised to be mostly a cultural experience and an exotic high-country trek, and these were not Jim's specialty. He was most interested in extremely difficult climbs. Would he be restless as we junketed about the mountains on a more pedestrian excursion?

This was Rick's first expedition. I had invited him because we expected cross-country skiing to be an important part of the Tibet half of the circle, and he was one of the finest back-country skiers in America. We had worked together teaching skiing in Vermont, and I had appreciated his ready laugh and his ability to work with other people. Although he was not well traveled, I felt he would adapt easily to whatever situation we might meet.

He thrived on short skirmishes in the mountains of Idaho and the Sierra—skiing versions of his days as a California surfer. But he was to find that expeditionary life was very different. Sometimes you traveled halfway around the world—all the while fighting through ponderous logistics and bureaucratic blockades—for a few brief ski runs. During that time you lived like primitives and risked your necks daily.

JAN: As we were unloading and organizing our 39 bags in the dry, dusty air at the Lhasa airport, I heard Chang coughing hard behind me. "Not quite like Beijing here in Lhasa, huh, Chang!" I said over my shoulder. When I wheeled around to look at him, he appeared so disheveled and miserable that I began to laugh aloud, though I tried not to. Luckily the humor was infectious, and Chang began to giggle. When he grinned, his chubby face became all teeth and no eyes.

"The Chinese have a saying," he told me. "Laughter makes you 10 years younger. This expedition will make me many years older, so I must keep laughing."

Chang had the right attitude. He'd opted to study English in his homeland, China, and had become an interpreter because what he read about the West had fascinated him. He'd done so well in his studies that he was in constant demand as an interpreter for American and British tourists. Chang told me that he enjoyed traveling with tourists, but he had never imagined he might be thrown in with a bunch of American mountaineers and have to spend a couple of months at 17,000 feet in Everest Base Camp. Right now, life was a bitter pill for Chang, but he was doing his damnedest to swallow it.

He was upset because there was no bus or truck to pick us up at the barren airport. We had yet to meet up with our liaison officer, who would be in charge of such details from now on, so Chang was frayed from doing double duty as shepherd and translator. An important-looking man left the plane shortly after we did, and went directly to a car that stood waiting for him. Chang ran up to one of the vehicle's windows, speaking rapidly. He motioned us all to come with him and leave the bags behind. He'd found someone kind enough to give us a ride to our accommodations.

NED: The official vehicle of the Commander of the People's Liberation Army, Lhasa District, was a well-shined Toyota Land Cruiser. A starched young man wearing white linen gloves drove us at top speed, crouched behind the steering wheel as if he were stalking a wild animal. The vehicle jittered and jumped on the gravel washboards—scattering walkers, draft animals, and bicyclists, then blanketing them in a dust cloud.

I gripped the back of the driver's seat, and tried to pay attention to the words of the Chinese Commander.

"You are the third expedition through Lhasa on the way to Chomolungma," he said.

The Commander lounged in the front seat, his arm draped over the seat back. A bright red star glistened on his visored cap. He was amused at the translation of our plans to ski near Everest.

He chatted back and forth with Mr. Chang, our translator. Chang turned to me. "He says this is the wrong part of China to come to ski. He used to be stationed in the northeast of China. There are many ski troops along the border areas. The snow is good there."

"Yes," I agreed. "Jan and I have skied in the northeast of China, and also in the far west. So now we'll see if we can ski in the south—in Tibet."

We drove toward Lhasa, 65 miles away from the airport, along the banks of the Tsang Po River. Here, flowing eastward from its origins near the sacred peak of Mount Kailas, it was wide, tranquil, and turquoise. Eventually the river would bend around the base of 25,442-foot Namcha Barwa, then churn southward and become the Brahmaputra before emptying into the Bay of Bengal.

I caught a glimpse of a band of Tibetans who had hauled their coracles out onto a sandbar. The round boats, which looked like walnut-shell halves, were made of raw, uncured yak skins stretched over a framework of willow branches. One end of each craft had been propped up by a stick so the hull could dry.

Now halfway to Lhasa, we sped across a new bridge that spanned the Tsang Po. A sentry saluted the car, and we headed north up the Kyichu River.

Chang and the Commander chatted on and on. Jan, beside me, stared out the window. I turned to look at Jim and Rick. They were hunched in the third seat. Jim's face was set and stoic. His appearance reminded me of the immensely uncomfortable night we had spent on Pumori, with four of us crammed into a single tiny tent. Each time the Toyota bucked on the rough road, Jim was launched into the ceiling, then dropped onto the unpadded seat.

The Chinese Commander whose car we shared was in charge of the largest contingent of Chinese regulars stationed in Tibet. They are there to ensure that Tibet remains integrated into "the big family of the motherland."

Fifty-four minorities live within China's boundaries. They are only six percent of the nation's population, but that adds up to nearly 60 million people. More significantly, they occupy more than half the land area of China, much of it in the strategically critical border areas.

China made its military move into Tibet on October 7, 1950, to establish a buffer zone between China and India. Government officials did not consider their action the invasion of a foreign country. "Tibet is an inalienable part of China," state Chinese leaders. Their claim is based on periods when it was a vassal state dating back to Kublai Khan and the Yuan Dynasty of the thirteenth century, and Chinese emperors were officially represented in Lhasa as early as 1736. No country in the world has ever formally recognized Tibet as an independent country. Following the occupation, Beijing granted Tibet token autonomy under the fourteenth Dalai Lama.

Many Tibetans see the situation in a different light. Regardless of distant history, they maintain that they won their independence when they began self-government after the collapse of the Ch'ing dynasty in 1911. Sealed off from China on the northwest by the Kun Lun Shan mountains, on the north by the deserts of Qinghai desert, and in the east by the deep gorges we had flown over this morning—and sealed from the rest of the world by the Great Himalaya to the south—the land is a geographic entity. Tibetans also claim that they are ethnically and culturally distinct from the Chinese.

In 1959, after years of escalating turmoil, the 24-year-old Dalai Lama—disguised as a rifle-toting soldier and barely able to see without his spectacles—fled southward over the Himalaya to India. In the months that followed, 100,000 refugees joined him in exile.

Mao quickly abolished the old system and replaced it with the "democratic reforms" already adopted throughout the rest of China. Landlords and high monks were denounced, then imprisoned or driven into menial occupations, and estates were distributed among the peasants.

During the Cultural Revolution of the late 1960s and early 1970s, all but 10 of 2,500 monasteries—the treasure houses of Tibetan scholarship—were destroyed, religious worship was banned, and the monkhood dismantled. Tibetans were ordered to grow wheat instead of their traditional barley, then obliged to sell it at a low price to support the 120,000 Han Chinese cadre and 250,000 soldiers. Mao seemed determined to erase Tibetan identity, which irrevocably alienated the Tibetans from their Chinese overlords.

After Mao died and the Gang of Four was rounded up, the Chinese government embarked on an era of more open understanding. Tibet was given a chance to recover and redefine itself, to combine the best of Buddhism and communal philosophy. In 1979 a delegation of Tibetan exiles representing the Dalai Lama was allowed to tour their homeland without restriction. Scenes were so emotional that their escorting Chinese hosts were repeatedly moved to tears. The visit set in motion a radical shift in Peking's minority policies and subsequent programs.

We turned a corner, and the road funneled down a line of willows and poplars toward the Tanglo Hills that hung above the treetops like a purple shroud. At a second corner, the Potala, lime white and vaguely luminescent, rose in the distance and seemed to dominate the higher hills. This was the former palace of the Dalai Lama, and was said to contain over 10,000 rooms and shrines.

We had arrived at last in the Forbidden City. In the old days, only the most determined trespassers had braved hardships and hostile guardians to journey toward the "City of Sun." We had simply bought tickets.

Still, we were in for an experience shared by few others. I determined to put myself back in time as much as possible. I had read James Hilton's *Lost Horizon,* in which the narrator's arrival in the mystical city is vividly described:

> To Conway, seeing it first, it might have been a vision fluttering out of that solitary rhythm in which lack of oxygen had encompassed all his faculties. It was, indeed, a strange and half-credible sight. A group of colored pavilions clung to the mountainside . . . with the chance delicacy of flower petals impaled upon a crag. It was superb and exquisite. . . . it looked to Conway a delightfully favored place. . . . [He] experienced, as he gazed, a slight tightening of apprehension; . . . but the feeling was only momentary, and soon merged in the deeper sensation, half mystical, half visual, of having reached at last some place that was an end, a finality.

The Toyota swerved from the idyllic tree-lined road—breaking my daydreams—and wove violently among chuckholes. Jim groaned. A factory belching black smoke blocked out the Potala.

"What is *that*?" I asked.

"The Lhasa cement plant," Chang explained. "There are more than 250 small industries in Tibet since 1950. We have built wool and textile and carpet and match factories. Opened quarries and mines. Without Chinese technology, Tibet would still be in the dark ages."

A couple of miles farther, we pulled into a neat complex of stone buildings and stopped in the courtyard of one. This was the state guesthouse, and our home for the next three days.

JAN: I was taken aback by the style and comfort, as well as the price of our lodgings, in Lhasa. I'd expected something rudimentary, in keeping with the local lifestyle. But Tibet belongs to China and it was the Chinese who allowed us access to the roof of the world. So it was fitting that we were put up in the Han Chinese section of town, in a military compound remodeled for tourists who could afford to pay Lhasa's prices of up to $200 per night.

We had a suite with two bedrooms and a bath—my heart leapt when I spotted the gigantic white porcelain tub. I was elated to think that I could enjoy one of my favorite pastimes, lolling in a hot tub and daydreaming, in ancient Tibet.

"What's that thing over there by the beds, Ned? It looks like something to extinguish unpleasant guests," I laughed. I examined it more closely and realized it was a tank to provide "oxygen cocktails" to those suffering from the altitude after the jump from sea level to 12,000 feet in only a few hours. Seeing it made me realize the incredible expense of supplying Lhasa, where almost everything had to be brought in by air or hauled in overland. These complicated logistics carried a heavy price tag.

Of the four of us, only Rick was feeling the effects of the swift change in altitude. I hoped that his nausea would pass quickly, so that he could begin to enjoy our surroundings. Considering that he was the new boy on the block, he had done an admirable job of fitting into our close society. This was no easy task—both new and old relationships are often fragile and tentative at the beginning of a trip. Ned and I were going through our "neutralization" phase, when we each become just one of the crew. Jim and Rick, who had never met before, were trying to get to know each other.

Rick was a good sport and a stoic, so he probably felt much sicker than he told us. Our goal-oriented endeavor was a long way from his usual freewheeling California style, but Rick seemed like someone who would adapt to the circumstances he found himself in. I remembered hearing Rick tell a friend how he had signed on for our expedition. "Yea," he said. "Ned's smart. He sold Bridwell the expedition as a climbing trip. He sold me the expedition as a ski trip. And he sold Jan the expedition as a vacation." With perceptions that keen, he should do just fine.

NED: After our confining ride in from the airport, we were ready to see the sights of Lhasa immediately. Chang knocked on our door.

"Time for *xu xi*," he informed us. "We must rest."

Immediately I was on guard. I had heard this many times before during our two previous trips to China, and I was ready. It was the opening move of the reluctant-guide game.

"We are not tired," I retorted politely but firmly, covering his opening. We had no intention of wasting half the afternoon. "If we sleep now, we will not sleep tonight."

Chang looked crestfallen, then brightened. "Lunch must be specially prepared. That will take an hour. Time for rest. Xu xi."

"The other guests just left the dining hall. I'm sure there will be food remaining," I suggested. "We are not particular." I was determined to visit old Lhasa during the afternoon, regardless of Chang's sleepiness. We had not come halfway around the world to nap.

"The driver assigned to you may be incapacitated," Chang said, shaking his head.

"Let's find another driver," I suggested.

"That is possible, yes," Chang nodded. "But your guide for the town is not expecting to be with you today."

"We are happy to walk in the streets alone," I answered.

I had learned that polite, unrelenting pressure usually works in bureaucratic China, and that it was necessary to be insistent if you wanted to mix with the people on the streets. Otherwise one's travels were likely to be full of factories, museums, and monuments. I knew where the people were—they were in the alleys and alcoves of the city, or at the end of a path followed into the country.

We walked to the dining hall and were served a quick but delicious lunch with cold beer.

"Mr. Chang," I said, "will you join us in old Lhasa?" My invitation was serious. We were growing fond of our Chinese shadow.

"No, I have seen it," he replied. "This is my second trip. No Chinese wish to come here. Tibet is a very poor place. But it is my job, my duty."

I looked at him in surprise. "But this is Lhasa, the most sought after, most magical city in the world!"

"Not for Chinese," he replied sadly. "For us it is duty. How will you understand?" He paused. He was very intelligent and well read. "Ah, you live in the north in America?"

"Yes."

"Maybe . . ." he said thoughtfully, "maybe you would understand if you were told to live and work in the deep South, or Appalachia."

We left the dining hall and piled into a Toyota.

"Remember!" Chang admonished us. "Do not buy any relics. Officials in Beijing will confiscate them." We waved good-bye to him and drove to the outskirts of old Lhasa.

At last on our own, we walked 100 feet down a broad avenue banked by functional gray buildings with tin roofs that housed Chinese stores and offices. Then, in a dozen steps, we passed out of new Lhasa and into the Middle Ages along a maze of curved, cobbled streets. Nothing was symmetrical, but everything fit. Two-storied whitewashed houses of stone blocks and clay bricks crowded shoulder to shoulder. In the old days, it was considered blasphemy to build higher than two stories and so compete with the Potala or Jokhang temple. The houses had deep-set doors and windows overhung with eaves of blue, black, and green blocks of wood stacked one on top of another. Most sills were decorated with potted flowers. Electrical wires criss-crossed overhead like tangled cat's cradles.

Within minutes we were surrounded by hordes of Tibetans who tugged at us and pressed against us insistently. We each moved along in the midst of private entourages. It felt benignly suffocating. The women wore dark tunics, colorful blouses, and jewelry of silver, jade, coral, and turquoise. They reminded me of the Sherpa women we had trekked with in Nepal. Some of the men wore cotton Mao jackets, others woolen robes dyed to dark reds and browns. The ones we noticed most swaggered in sheepskins that left one shoulder bare. They sported fur-lined hats angled jauntily, with one ear flap half down, and carried knives tucked under bright waistbands. Tibetans considered the absence of color a sign of poverty. Some wore charm boxes that contained personal prayers; others wore long strings of polished prayer beads.

The atmosphere was that of a country fair. Shops sold all manner of things, for Tibetans take a special pleasure in trading and bargaining. Before the arrival of the Chinese in 1950, one could find here Australian butter, English whiskey, Elizabeth Arden products, and Bing Crosby's latest records. Many people clowned and danced for us when we turned a camera toward them; others assumed serious, dignified expressions. Later, Jim told us that many people had delighted in sliding his shirtsleeves up to his elbow, then stroking his hairy forearms. He believed their fascination was due to their relative lack of hair. Tibetans love to laugh and poke fun both at themselves and at others. Throughout the centuries, travelers who managed to get to Lhasa invariably described the Tibetans as kind, generous, hospitable, and pleasantly open.

We had expected insistent begging, but here it took a new twist. A hundred times we heard pleading words spoken through clasped hands: "Dalai Lama! Dalai Lama! Photo. Dalai Lama! You have?"

We were approached repeatedly by peddlers who sidled up to us to sell rings, bracelets, knives, and little statues. They hid their wares inside their garments and pulled them out furtively to show us. I thought of Chang's warning, then purchased a tiny statue.

Jim emerged from a crooked alleyway towing a Tibetan who was dressed in a checked Western suit coat. "This is Chester. He's from Oregon," Jim said in explanation.

We followed Chester back into the maze of old Lhasa, the heart of the city before the arrival of the Chinese. A stooped woman sweeping the pressed-earth path sent a chicken into flight with a flick of her broom. We entered a miniature courtyard, ducked under a circular stairway molded of adobe, and stepped into a well-ordered house.

"These are my friends," Chester said to us, sweeping his hand as introduction to three Tibetans who smiled, nodded, and left. Soon a woman returned with five cups of tea. "I rode in the back of a truck from Kathmandu," he said. "I'm staying here for awhile, waiting for permission to go to eastern Tibet. My mother lives there. I used to live there. I have not seen her for 27 years."

"Why did you leave Tibet?" Rick asked.

"My family is Khampa."

That was answer enough for me. I knew that the Khampas—tall, fierce fighting men—were heavily involved in the first violent outburst against the Chinese in 1956. Many had been trained by the C.I.A. at the mountain winter warfare center in Colorado. Since then, they had carried out hit-and-run guerrilla skirmishes until the late 1960s.

"When things got bad in Tibet, I decided not to return," Chester explained. "I am a carpenter in Oregon. I came back after the Chinese relaxed control and opened the country to visitors."

"To stay?" I asked.

"During the first few days, I thought maybe so," he replied. "But I have been waiting three weeks for a permit to travel to the east. It is not so good as the Chinese say."

Curious, I nosed about the house while Jim and Chester puffed clouds of blue cigarette smoke at each other. It was worth a polite snoop to see how a Tibetan family lived—this was no model house into which we had been ushered by our Chinese hosts.

There were three and a half rooms: a family sleeping chamber with beautiful rugs on the beds, a combination sitting room and chapel, a kitchen with big brass kettles, and a storage alcove. Seven people lived here. I returned to the small chapel, which was lit by a single bare bulb. Silver water cups and painted prayer wheels adorned a cabinet of wood and glass. A portable radio-cassette machine occupied the center of the table that the others sat around.

"It looks like your friends have a comfortable house," I said to Chester.

Chester looked about him as if he had never been in the room before. "Yes," he said reluctantly. "Yes, it is good, because things are more even than before. For my friends it is better. Their children are going to school, although many of their teachers have only six years' education. After the first grades, all education is in Chinese, not Tibetan. I don't know any Tibetan who has a university education." He poured more tea. "My mother used to be very rich. Now, she has barely anything."

I looked at my watch. We were late in getting back to the Toyota, so after a few more words we took our leave. The driver had been waiting, and seemed to reprimand us with his eyes.

We returned to the guesthouse. Waiting for us was Losan, our liaison officer, and Laba, our truck driver. Both were Tibetan and worked for the Chinese Mountaineering Association. Losan, dressed in leathers, sat on an ancient motorcycle with one leg cocked up on the gas tank. Laba, who was wearing a long oiled-canvas coat, had sparkling eyes and a ready grin. We all went into our room and talked about our plan and logistical needs. During the next two days we would go over every aspect of the plan in detail.

JAN: We were given a special Han Chinese interpreter to guide us while in Lhasa. Her name was Tsao, and she had been specially briefed in the history and culture of the area. I suspected that much of what she told us would be the "party line." She had lived in Lhasa for 10 years, yet spoke no Tibetan. At first, I didn't understand why, but after spending some time with Tsao I began to see what got in the way. One day as we watched religious pilgrims circling the great Jokhang monastery in the center of Lhasa, Tsao said, "But you know, they are peasants, just masses. They are ignorant and dirty." I doubted then that Tsao often mingled with the locals.

NED: We stood in front of the Jokhang, or House of Wisdom, the holiest temple in all Tibet. It was 1,300 years old, and housed the Sakyamuni Buddha, or Jawa Rinpoche, said to have been brought to Tibet in A.D. 630 by Princess Wen Ching of China, one of two wives of King Songtsen Gampo. She talked the king into adopting Buddhism, probably as a superior form of magic and healing.

The flagstones that paved the entry had been polished and hollowed by centuries of bowed prayer. Beginning in 1980, the Chinese had once again permitted worship. Today, as on every day since, softly chanting pilgrims shuttled up and down in endless prostrations on the stone terrace. Towed by our Chinese guide, Tsao, we stepped carefully around the praying figures, tugged open great red double doors, and passed into the Jokhang. Then the doors thudded shut behind us and we found ourselves alone.

"I thought it was open to worship." I spoke to Tsao.

"Certainly. But today it is closed for repairs," she replied.

We walked silently through a dark passage guarded by frescoes of hideous demons with round stomachs, tiger fangs, and snake tongues who were gnawing the skulls of helpless humans. In the old days, the monks had ruled through fear and superstition. To devout Tibetans, these demons were as real as the trees and rivers around them. Bad behavior, including disrespect for the monkhood and nobility, or refusal to pay taxes, were punishable by the hells depicted in the frescoes.

We entered an open-air courtyard. It was an enchanted place of yellow walls and bright red columns that supported golden roofs. Golden dragons and mythical birds erupted from the corners, and silk banners hung from the eaves. Doors and windows had been newly painted with meticulous designs. I looked around, but saw no workmen. The buildings were in fine repair. The Chinese have spent hundreds of thousands of dollars fixing the damage of the Cultural Revolution.

The Jokhang was not closed for repairs today, it was simply closed. But by whom?

Two monks in crimson robes greeted us. In 1959, there were still 120,000 monks in Tibet. Earlier, they had numbered 300,000—at least one son from every family. Having a son enter the monastery brought good karma to the family and a chance for education to the boy. The population of Tibet, which had been declining since the seventeenth century, is now on the upswing (currently nearly two million) and there are fewer than 2,000 monks, who serve as caretakers in the few remaining monasteries and temples.

Tsao introduced us to the monks. "They will escort us."

A man in a Mao suit tagged along. He was a member of the Department of Cultural Relics. "No photographs," he said in greeting. A few minutes later he said it again.

We entered the central hall. A colossal Future Buddha, gilded and draped in brocade, raised his hands high above our heads in benediction. We walked from shrine to shrine, then waited while the monks unlocked a huge padlock and hauled a heavy chain curtain aside so we could stand before the Sakyamuni Buddha. The monks were practiced curators giving us a tour of a stuffy museum.

"This is the Water Dragon shrine," Tsao said, as if she were repeating a memorized lecture. I turned to the older monk. "How many pilgrims come to the Jokhang when it is open for worship?"

"Over a thousand each day," Tsao translated.

"Why is it not open today?" I asked.

The monk smiled with a mixture of sadness and reality. "You must ask the Chinese."

Those five words summed up the situation in modern Tibet. There is greater religious freedom today than during the past two-and-a-half decades. But it appears to be precisely choreographed from Beijing. The Tibetan Buddhism that once controlled every aspect of life—cultural, economic, and political—is on display as in a museum.

As we climbed the stairs onto the roof of the temple, I knew the answer to my earlier question. The Chinese had, for whatever reason, closed the Jokhang today. If they so chose, they could close it tomorrow and the next day. The man in the Mao suit who shadowed us—not the abbot—was the boss.

As we emerged into the sunlight, the "Mao man" said, "Photographs now okay."

In a sun-drenched corner two monks, an elder standing, a younger man seated, chopped and swept the air with their hands. Other monks watched, laughing and pointing. "What are they doing?" I asked Tsao.

"Searching for truth using logic and language," she replied.

The two monks whirled, leapt, and flung their arms as if they were in strenuous athletic training. They shouted. They crossed fingers and sliced hand gestures in flamboyant punctuation—all to make critical points in this spirited debate. We were witnessing dialectical inquiry into the nature of existence, and it seemed joyfully sincere. I had no idea of the nature of the debate, but it would be something difficult for me to grasp—maybe an investigation into a statement made by the monk who was standing, such as "Form is always a shape."

◆ ◆ ◆

The next morning we toured the Potala. It, like the Jokhang, seemed like a sterile museum—a huge, haunted edifice filled with the remains of past Dalai Lamas and gilded shrines coated in dust. That afternoon we embarked on a spree of guerrilla tourism after canceling our scheduled tour of Drepung monastery. It had once housed 10,000 monks, but is now primarily a museum. Instead, we set off on our own cross-town and cross-country. I had read about the Tibetan custom of air burial, and knew there was a site near Lhasa. I was determined to see it—and doubly determined when Tsao insisted it was no longer practiced.

We walked beyond Lhasa, out along the base of the Tanglo Hills, whose knobby summits were still daubed with snow. As we rested against a tree that shaded a stone house, a woman offered a cup of *chang,* or barley beer. As thanks, we gave her a Polaroid picture of herself. She gaped in toothless amazement. We continued on, weaving in and out of dry ravines.

Each vulture that soared overhead seemed to be the final clue to the whereabouts of the burial location we sought. Vultures are considered sacred birds, and are the final recipients of celestial burial, which is the most common form of burial in Tibet. The ground is hard and frozen much of the year, and wood for cremation is scarce. After death, monks chant to release the soul from the body. Then an undertaker, who is always of low caste, carries the body to a special rock, where he dissects the corpse and crushes the bones, mixing them with mashed barley. Every morsel is fed to the vultures, so that even in death the body is of use to fellow creatures.

After two hours we found what we were looking for—a huge rock embedded in a shallow alcove. The place was deserted and eerie. Scraps of clothing from the deceased lay scattered about, and clumps of vulture feathers. We climbed up on the rock, which was pockmarked and chipped. Knives, hammers, axes, and saws littered the surface, which was black with dried blood. The place both attracted and repelled me. The very foreignness of the custom provoked my curiosity, but its distance from our own rituals was also shocking. We walked back to the guesthouse not sure how we would have felt if a ceremony had been going on while we were there.

That night I asked Chang when the Jokhang would open again for worship. I wanted to be there when it was alive with pilgrims.

"Tomorrow. But if you wish to take photographs, you must pay—150 yuan." I calculated that to be $90, and reluctantly agreed. "It doesn't matter," Chang chirped. "Money. It is just like water. You fetch it, you use it. It doesn't matter. We are all the same. Friends."

The next morning I walked to the Jokhang and as I stepped through the great doors I was immediately swept through a dark passage in a jostling current of humanity that smelled of greased wool and charcoal. In the broad courtyard the crowd slowed, then stopped. Here hundreds of worshippers waited in reverent calm to enter the inner sanctum and pray at the shrines that we had so clinically examined two days before.

The man in the Mao suit from the Department of Cultural Relics was lying in wait for me. I slapped the required yuan in his outstretched hand, then passed under a sign that said "No Photos." The "Mao man" followed.

It didn't matter. Once in the central hall, I entered a world that obliterated thoughts of anything else.

Smoky blue daylight filtered down from slit windows four stories above. It lit the great central Buddha's benign face, and the brocade banners that framed it. The eyes seemed unfocused but all-seeing. Lower, the meditative pose reflected a golden light. Hundreds of yak-butter candles were burning, some in demitasse-size chalices, others in banquet-size silver bowls decorated with copper-colored dragons. I was immersed in heavy fumes and endless deep chanting.

Rows of dark-robed devotees sat on the floor beneath the Future Buddha. They chanted, "Om mani padme hum, Om mani padme hum." The words rose from so many mouths that individual syllables were lost in the general benediction. Their eyes were unfocused, as if they were peering into their own being. Many leafed through piles of long rectangular papers held by wooden binders—sacred texts of Buddhist scripture. One man fixed me with a white-eyed stare that should have been frightening, but was not.

I joined the slow procession circling the hall. It wound under low peripheral balconies supported by ancient painted beams. Young and old alike were here to worship. A woman beside me suckled her baby. The roots of religion seemed to run deep. I was never jostled, and nobody shied away from me. There was a mutual respect that seemed to deter any anger or contentiousness. In line, I squeezed into tiny side-chambers to witness the worship.

Here, before the shrines, control slipped away. The air was loaded with superstitious fervor and buzzed with electric energy. The faces of the pilgrims glowed with emotion. They reached—almost lunged—to touch the statues; laid offerings of flowers, barley, and money. Each "Om mani padme hum" echoed off leering figures clothed in silk that lined the walls. Monks standing bare-armed and glistening with sweat dispensed oil from silver pitchers. They herded the faithful on, shoving and shouting at the crowd as if they were naughty children.

Somehow I was not feeling claustrophobic, although the fumes and the bodies and the fervor made me giddy. But I touched something real. Here was the essence of Tibetan Buddhism: a combination of ancient belief in shamanism and blood sacrifice, tantric magic and sexual rites, and the attainment of nirvana through the help of enlightened, living Buddhas. The Jokhang, filled with pilgrims, symbolized an entire culture.

JAN: I stood outside the Jokhang, absorbed in watching the circling pilgrims. Many were dressed in dark tatters or in sheepskin. There was a continuous droning hum of "O mani padme hum" as the people prayed on their strings of 108 beads and spun their hand-held prayer wheels. My attention was drawn to those who had pads on their knees and wooden blocks strapped to their palms. They were performing *kyan chehak*, meaning "like silkworms." The pilgrims would prostrate themselves, stretching their arms before them as they lay face down, then would stand again where their hands had reached, all the while repeating their prayers as they moved forward. Tsao told me that she had seen many people traveling to Lhasa from miles away in this fashion.

I began circling too, although I looked like a freak to the Tibetans because I was a woman dressed like a man and had fair skin. But they merely acknowledged my presence and continued on, round and round. Some did stare and follow me, but they never stopped going around. Tsao told me that they continue through the night: there is always someone beginning when another is falling asleep.

13

ON THE EVEREST ROAD

"In China you need permission for everything."

Ned Gillette

JAN:  We left Lhasa before daylight on April 22 for the three-day, 800-kilometer drive to Everest. The day before we had loaded the four-ton army "liberation truck" (designed in 1949) with all our food, base camp equipment, and mountaineering gear, plus two 55-gallon drums of gas. Losan, Laba, and Chang crowded into the heated cab; we, bundled in parkas and windproofs, climbed over the tailgate and into the back, which was covered with a canopy tied over metal bars. We nestled in among the baggage as best we could, and settled in for the next 13 hours. Laba leaned on the gearshift and ground his way into first gear. We chugged away from Lhasa, through villages that had not yet awakened, then across the Tsangpo River.

Despite the heavy green canvas covering the overstuffed truck, a cloud of dust and dirt drifted around us, so we put on white surgical masks to keep our breathing passages clear. The ride over the rough road was so bumpy that I found it was good passive exercise trying to keep myself from colliding with the others and our packaged supplies.

How unlike our approach to Everest from the south, in Nepal, I thought. Our trek in there on foot over forested hill and dale had been romantic, and had prepared our muscles as well as our psyches for our winter climb. The Khumbu and its people had been both charming and welcoming. Our present approach to Everest by truck, in the barren rain shadow of the Himalaya, was a sharp contrast, and the people here seemed to be more reserved and skeptical.

Underneath our masks the air became hot, stale, and sticky, but if we tried riding without the masks, we ate too much dirt. As we drove higher and the air became thinner, we began to feel as if we were slowly suffocating beneath our masks.

Because we'd flown to Lhasa, at 12,000 feet, from sea level and were rising up to 15,000 feet two days later, we were all feeling lethargic with altitude hangover. It was an effort just to move. I put on the earphones of my cassette player and tried to drift away from the uncomfortable surroundings. Rick, still pale and weak from altitude sickness, pulled on my second set of earphones to do the same. When I turned to look at Jim, I began to laugh. He was swaddled in down clothing to ward off the cold and snuggled up to the unwrapped dried sheep carcass that would feed us in Base Camp. He, like the rest of us, was coated with gray dust that had changed the color and texture of his hair and skin.

"Bridwell, you dirtbag," I laughed. He just rolled his head toward me and returned my grin without a word.

NED: In some ways we felt like trespassers in Tibet, for we were guests of the Chinese, not the Tibetans. Long ago, Tibet was an open country—at least politically. The great mountains, windswept plateaus and river gorges inhabited by murderous bandits that ringed Tibet were natural barriers to travel. Only a handful of foreigners, mostly Jesuits and Franciscans drawn by reports that pockets of Nestorian Christians still existed in the mountains, had managed to visit Tibet. In 1661-62, Fathers Johann Grueber and Albert D'Orville traveled on foot from Peking to Agra, and were the first Europeans to visit Lhasa in more than 300 years. Later, Tibet was invaded by the Gurung and then the Chinese. Alarmed because of the threat to their way of life, their religion, and their gold fields, Tibetan regents sealed the country's frontiers.

Trespassers were often imprisoned, tortured, and even put to death. As late as the middle of the nineteenth century, Tibet was still largely unexplored and certainly inaccurately mapped territory. The latitude and longitude of Lhasa, for example, were not known. Concerned that the Dalai Lama might side with the Russians who were vying for control of the region, the British were desperate to obtain accurate geographical information of lands to the north of India. They came up with an ingenious solution: they trained Indians of the intellectual class called "pundits" in surveying techniques. Disguised as traveling holy men, the pundits made solo journeys of thousands of miles and several years' duration. Counting each precisely paced stride with unvarying accuracy, they summed them on rosaries that held an even 100 beads instead of the customary 108. They recorded the results on scraps of paper hidden in prayer wheels. Small compasses, sextants, and thermometers were hidden in false compartments built into baggage cases and walking sticks and tucked into folds in robes. Had the pundits been exposed, they would have been executed on the spot as spies. For this risk and hardship, they were paid 20 rupees per month. In the history of exploration, there are few who can match their achievements.

In 1871 a pundit named Hari Ram, code-named "MH" or "#9," made a half-circumambulation of the Everest group, although he was far enough away so that he never saw the mountain itself. Starting in Darjeeling, he crossed the border and journeyed to Shigatse. Turning south, he recrossed the Himalaya to the west of Everest on his way to Kathmandu. We were headed toward Shigatse, and would follow some of the roads which "MH" took to the Himalayan crest.

JAN: As we bumped and banged along in the truck, on the first leg of our three-day drive to Everest Base Camp, it seemed funny to me that we were paying more than four dollars per kilometer to the Chinese to suffer this ride. We were all tumbling in the back with the cargo, while Chang and Losan, our liaison officer, rode in the warm, comfortable cabin up front with Laba, our driver.

Both Losan and Laba were Tibetan. Laba, a wiry wisp of a man, was good-natured, but tended to shy away from us since we were foreigners. He was a sensitive, devout Buddhist. I once watched him catch trout with his bare hands, but he always threw them back.

Losan, on the other hand, was short, stocky, and full of unabashed mischief. He was a climber himself and had gone quite high on Everest back in

1975. The two of them became fast friends, leaving Chang as the odd man out. It wasn't that our crew or the Tibetans didn't like Chang—he just didn't have anyone to pair off with, so he became a bit of a loner.

Jim came up with a partial solution to the dust problem: by rolling back the canvas just a foot or so behind the cab, we could see out and stand up in the breeze if we wished. The force of the wind whipped most of the dust by the opening in the canvas before it had a chance to blow back into our cargo hold. Jim was in his glory. He loves people and he loves attention. He stood up, waving his arm with broad strokes to any locals he saw when we passed through their rough stone villages on the flat, treeless plateau. Sometimes small children would run out to chase our slow-moving truck, and Jim would toss bits of candy to them when they got close. Jim had come to life and was even talking about what he'd bring "When I come back to Tibet."

NED: It was surprising, in a way, that our truck received such a friendly welcome. Prior to 1950, wheels were virtually unknown in Tibet, and were believed to release evil demons by scarring the earth. The absence of the wheel was another example of the extraordinary stability of life in old Tibet: the lamas resisted any change that might reduce their status and power.

Driving along the flat river valley, we began to feel more affectionate toward our dilapidated vehicle, and nicknamed it "Mister Truck." We turned at a fork, and Laba shifted down into second, then first gear for the long, slow climb over 15,840-foot Khamba La. Now we learned of the truck's true, gutless character. The engine vapor locked regularly, and we stopped repeatedly to let it simmer down. Once, when the hood was propped up, I saw Laba pour water into a weird contraption. I looked more closely: a mud-filled tin can had been wired onto the fuel filter to serve as a fuel-line cooling system! Watching my amazement, Chang chuckled, and said, "Here in Tibet, high altitude makes it a two-ton truck, not four tons."

By the end of the expedition we would have pushed Mister Truck over 2,400 kilometers of tortuous mountain roads. After depositing us back in Lhasa, it would stagger only 100 more yards before the main steering bearing went out.

We came to a heaving, sputtering stop at the top of the pass. The ridge was speckled with colorful prayer flags flapping from thin poles that bobbed in the wind. We started up again and dropped down the south side to a magnificent turquoise lake, Yamdok Tsamdo, whose waters shelter numerous species of migrating water fowl. When we stopped to eat lunch on the far side of the lake, Chang offered us tea from a thermos he called a "water hotter."

Pulling our masks on, we climbed back aboard and struggled over a second, higher pass of 17,160 feet called the Kharo La. Near here, in 1904, British troops led by Colonel Francis Younghusband fought a pitched battle against outgunned Tibetans, killing 600 in "a terrible and ghastly business." Younghusband had been sent in to show the flag and keep the Russians out.

After Younghusband occupied Lhasa, an agreement with the Dalai Lama gave special privileges to the British—including permission to attempt Everest in the 1920s and 1930s. Later, Captains C. G. Rawling and C. H. D. Ryder rode into western Tibet and saw Everest from a distance of 60 miles.

In 1913 John Noel, a romantically adventurous British officer, disguised himself as a Mohammedan from India and got to within 40 miles of Everest before Tibetan soldiers turned him back.

We drove on to Gyantse and stopped for gas at an adobe building with barred windows. A disembodied hand stretched through the bars and scooped up the ration tickets Laba held out. The hand disappeared, then presented a hose and nozzle.

From our vantage point on top of the truck we caught sight of the Gyantse Kumbum (place of 100,000 images), the largest *chorten*, or building for worship, in Tibet. It rose in seven white and gold circular tiers like an outlandish wedding cake. We asked Losan to drive to it for a visit, but he said we must hurry on. We asked more strongly, then insisted. Grudgingly, he allotted us 20 minutes. Inside the walls we found that most of the monastic city had been destroyed during the Cultural Revolution. But some official Chinese decree—or maybe some powerful, holy force—preserved the great chorten. Next door, in a small temple, workmen using mud and straw were repairing two huge statues of Buddha, then applying bright paint.

Laba leaned on the horn, calling us back to the truck as if we were errant school children. All afternoon Mister Truck toiled through the bleak, brown landscape. Just before dusk we arrived at Shigatse, Tibet's second largest city, and pulled into the courtyard of the government rest house. There were many Chinese officials and drivers staying in the concrete rooms, but no other tourists this early in the season. We planned to spend a day here, exploring and acclimating.

In the morning we toured the Tashilhunpo monastery, the name of which means "lucky firm place." It was founded in 1445 by the first Dalai Lama. After the second Dalai Lama moved to Lhasa, it served as the seat for the reincarnate Panchen Lama, or "highest scholar." By the Chinese emperor's decree, the Panchen Lama ruled over a portion of western Tibet and the Dalai Lama over the eastern part of the country. The Dalai Lama considered the Panchen Lama to be a subordinate. There was continual strife between the two rulers.

Our guide told us that there were now 600 monks living at the monastery, and that children were being inducted as apprentices. We attended the morning service in the great Chanting Hall. The pillared room, hung with huge, umbrellalike tapestries and lined with silk-clad figurines and golden statues, was filled with seated monks. They were dressed in yellow robes and uttered nonstop, rumbling prayers. I paid 150 yuan to the government guide for the privilege of taking pictures.

Afterward, we visited the Scripture Room. Two monks with shaved heads read prayers beneath a colorful wall stacked with prayer books. In the old days any Tibetan might make an offering to the community of monks in return for the recitation of prayers and texts—such as the "Perfection of Wisdom"—to benefit his family. The usual offering was the *mang-ja,* or general tea ceremony, often accompanied by a contribution of money. This kind of action was believed to build up merit, offset bad deeds, and ensure a happier rebirth.

I couldn't resist taking a photograph of the two monks, but was sick of paying. Nonchalantly leaning against a post, I surreptitiously clicked the shutter. Our guide must have had well-tuned ears—although he stood on the other side of the room, he fell upon me instantly, speaking rapidly and pointing accusingly at the offending instrument. Mr. Chang sighed and interpreted: "You must pay. Eighty yuan."

While Jan, Jim, and Rick headed to the market area, I joined the lines of ragtag pilgrims circumambulating the outer wall of the monastery. They scuffed along, tapping the ground with staffs and spinning prayer wheels. One man, his hands protected by wooden pads, climbed the stairs of a steep section by a series of prostrations, moving like a caterpillar.

As a member of this pilgrimage, I was participating in a practice thousands of years old. Long before the time of Christ, Hindu and then Buddhist pilgrims crossed the Himalaya from the Indian plains while tracing the rivers of the subcontinent to their sources. Somehow they must have realized that the fertility of their crops depended on the lofty snows to the north, and came to worship these places. They penetrated into Tibet, and may well have been the first to see many of the river sources and peaks that later explorers claimed to have "discovered."

Continuing on around Tashilhunpo, I passed entrepreneurs who sat on the ground beside the path. With wooden mallets, they stamped holy plaques out of clay, then sold the final sun-dried images. Along the upper portion of the circular route stood several shrines—statues, adobe "beehives," ovenlike alcoves cut into the wall, and unusually shaped rocks. The faithful daubed yak butter on the shrines as offering, and prostrated themselves. They also laid tidbits of incense on smoldering piles and touched prayer flags.

I watched several Tibetans assume a stance in front of a large rock, close their eyes, stretch their right arms and point their index fingers. Then they walked four steps until their fingers touched the rock. Opening their eyes, they laughed, and so did their companions. It seemed to be more of a practical joke than a holy act. Then one good-natured Tibetan dressed in a Mao uniform took me by the arm and, with a sweep of his hand toward one particular well-worn spot on the rock, invited me to try. "Touch here, best luck," he said in halting English. I missed by the width of my hand, "Okay luck," my new guide judged.

I finished my walk-around, and started back into town. While taking a shortcut through a grove of trees, I heard music, and soon I came out into a grassy park that looked like the location of a flea market. Families of Tibetans had set up cloth-walled booths, and were lounging about enjoying the midday sunshine. While the adults ate, drank, and talked, children frolicked. They immediately spied me, and ushered me into the center of the fair, giggling and holding exaggerated poses for my camera. The music blared from half a dozen portable radios. At each booth, a cup of chang was thrust into my hands. After an hour I walked away, happily soused.

JAN: Jim, Rick, and I were lured to the open-air market along with most of the locals. We fanned out to do our bargaining independently, in our separate styles. Jim liked markets more for the sport of aggressive bartering than anything else, and his purchases were mere by-products. I found it easy to spot Jim at a market because of the crowd around him enjoying the show.

Rick was happy just to be out of the truck and feeling a bit better. I was concerned for him—we were as high as Rick had ever been before, and we hadn't reached Base Camp for our climb yet. We were all optimistic that a little more time would do the trick and Rick would come around. Rick had already considered the possibility that he might not be able to go high, but we all knew it was much too early to tell. He seemed to like standing back and watching, trying to discover something about the inner workings of Tibetan culture.

I just liked shopping—I went to the market to see what was for sale. I have four sisters, and a mother who took us shopping every spring during sales, so I'm a trained buyer.

I had many things for trading tucked under my arm, including a cowboy hat that I thought would be a hot commodity. I walked down a back street with only a few tables and around the corner to the courtyard that was alive with commerce. Some men sat on the ground, with blankets spread out before them displaying their wares. Others had rickety wooden tables with knives, pots, turquoise jewelry, buttons, snuff boxes, and countless other objects laid out on them. Some merchants had fashioned squares of material for overhead awnings, while others stood right out in the harsh, penetrating sun. Although the market was dry, dusty, and not very colorful, the mood was definitely upbeat. Tongues were wagging and hands were flying.

One of my finds at the market was an Australian named Ian who had been traveling solo throughout Tibet. I asked him to have dinner with us in hopes of hearing some of his experiences.

NED: Ian, who spoke Chinese, had been traveling in China for five months. All that time he had avoided the jurisdiction and expense of the Chinese Travel Service, which organizes and guides all visitors. He had done it first by obtaining a special entry visa in Hong Kong, then by gathering permit stamps from local officials along the course of his travels. Each of these constables was persuaded by the stamp of the last official to add his own.

He was worn out from battling the world's biggest bureaucracy. "China is a funny place," he said, "but I've stopped laughing." He had hitchhiked from Mongolia to Lhasa, then on to Shigatse. To slip through major checkpoints on the road into Lhasa, he had persuaded Tibetan truck drivers to hide him under a cargo of rugs. "You know," he said, "Tibetans have no love for the Chinese. It was all a grand joke to them."

He also educated us in the rate structure that the Chinese have established for foreigners, after I admitted paying 240 yuan ($160) in Lhasa and 120 yuan ($80) in Shigatse for room and board at the government rest houses. He chuckled knowingly. "In Lhasa, I stayed in a local tea house. A bed and two meals cost one and a half yuan. Of course, as an official expedition, you have no choice."

Six months later, he wrote us in the United States. After Shigatse, he had tried to follow us into Everest Base Camp, but a yak he bought had run off with much of his gear, and he turned back. Then he left Tibet over the Friendship Highway into Nepal. At the border, which was closed to foreigners at that time, the guards were asleep in the early morning—so he simply walked across. His jaunt may well have been the first crossing by a Westerner of the main Himalaya since 1950.

The next day we were back on the Friendship Highway, driving through broad valleys that led into winding, rocky defiles and up over high passes. The countryside was stark, as if the bones of the earth had been laid bare. "Tibet is like a defoliated Nevada," Jim said. The hills were a thousand hues of brown, and rare rainfalls had raked them with gullies. Striated rock lay in enormous folds, and the standing rubble of destroyed monasteries and shrines poked out of many prominent nobs and outcrops.

The monotony was relieved by small villages of whitewashed adobe and rock houses that were painted with green and red stripes. Sticks of firewood and disks of dung were stacked to dry on the flat roofs; prayer flags fluttered. In the fields, teams of darkly dressed men guided shaggy yaks that pulled single-pronged wooden plows. Colored cockades and sometimes red flags adorned the yokes. Women walked behind, sowing seeds. Later, after the irrigation ditches had been opened, the first sprigs of green would dot the landscape. Some fields were plowed in a circular pattern. This was an ancient strategy intended to force demons out and bring in a good crop. In the center of each field, a stone painted white and turned on end stood for good luck.

Ten hours later, before we saw the town of Shekar, or New Tingri as the Chinese call it, we were captivated by the sight of a leaning tower of conglomerate rock that rose straight out of the flat-bottomed gorge in which the town lay. We could discern a line of walls and turrets that snaked up the tower, rising almost vertically. Once they had connected a monastery containing over 400 monks with a Gothic-like fort on the very summit. The structures we saw were the skeletal remains of what John Noel had described as "the fantastic dream castle of Shekar-Dzong—'The Shining Crystal Monastery.' " *Dzong* means "fort." Like many other monasteries in the old days, the Shining Crystal had been designed by the warrior-monks for defense and battle, as well as for religious rites. When Noel visited the monastery in 1921 it was presided over by a one-toothed head Lama who was considered a saint. Like most shrines, it had been destroyed during the Cultural Revolution.

The process of obtaining permission for the 1921 British Reconnaissance, the first party to search for the most logical route up Everest from the north, was initiated by Noel and Lt. Col. C. K. Howard-Bury. It was concluded by Sir Charles Bell, the British political officer for Bhutan, Sikkim, and Tibet, and a close friend of the Dalai Lama. Not that the Dalai Lama was much interested in mountain climbing. His real motive was to obtain weapons and ammunition from the British to fight the Chinese on Tibet's eastern frontier.

The 1921 expedition had taken nearly a month to travel the 210 miles from Darjeeling to Shegar across the windswept Tibetan plateau. A hundred mules carried the provisions and equipment for the nine Englishmen.

When he caught his first glimpse of Everest, expedition member George Leigh Mallory described it as "a prodigious white fang excrescent from the jaw of the world" (Howard-Bury, 1922).

The team surveyed an area the size of Switzerland. Author Walt Unsworth described it like this:

> What immense and exciting opportunities the 1921 expedition had for exploration! To the south of them, between Tingri and the Nepalese border (beyond which they could not venture, of course), lay a vast tract of the world's highest mountains virtually unknown to

Members of the expedition. Reprinted from Mount Everest, The Reconnaissance, 1921, *by Charles K. Howard-Bury.*

civilization. They were the first Westerners even to approach as near as Tingri, and the country to the south was their oyster, of which the pearl was Everest. The pearl was not for them to snatch, of course—that would be too much to expect—but their reward was almost as great, and some might say greater: to tread the untrodden glacier, to see for the first time what lay around the next spur or beyond the next blue mountain.

◆ ◆ ◆

The new Tingri rest house we checked into was a cold, stark, concrete motel, and the charge was 60 yuan ($40) per person. There was no central heating, but the narrow cots were piled high with blankets. To wash the day's dust from our hands and faces, we poured warm water from a thermos into a tin dish and soaped up—all goose bumps in the chill air. There were no other guests, and we talked in echoing tones at one end of a 100-foot-long dining room. At dusk, a loudspeaker blared announcements in Chinese and music over the village.

In the morning, a heavy frost coated the ground. Shivering, we shuffled to breakfast. A man in a dirty Mao suit served us tinned fish, a relish we didn't recognize, and garlic soaked in vinegar marinade. No tea was available.

Outside, Laba had ignited a huge blow torch and set it under the truck, aimed up at the engine block. At every moment I expected Mister Truck and all our gear to go up in a ball of flames. Instead, the engine started at the first touch of the starter. We piled in, then sat waiting. I asked Chang why.

Photo-surveyor Wheeler (left), a member of the 1921 British Reconnaissance, with Tibetan porters. Reprinted from Everest—A Mountaineering History, *by Walt Unsworth.*

"They are checking to make sure all furnishings are still in rooms," he answered.

I was puzzled. Soon the manager emerged, very agitated, and addressed Losan. Chang turned to us, sighed as he always did at the announcement of bad news, and said, "There is a soap dish missing from your rooms."

Rick grinned, fessed up, and produced the missing dish from his duffel. He had left his soap dish back in Lhasa, but apparently this was not the place to replace it.

We chugged down the Friendship Highway. Rick began to feel the altitude again, and moaned that it must be the karma of the soap dish catching him. We turned off the highway, and started up a primitive road. Losan told us that the road had been built especially to move gear into the mountain for the first Chinese ascent in 1960—an expedition composed of 214 members!

Toward the top of the 16,700-foot Pang La, we encountered snow. The switchbacks were tight, and slowed our momentum until we finally lost traction and ground to a halt. We jumped out when the truck slewed in an alarming manner toward the edge of the roadbed. The rear wheels, which were bald, had stopped a foot from the edge of the roadbed. Below, the slope plunged steeply. Jim suggested putting on chains, but there were none. Nor were there shovels. We transferred much of the gear over the rear wheels. Then, while the rest of us walked behind, Laba nursed the truck to the top.

There we had our first view of the main Himalayan chain from the north: Makalu, Lhotse, Everest, Gyachung Kang, and Cho Oyu. Losan was impatient to proceed, so we roared off the south side of the pass, which was clear of snow.

Laba coasted in neutral much of the way to save gas. The four of us hung on in back, bug-eyed and terrified, until we arrived at a small village on the valley floor. We stopped to obtain a permit from the vice chairman of the county government so we could hire yaks for transportation beyond Base Camp.

"In China you need permission for everything, don't you?" I said to Chang.

"Yes," he agreed, "the stamp is very important." Many villagers had gathered around us. Chang continued. "Today the commune system is good. The peasants give a far smaller percentage of their production to the state than they used to give to the landlords in the old days. Then they were slaves."

From what little I had seen in Tibet, the former terrible poverty had been removed by the Chinese—at the price of the country's spiritual leadership. In Shigatse, a few tractors and combine harvesters had been available for working the fields of barley and potato; here, I saw only one tractor. The villagers who milled around us looked to be reasonably healthy and, judging from the houses in the village, all had decent roofs over their heads. In this remote corner, the spiritual life and customs of the people remained little changed.

I asked Chang how the system of government was divided. "We have province, county, district, commune, brigade, production team," he answered.

"You forgot one," I responded lightly.

"Oh?"

"The individual."

"Ah, you mean the family!" he concluded triumphantly.

We turned out of the village onto a road that was little more than a track, then started up alongside the river that flowed from the Rongbuk Valley and carried meltwater from Everest's glaciers. This river would eventually turn south, join the Arun, cut through the Himalayan crest, pass through Nepal, and empty into the Bay of Bengal. The Arun was the river along which we had walked out from Makalu at the end of the Nepal half of the circle.

Farther up the valley there were no bridges, and we had to ford the river. The truck stalled precisely in the middle; there we sat, marooned, with the water surging over the running boards. When Laba restarted the engine, the truck refused to budge. Wading about in the icy waters, we removed the biggest rocks and completed our amphibious assault—at great cost to the clutch plate.

The last village was a maze of rooms, courtyards, and alleys—all interconnected for protection from the winter winds, and built of small, roundish gray and brown rocks. It looked like a dot-matrix printout picture. Gaining elevation, the heavily laden truck crabbed sideways across streams that were still frozen; crept along a narrow cut in a gravel bank—after we had shored the roadbed with rocks, and by hanging one of the double-drive wheels over the river 50 feet below; and detoured around a great slab of rock that had fallen onto the track. Twice we jumped from the back as the truck canted dangerously close to capsizing.

JAN: Our canvas covering was rolled back so Ned, Jim, Rick, and I stood on our cargo in the back of the truck with our bellies leaning against the cab as we gazed forward. We were lined up shoulder to shoulder, close because there was just enough room for four to stand. Close to dispel the chill. Close because we could see Everest in all its solitary splendor, and its magnitude made us gather together as if to remind ourselves that there is safety in numbers. We needed each other to do what we had set out to accomplish.

The winds had swept the summit clean of snow—as they have been doing since people began recording Everest and her moods. So, even though we were probably as much as 20 miles away, we could see the distinctive yellow bands of limestone slicing the summit triangle horizontally.

On June 25, 1921, Mallory and G. H. Bullock entered the Rongbuk Valley. They were the first Westerners ever to do so, walking beyond "the clean fragrance of mountain plants" up the cruel and "monotonously dreary" moonscape through which we had just driven. They mounted a rise crowned by two chortens. Mallory wrote:

> We paused here in sheer astonishment. We forgot the stony wastes and regrets for other beauties. We asked no questions and made no comment, but simply looked. It is perhaps because Everest presented itself so dramatically. . . . The Rongbuk Valley is well constructed to show off the peak at its head; for about twenty miles it is extraordinarily straight and in that distance rises only 4,000 feet . . . to the very head of the glacier from which the cliffs of Everest spring. . . . Everest rises not so much as a peak as a prodigious mountain-mass. There is no complication for the eye. The highest of the world's mountains, it seems, has to make but a single gesture of magnificence to be lord of all, vast in unchallenged and isolated supremacy. (Howard-Bury, 1922).

NED: As the daylight faded, our truck finally ground up the final grade to 16,900 feet, then rattled across a windswept gravel plain toward a cluster of tents pitched just below the terminus of the Rongbuk Glacier. It was the Base Camp for two climbing teams—one British, the other American—that we knew would be here. The truck stopped and we jumped down to introduce ourselves.

14

RONGBUK BASE CAMP

"The yak drivers must have dark glasses and walking shoes.
Otherwise the regulations say they cannot work."

Losan

JAN:

As I tasted the last sips of my sixth bottle of Hennessey Cognac, I tossed my head back and laughed out loud. "The last thing I expected to find at Everest Base Camp was a fully equipped bar."

"Just a minute, I'll hatch you another one," Joe Tasker said, grinning demonically.

He rocked to one side of the large box he was sitting on, reached between his legs into the box, and pulled out yet another airline-size bottle of cognac.

"Ta da!" he sang proudly, as he lifted the bottle over his head and wrung the cap off for me. The caps had mysteriously become more and more difficult for us to twist off as the night wore on.

Joe was one of four British climbers fashioning a route up the unclimbed, difficult East-Northeast Ridge on Everest.

They had carved out two snow caves for shelter and had run up fixed ropes above the higher cave at 23,800 feet, but had just returned to Base Camp for rest and replenishment. As they put it, "We're down here for four days to stuff ourselves with food, three huge meals a day."

We had driven in to the 17,000-foot-high Base Camp on April 25, the evening following their return.

I sat on a storage box pushed up to a splendid folding table from Hong Kong, which was littered with crushed beer cans and empty wine and cognac bottles. The lantern swung gently overhead, casting a wavering glow on our celebration as the large canvas tent shivered in the breeze. Despite the kerosene heater, we had to huddle close, wrapping our coats around us as we drank. Dick Renshaw sat beside me, drinking his fair share and soaking up the scene in silence. Across from me sat Chris Bonington, the expedition leader. Chris was quick to put me at ease and share a laugh. I was pleased to find that the person whose mountaineering achievements I had read about and admired was so warm and friendly.

Jim pushed through the canvas flap, letting in a cold blast of air with him.

"Listen to this stuff! You guys need some new tapes."

Peter Boardman scanned the plastic tape cases that Jim had handed him and flipped a new tape into their expensive cassette deck, bragging, "We even have champagne." Considering all their efforts to be a small team going light, they had managed to bring a great deal of "liquid refreshment." They also had a doctor, Charles Clarke, and a Base Camp manager, Adrian Gordon. The British plan was so well thought out that only the climbing was left to the climbers.

Our camaraderie with the British was instantaneous. The tent was filled with hearty laughter, and the party rolled on until three o'clock the next morning, when we reluctantly called it a night. We staggered out of the tent into the crisp, sharp night and melted into inebriated slumbers, all wrapped in down.

I woke slowly the next morning, missing my Sherpas. There was no smiling face serving me hot, sweet tea in bed. I poked my head out of my tent. The rock-studded plateau was sprinkled with tents, yet the wind whispered through the camp as if it were a ghost town. Three expeditions shared Base Camp: the British, ourselves, and another American expedition that was climbing the central couloir directly, led by Lou Whittaker. Lou's expedition involved 16 climbers, none of them than at Base Camp.

Again I thought of the contrast between our adventure in Nepal the previous winter and the closing of our circle here in Tibet this spring. There we had been alone, but here it was truly a case of social climbing. English-speaking people were spread from ridge to ridge on the north side of Everest, and the Russians were on the south. It was a gathering, a climbing jamboree.

I crawled out of the tent and stood up. I couldn't understand why I felt quite all right after everything I had drunk the night before. Perhaps I couldn't distinguish altitude adjustment from the morning after—I'd often used a hangover to describe the sensation of acclimating. I shuffled over to breakfast.

NED: Our first morning at Base Camp, April 26, was windy and cold. My head throbbed—a little from the altitude of 16,900 feet, and a lot from our introductory drinking bout with the British the night before. I lay in my bag until the sun hit the tent, then struggled over to the truck. We had set up a temporary kitchen in the back.

"We have a big problem," Chang said in greeting. "We have no mess tent. The bag for it contains extra duffels, not a tent."

I protested that there must be some mistake, but when I checked through our dunnage, I found that he was right. Jim, who had gone to a special storeroom in Peking to borrow the tent from a travel agency, had grabbed the wrong bag and had not checked its contents. It really was a problem—not only for cooking, but for the day-to-day living comfort of Chang, Losan, and Laba during their long vigil at Base Camp. They were far from home, assigned to a boring job they disliked—the comfortable shelter and good food we had promised to supply were critical for maintaining their positive attitude. Losan responded with a disgruntled look when I suggested setting up a much smaller tent, but there was no alternative but to improvise.

Rick, Jan, and I set up our biggest dome tent as a mess tent, but it was still too small to stand up in. I left to let Losan cool down. This was no time to sort out logistics and travel plans with him, as I had planned.

It was also no time to get Jim to help with the mess tent mess, even though he was responsible for it. He had settled down with a book, and made it clear that he didn't want to be disturbed until he had finished his reading. There was a touch of the prima donna in Jim—a feeling that his expertise as a climber should exempt him from some of the more mundane tasks necessary in camp.

The attitude was not peculiar to Jim, although he excelled at it. Bonington had defined it in 1982 as "the jockeying for position in the pecking order of decision making and day-to-day living." If Jim could manipulate the situation so others would do the work, he would—and see himself as the winner. He was points ahead in this game if he garnered the most comfortable position in the tent—as he had done during the epic night we four had spent crammed into the tiny tent on Pumori. Over time, such behavior can become divisive and cause stress. It put me, as leader, in an awkward position—forcing the issue would alienate the gamesman, while ignoring it would alienate the rest of the team. I chose to overlook it for the time being, hoping Jan and Rick would understand.

Later in the day I visited the British mess tent, which was pleasantly spacious and outfitted with tables, chairs, heaters, lanterns, and a cassette tape recorder. A powerful radio brought in daily updates from the BBC on the Falklands crisis. A cardboard placard hung from the ridgepole of the tent, with a ditty written on it entitled "Everest's Flag Clouds":

Wind from the northeast
The summit's your feast

Clouds at night
p'haps two day's respite

Southeast from Nepal
Snow will fall

Clouds blowing all over
run for cover

Charlie Clarke, the doctor with the British expedition, was the only other person in the tent. He was intelligent, energetic, and fun-loving, and I had taken an instant liking to him. Right now he was as immensely hung over as I was. To get his mind off his own misery, he told me about an important discovery he had made a couple of days before. To see it, we would have to walk a mile down the valley. "Anyway," he said on a professional note, "you've come from sea level to almost 17,000 feet in less than a week, and a little exercise will speed your acclimatization."

We strolled down the pebbly outwash below Base Camp, then turned right toward an inviting patch of grass that was tucked behind a low moraine. Here, we were sheltered from the wind. It was the site of the 1921 Base Camp, as well as the six subsequent British expeditions through 1938. A few rusted tins lay about, and I could imagine gentlemen in tweed jackets dining on chicken in aspic and sipping champagne, as they did in 1922. But the memories were not all bubbly. In 1924 a memorial cairn had been built on the moraine mound above camp to commemorate those who had died on the first three expeditions of 1921, 1922, and 1924; but especially for Mallory and Andrew Irvine, who had been lost just a few days before the construction of the cairn.

Later, angered by the disruption of the countryside caused by the expeditions, Tibetans pulled down the monument. Charlie Clarke and Adrian Gordon had been determined to find the remains. As we walked to the top of

Above, *Memorial cairn.* Right, *George Leigh Mallory. Both photos reprinted from* The Fight for Everest: 1924, *by E. F. Norton.*

Mallory and Norton approaching their high point of 26,985 feet. Reprinted from The Assault on Mount Everest, 1922, *by Charles G. Bruce.*

Mallory and Irvine preparing to leave Chang La camp for the final attempt on Everest. Reprinted from The Fight for Everest: 1924, *by E. F. Norton.*

the mound, Charlie explained the systematic sleuthing they had done. "It took hours of searching, aided by prewar photographs and a set of hand-colored slides lent by John Noel from the 1924 expedition. Just as we figured there was no hope, I kicked over a slate fragment and the light fell on it obliquely, throwing a shadow around the numerals 192. Encouraged, we turned up further shards."

At the top he showed me several pieces of grayish green stone tablets clearly carved with letters. The largest weighed over 40 pounds, and read:

IN MEMORY OF
THREE
EVEREST EXPEDITIONS

The British expeditions of 1921, 1922, and 1924 were pioneering efforts. No mountaineers had ever been to such heights. In 1922, when Camp IV was established on the North Col at 23,000 feet, nobody had ever camped that high. Much of their food was suddenly unappetizing, stoves were inefficient, canned goods froze, tents blew down, clothing and boots were inadequate. Supposing that snow on Everest evaporated rather than slid, they discounted avalanches as a threat until seven Sherpas were swept to their deaths in 1922. Climbing strategies were also naive. Mallory's 1922 plan above the North Col was to establish a camp at 26,000 feet, then dash to the summit the next day. In reality, it turned out to be far more difficult.

Mallory provided the driving force during the first three expeditions. He was identified with Everest, and became a symbol of man's ultimate achievement. Although he was handsome, articulate, and refined, he was a most unlikely hero. After college, romantic and uncommitted to anything in particular, he had drifted into teaching, marriage, and family. He thrived on athletic action and was a strong, graceful climber; but his climbing record was marked by "unfulfilled achievement." Then everything changed. When he stepped onto Everest for the first time in 1921, the summit became his overriding ambition. At 38 years of age, he realized that it was now or never. His sense of his own destiny, and of the mountain's role in it, shaped the rest of his life.

At the site of the memorial, buffeted by the ever-present wind that funnelled down the Rongbuk Valley, Charlie and I crouched to touch each piece of carved slate. On one triangular fragment, obviously broken from a larger slab, I deciphered the numbers "192" and the letters "MA." The letters had once spelled "MALLORY." I looked up at Everest. It had been clear all morning, but now a snow squall was settling on the summit.

On June 8, 1924, Mallory disappeared into just such a squall as he climbed upward less than 1,000 feet from the summit. His partner was Andrew Irvine, a 22-year-old Cambridge undergraduate who had shown strength and endurance on an Arctic sledging expedition but had little mountaineering experience. Four days earlier the leader of the expedition, Edward Norton, had struggled without the aid of bottled oxygen to 28,125 feet before retreating from exhaustion. But Mallory had decided to use oxygen, and felt confident of making the summit.

At 12:50 P.M., the clouds parted momentarily and Noel Odell, a geologist with the team, looked up from an altitude of about 26,000 feet to see Mallory and Irvine. "I saw the whole summit ridge and final peak of Everest unveiled. I noticed far away on a snow slope leading up to what seemed to me to be the last step but one from the base of the final pyramid a tiny object moving. ... A second object followed, and then the first climbed to the top of the step. ... I could see that they were moving expeditiously as if endeavoring to make up for lost time" (Norton, 1925).

Odell was surprised by the late hour—Mallory and Irvine were almost five hours behind schedule. Then clouds enveloped the mountain, obscuring Odell's vision. Soon a vicious two-hour storm struck, wrapping the fate of the summit climbers in misty speculation. When it cleared, Mallory and Irvine had vanished.

The question remains of whether Mallory and Irvine reached the summit before they died. There are compelling arguments on both sides, but no conclusive evidence.

Hard facts tell us it is possible, even probable, that Mallory reached the summit—maybe climbing solo if the inexperienced Irvine had encountered difficulties. When Odell sighted the pair, they were 600 to 1,200 feet below the top, depending whether it was the "first" or "second" step they negotiated during the brief clearing. Mallory was in excellent physical shape and using oxygen. He would have been required to climb only 240 feet per hour to reach the top by nightfall. Undoubtedly Mallory's oxygen would have run out before the summit, and darkness would have fallen. But on the brink of achieving his greatest dream, he would have concentrated all his energies on a final push toward the summit. So there is a chance that he, with or without Irvine, won the summit and was returning when he died.

Whether they made it to the top or not, they did what they did because they wanted to climb. It was not suicidal, but a joyful attempt to fulfill what they were best at. The spirit of Mallory and Irvine fit the time. Everest was a blank on the map, just as the polar regions were. It demanded exploration and presented a challenge that pushed men to their limits—and beyond. Historian Audrey Salkeld concludes, "What makes them heroic figures is that they went too far . . . when Polar explorers such as Scott and Nobile went too far, they became heroic; if they went so far as not to come back, truly heroic."

◆ ◆ ◆

Charlie and I walked back to camp. On the way he told me he and Adrian had decided to leave the stone tablets where they had found them—collected in one place, but otherwise unaltered. He had written the expedition sponsor about the discovery, finishing the letter: "Assuming one of us doesn't join the In Memoriam, God forbid."

JAN: Rick, Ned, Jim, and I assembled in the small tent to determine a plan for the next four days in Base Camp. Rick had retired from the party before the rest of us the night before, yet he seemed vacant and slow this morning. He still hadn't recovered from our gain in elevation, and though he tried to hide his discomfort, his dull eyes gave him away.

"The two major things we need to do are mount the bindings on the skis and sort all the food into caches," Ned said, as he reached across Jim's legs and mine for his porridge.

Jim appeared uninterested in our discussion of the chores ahead of us during preparation at Base Camp. I suspected that he felt a twinge of envy—the ambitious route that the British were tackling was just his style. Our half-circle in Tibet emphasized logistics rather than intensive climbing. I wondered if Jim would become restless skiing with us, considering the caliber of climbing and climbers in this heart and soul of the Himalaya. Although Jim had come along to improve his filming skills and to see Tibet, when it came right down to it he needed more—he needed to climb.

After breakfast, we all moved outside. Rick and I began to sort food for the caches, while Ned worked out our specific climbing and skiing plan in terms of the food and equipment we would need at each point. Jim lay back in his tent to read a mountaineering book one of the British team had given him.

The weather had been clear in the morning, and had even begun to warm until the wind kicked up in the afternoon. This became the pattern during our stay at Base. A strong wind seems to suck out my strength, since I have to push my way through it, and the constant noise is wearing. With no vegetation as a buffer zone, the wind played hard and maliciously anywhere it wished, up and down the Rongbuk Valley. We were all tired by afternoon and called it a day of work. Escaping the wind in our tents, we all napped away the rest of the day.

The next day we hauled out the skis, bindings, screws, glue, heel plates, skins, safety straps, and other assorted ski paraphernalia for assembly. Rick took charge, since ski equipment was his area of expertise. Although he was still having trouble keeping his food down, he gallantly directed the rest of us and did the bulk of the work himself.

Our work conditions were not the best. Instead of standing up beside a workbench with our tools hung neatly, we knelt down on the rocky ground, straddling our skis, hunched over with effort. Tools were scattered around the rocky moraine we were camped on, and we tossed them back and forth as we needed them.

"I haven't skied on these skinny skis before," Jim said. "I've done plenty of serious skiing, but it was always on wider boards."

"It's the same thing," Ned assured him, as he wiped the glue from his fingers. "Don't try to telemark. Forget that there are only three pins holding the boot to your binding and that your heel is free. Ski just as if you were on your alpine gear at home. These boots are stiff enough so that you don't have to change your style."

Ned is a strong man on skis, and can bash through any type of snow, even with a load on his back. Rick has quick finesse, a clean style. And me—I can get down anything. I don't often win any style points, but I get where I'm going. If the route looks tricky, I stuff my pride in my pocket, traverse the slope to lose elevation, and kick turn to come around. As we worked with the equipment, it was obvious that Ned, Rick, and I were anxious to do some skiing, to have gravity working with us instead of against us. After all, the Everest Grand Circle was originally supposed to have been a ski trip. Jim seemed less enthusiastic. I noticed his glance often drifting upward toward the summit of Everest, and I assumed he was tracing routes up the mountain, perhaps memorizing them or imagining himself on them. We were closer to Everest here in Tibet than we ever had been in Nepal, and I thought that very closeness to the peak might be frustrating, since he wasn't going to climb it. That would explain why his morale and enthusiasm appeared uncharacteristically low. There was no sign of the banter and good-natured play he and Ned had exchanged the previous winter. I couldn't figure it out: Rick was sick, Ned was abrasive, Jim was restless, and I was low. Only our newfound British friends were keeping our spirits up.

I pulled the hood of my anorak up tight around my head to keep the wind from blasting my ears and blowing down my neck. I'd just finished cutting my climbing skins, which I'd use for grip when we were ascending, to the right length. I laced my ski boot up tight on my foot and slipped on my overboot to check the fit on the binding—and discovered that the custom-made overboot wouldn't quite fit under the bale of the binding.

"Hey, you guys. These overboots are going to need some modification if we're going to use them," I said, holding an overboot up as I clumped around on the moraine with a bare boot and ski on my right leg.

"Well, why don't you modify it then, Jan? I'm not going anywhere without an overboot," Jim stressed. Jim's feet had been freezing on the summit of Pumori and apparently the memory was still fresh.

I figured out that by using a bit of "home-ec" I could get the overboot system to work. I collected everyone's overboots, dove for my tent—out of the wind—and set to work. But sitting alone in the tent made me aware of just how much I was coughing. My throat was raw and dry from the parched, thin air.

I thought for a bit and decided from then on to try sleeping with a dampened bandanna tied over my mouth to moisturize and warm the air before I breathed it in.

NED: As soon as Losan had simmered down over our failure to provide him with a mess tent, I started working with him on a practical plan to support our travels. It was really double-checking. In Lhasa, I had gone over every aspect of our plans with him to ensure that there would be no unpleasant surprises in the field. We needed his cooperation, because our cross-country trek was the first of its kind in Tibet under the auspices of the Chinese Mountaineering Association. Unlike an expedition to climb a peak, which works out of a fixed Base Camp, we planned to move from point A to point B. Our Chinese support personnel would have to remain flexible and mobile. But Losan turned out to be maddeningly obstructive. I was surprised, especially since he had once been a mountaineer himself.

"The yak drivers must have dark glasses and walking shoes," Losan informed me through Chang's interpretation. "Otherwise, the regulations say they cannot work."

The timing of this demand was puzzling, since Losan surely had known of the regulation before we left Lhasa. There was no place short of Shigatse—two days' drive away—to buy glasses or shoes. I had no choice but to find some way to supply the items. One solution was easy: the British had spare glasses; the other solution was touching: Chang and Losan themselves donated the shoes we had given them. Given his earlier recalcitrance, I was dumbfounded by Losan's generosity.

Our liaison officer was a complicated man. He was one of many Tibetans who had chosen to work with the Chinese, having realized that any career advancement lay with them. Losan had been in Beijing to work with the C.M.A. and had learned to speak Chinese. Somewhere along the way he had acquired a chip on his shoulder—perhaps he felt torn between his Tibetan past and his Chinese present. Whatever the reason, at the moment we bore the brunt of his dissatisfaction. The Chinese are perfectly open about the high cost of expeditions in their country: the government needs the foreign exchange. In return, however, we expected good service. I determined to be firm, but polite and careful with my words to Losan. The C.M.A. in Beijing had granted us full permission for our proposed itinerary, and Losan was the organization's delegate. It was his duty to facilitate the expedition.

This turned out to be the first in a long series of problems, and Losan seemed to derive more satisfaction from announcing them than from finding solutions. "It will be necessary to pay the yak drivers in cash," he said next. And then, when that one was behind us: "We do not have enough petrol to drive to Kharta to pick you up at the end of your walk, then get back to Rongbuk." That one took longer to solve, but we finally managed, with the help of some ration coupons from the British.

Eventually, over the days and weeks ahead, Losan provided the logistical support we needed. I had to remind myself that he didn't have an entirely free hand himself, since the Chinese have less control in Tibet than in the other autonomous provinces. But I wanted him to try willingly, without being badgered. His sullen, obstinate attitude was in total contrast to the support we had received on our previous expedition to China in 1980, when we had climbed Muztagata. Then, our liaison officer had been Chu Ying Hua, an energetic, vibrant man who accomplished the impossible as a matter of course. He had been one of three Chinese to make the first ascent of Everest from the north, in 1960.

Concluding my conversation with Losan, I told him that we were planning a picnic with our British friends at the Rongbuk monastery, six miles down the valley. Chris and I had agreed that his team would supply the food and drink, we the transportation. "Could we," I asked Losan, "have Laba drive us there in our truck?"

"No," he answered.

I couldn't believe my ears. I scowled at Losan, exasperated. To ease the tension, Chang turned to me and said, in light-hearted English, "Maybe Mr. Losan went high on Everest too many times!" It was Chang's way of apologizing for Losan's stubbornness.

JAN: I was delighted that the British had invited us to a picnic—the event seemed somehow in keeping with their sociable, hospitable style. They would bring some surprise delicacies and plenty of wine. The only thing they asked from us besides our company was the use of our truck to take us to a grassy spot out of the wind.

I danced around, excited, told Jim and Rick about the invitation, then rustled into my tent to find something to wear. My wardrobe was considerably limited, but I did find a clean scarf to tie around my neck and I plaited my hair into a fresh braid. I must admit the lopsided ratio of males to females probably gave me more attention than I deserved, but I liked it.

Ned came back to the tent looking as disappointed as if we'd been told part of our expedition was off.

"Losan says our truck isn't to be used by the British for anything, even if we're involved. He also said we don't have enough gas. I guess the picnic is off."

I was let down, but realized Ned was so frustrated with Losan and embarrassed about telling the British we couldn't offer the truck that I acted very nonchalant about the whole thing and tried to cheer him up.

"The wine and dainties will taste just the same inside the Brits' big canvas tent, Ned, it doesn't really matter."

Ned left, then returned a few moments later, brightened, to announce that the picnic was still on. Charlie and Adrian had gotten permission to take the jeep used by the British team—not as far as the monastery, but to the site of the prewar Base Camp, only a mile away. The rest of us would walk down.

There was grass—brown and strawlike as it was—at our picnic site, and we were sheltered from the wind by a moraine. The sun was out, making the scene as warm and pleasant as it could be for this elevation in Tibet in the spring.

We settled ourselves against rocks and curled up on the grass as the tape player echoed music down the open plateau. While Charlie manipulated his two-stringed black kite, Adrian acted as bartender and waiter. He laid out and distributed cheeses, biscuits, and salami, which we nibbled off real plates. We also drank out of real glasses. This impressed me because on our expedition we each used our one plastic cup for everything.

I wondered why I felt so immediately comfortable and at home with these British climbers. We'd known them only three days, but it seemed a much longer time. Perhaps it was our similar attitudes. We respected each others' styles of having small teams wrestle with big objectives.

Jim was in a storytelling mood, so he and Peter, the charming, self-proclaimed male chauvinist, traded tales. We laughed not so much because the stories were funny, but because we sensed the "improvements" Jim and Peter had made on the original versions.

Chris, still exhausted from work at their Advance Camp, slept a good deal of the afternoon. Joe, the needler, looked up from his book now and then to get in some teasing digs. Dick, in his usual quiet manner, continued to carve away at a piece of wood he was turning into a graceful swan.

We talked, snoozed in the sun, woke, and ate some more until the afternoon began to slip into evening. Our two teams walked back up the valley to Base Camp together, gazing at Everest standing solitarily before us, the magnet that had drawn us all here.

◆ ◆ ◆

We woke early the next morning under mottled gray skies stirred by strong winds. We were up to see the British off to begin their summit bid on Everest. Ned, Rick, Jim, and I signed one of the Frisbees we had brought with us for fun and staying fit and gave it to them. To our surprise, they had already pulled out expedition T-shirts for us. There was a different feeling in camp, a quiet, strong determination that emanated from Chris, Joe, Pete, and Dick. They were our friends. We wished them well.

Most of our chores at Base Camp had been completed, so we spent this last day investigating the Rongbuk Valley—"valley of steep ravines." We hiked down to 16,500 feet, and the site of the remains of a monastery destroyed by the Red Guard of the People's Liberation Army. According to legend, the monastery existed over 2,000 years ago. But the shrine I looked at now was crushed, battered, and roofless, and the frescoed walls were deteriorating in the sun and wind. I wandered around the ruin's walls, kicking stones and touching the paint. The silence was thick and my heart beat faster. The monastery had been a house of devil worshipers during the reign of the Bon religion over 2,000 years earlier. But when the King of Tibet, Songtsen Gampo, permitted his Chinese wife to introduce Buddhism to Tibet over 1,300 years ago, she called on the saint Padma Camblava. The Buddhist saint defeated the evil Lama in a race up Mount Everest by arriving at the top sitting in his chair, riding on a sunbeam. In the 1920s, the Tibetan Lamas feared that arriving climbers had come to steal the holy chair from the summit.

Ned, Rick, Jim, and I had all gone separate ways to explore privately. As I ambled through the monastery, passing by walls that had sheltered centuries of mystics, my imagination played on and on. Perhaps Mallory had indeed reached the summit of Everest. And, upon reaching it, had discovered the sacred chair. Mallory could quite well have rested on the throne of the world, which might have taken him to his mysterious "there." Mallory used "there" as a term for feelings he could not put into words. He had repeatedly been asked the question, "Why do you want to climb Everest?" But when he replied, "Because it's there," it wasn't a curt, trite answer from a tired lecturer. The statement had more meaning than his audience perceived.

For Mallory and his close friends, "there" was a term denoting anything that had a mystical quality. In their letters back and forth, certain books and paintings they valued were also deemed "more there." But for Mallory, personally, nothing was more "there" than the summit of Everest. Perhaps he meant that "there" is something felt in the heart, not seen with the eyes.

The four of us walked away from the monastery together, a little quiet and a little restless. Something about the Rongbuk monastery was disturbing. Ned and I stopped to look at a ruined nunnery halfway between the monastery and camp. As we explored, we found many kilns, still full of clay idols, and some yak horns with inscriptions carved into them. As we were poking around, we saw some yak herders approaching from the stream below, where they'd left their animals. As they moved through the rubble, they suddenly caught sight of us—then beckoned for us to follow them. I was intrigued and wondered what they wanted to show us. They stopped, and we watched them uncover and lift a wooden trapdoor in what had been the floor of the nunnery and descend down a ladder into the darkness. I hesitated briefly, then followed. By the time I'd gotten to the bottom rung, candles had been lit, and I could see small idols on rough altars. The smoke and heavy yak butter fumes filled the cellar. I was in awe, as I realized that the Tibetans were so devout they were willing to hide their religion to keep it alive. The yak herders spoke a few prayers and left some rice on the altar for the gods. Ned and I left while the candles were still burning.

Back out in the bright, dry sun, I had an idea. I walked back to the kilns, collected several of the clay idols that were lying on the ground, and wrapped them up in my bandanna. I was aware that foreigners aren't permitted to take relics from the country, but they weren't for me. I knew we would be driving back to Lhasa on our way out. If these shrines at the top of the world were important enough to be kept alive underground, then the devout pilgrims circling the Jokhang in Lhasa would value these religious pieces tremendously, and I would pass them along on my way out.

15

LHO LA

"If you guys are supposed to look like expert skiers, you sure did a good job of hiding it."

Jim Bridwell

JAN: 

I woke up on April 30 feeling terribly tired and groggy. Could this be the altitude taking an unexpected last stab at me? I thought it was more likely the drugs I was taking—one to keep the swelling and pain in my knees under control, another for my respiratory infection, and a third for nasal congestion. I laughed when Rick compared me to the jalopies the Mexicans drive in Baja, California. "No matter how many cylinders are out, they just keep limping along," he said.

My knees were an old problem, but this respiratory ailment was new and bothersome. I crept out of my bag and slowly began packing.

"Hey, Jano, Happy Birthday!" Rick was warm and cheerful. His smile lit up the tent when he looked in, and his energy spurred me on. Rick had begun to feel like himself again.

"Thanks, Rick. I forgot." I saw Jim's feet walk by my tent door, backtrack, and then his head poked in the door.

"Happy Birthday, Old Lady," he laughed, and went back to packing. I was pleased they had remembered my birthday, especially since Ned had seemed to have forgotten it and so had I.

By half past ten we had five yaks loaded with our skiing and camping gear and ready for our trek to the Lho La, the 20,000-foot pass we planned to ski. Three more yaks were all set to carry in supplies for a cache up on the east Rongbuk Glacier, a point farther along on the swing of our Tibetan semicircle. With whistles and time-honored calls from the drivers, the yaks poked out of camp like an old train trying to muster up steam. Ned, Rick, Jim, and I all brightened in spirit to be moving again en route to the border between Nepal and Tibet. We would be touching one end of our half-circle completed the winter before in Nepal. I remembered Pumori vividly. When I closed my eyes, I could still see its shape and envision our route. I looked forward to seeing the peak again, but this time I'd gone around the world and would be approaching it from the northern side.

We hiked for six hours along a lateral moraine of the Rongbuk Glacier. These residual rocks of varying shades of gray accented with black formed banks on either side of the long white river of ice, which was covered with white and blue seracs resembling sails cutting the wind. The scene was colorless and dreamlike. The skies were absolutely clear, and the thin air heated so intensely that it smelled scorched.

It felt good to be moving my legs again, and my head cleared with the exercise. I could breathe again. I felt alive. Time spent in camp dampens the spark of an adventure—I'm never so aware of this as the day I depart.

The moraine was undulating, and the glacier curled and turned as a river would. At one point the moraine took a steep dip for about 70 feet. The yaks balked, but the drivers were undaunted. They pushed and shoved the beasts and hurled small stones at their hooves. The yaks didn't have to climb down the slope—the scree was so loose and the incline so steep that they slid down under the weight of their loads. The yaks' ability to negotiate this rough, uneven terrain was impressive. I laughed to think that they place four feet correctly over this rocky ground to move ahead and I have trouble with just two.

The yak train settled down as the moraine leveled, and the drivers slipped back into their steady, rhythmical walk with their hands clasped behind their backs. These men must have been amused to see all the gear their yaks had to carry for us, since they travel with just a cooking pot, ladle, and sleeping robe. We did give them a tent, which seemed to please them.

When we reached about 18,500 feet, I spotted two tents large enough to stand up in. This obviously was the site of the American Everest team's Advance Base Camp. It was also the end of the line for our yaks and drivers, since the terrain was too rough for them to go any farther.

The camp looked and sounded empty, but we approached one of the tents and gave a call. Much to our surprise, two men appeared. They introduced themselves as Phil Ershler and Dan Boyd, and invited us in. They seemed both curious and slightly skeptical as we described our plans to ski around Everest.

Rick's back was bothering him a bit, Jim was tired and had a headache, and Ned was busy gathering information from Dan and Phil, so I got a couple of large plastic containers and lugged some water from the broken glacier below for tea and dinner. While I was fussing over the stove, Ned came up, grinned, and handed me a wad of toilet paper.

"What's this?" I said roughly, without looking up. I was a little annoyed that he hadn't helped with the water.

"Just open it." Ned was impatient. I stopped what I was doing and unfolded the crumpled white tissue. Inside was a bronze medallion, a hand-cast Tibetan calendar.

"Happy Birthday, Jano. I didn't forget."

I couldn't help it, I started to cry. I'd forgotten again that it was my birthday, so the gift was a true surprise. I was embarrassed to cry in front of the two people we'd just met, so I sniffled and stifled the tears as quickly as I could and went about my business with the stove. I was afraid my voice would crack if I said anything right then, so I hoped Ned would realize how pleased I was.

Our plan the next morning was to continue up the glacier a few miles to about 19,000 feet and stash our ski equipment and ropes on the edge of the snow slope at the base of Everest. I felt like hiking alone, so I packed up quickly and slipped off before the others were ready. I knew they'd be close behind me soon. I waved good-bye, saying I'd wait for them up higher.

I was hungry to be by myself, so I could absorb more of the richness of the surroundings. Everest was beautiful up this close, and that day we were going right to its base. I wanted to look at it undisturbed at least for a few moments. After I had meandered up the moraine for a couple of hours, I spotted some lumps that looked like painted turtles on the edge of the snow—the Americans'

Camp I. Two small figures emerged from the tents, and because I was so far away they seemed to be drifting over the snow on the path marked by the crevasse warning wands. This surreal vision made me aware of the fantasy world climbers live in. Perhaps some of us are drawn back to the mountains again and again because we can be in control there. We can design our own destiny, make our dreams come true. The very limitations of life in the mountains make it a playground for the mind and a testing ground for the body. It's living a fantasy, vivid and exhilarating.

I continued up to the tents and lay on a rock in the sun, looking right smack up at Everest. It looked large, but negotiable. The air was so hot it felt tropical, and the sun blazed off the snow as I daydreamed. By the time Ned, Jim, and Rick came into view I was glad to see them. I had had my few moments alone.

We cached our equipment before descending back to the Americans' Advance Base. Jim mumbled to me that he and his tentmate didn't always see eye to eye. I hadn't noticed, and I wondered if Jim was just having a bad day. This was as close as we'd ever get to climbing Everest, and that might have been frustrating him. I knew he could be moody, so I hoped this complaint was just a passing thing.

◆ ◆ ◆

On May 2, we rose early, and hiked back to our gear stashed at snow line. The weather was beautiful and I wanted to be skiing, so it seemed to take forever to put on all the paraphernalia: ski boots, skis, harnesses, ropes, prusik slings (devices used to escape in the event of a tumble into a crevasse), and safety straps. Finally we slid off, skiing in a "Volga boatman" rhythm and stride, roped together to guard against falling into crevasses. I felt like part of a chain gang.

We stopped after a few moments to tie bandannas over our faces as protection against the harsh sun. During the process of covering up someone suggested we do away with the rope.

"That's a good idea," Ned agreed. "We're running perpendicular to any crevasses, so we're pretty safe with our skis on. They're plenty long enough to distribute our weight over thin snow bridges."

I was ecstatic at being able to ski freely, and I took off fast. Rick and Jim weren't as interested in endurance sports as I was, and Ned was busy snapping photographs, so I just left them all behind. It was so hot I could have been skiing comfortably in a bikini if it hadn't been for the risk of an outrageous burn. I did take my gloves off for a while until I noticed a blister rising on my right index finger.

I reached the crest of the Lho La, just shy of 20,000 feet, glowing from exercise. I could look right down the rocky drop-off into Nepal and see directly into Everest Base Camp on the south side. To the west Pumori rose proudly, and my eyes traced our winter ascent. I could hardly believe I'd stood on top of the peak just a few months earlier. I remembered the strain and the cold. Our windy, frigid summit day contrasted sharply with the still, torrid weather today. Yet in January and now in May I'd touched the border between Nepal and Tibet. I saw our circle begin to take shape—our fantasy was becoming reality.

◆ ◆ ◆

Ned reached the top of the rise where I stood and yelled over to me, "What's it look like down towards the cliff?"

I told him I didn't know because I hadn't investigated. The layout was a little tricky: beyond the height of the pass where I stood it was possible to continue south dropping down toward Nepal a short distance before the slope broke off into a cliff. A fall there could be the beginning of a long slide over the cliff and thousands of feet down into Nepal. I wasn't tempted to try it, but Ned continued for another 200 yards.

Jim and Rick slid easily on up to me. Jim and I hugged each other and excitedly exchanged memories of Pumori. So Rick wouldn't feel left out, I reminded him that this next portion of the expedition was his forte, skiing back down off the pass.

Ned skied back up to us. "Hey, did you guys see the Russians' camp in Nepal?" When we looked, we could just see the huddle of their orange and blue tents. Our eyes began combing the southern exposure of the peak, and after a few moments we spotted what looked to be seven tiny figures moving up.

"There they are," Jim's voice jumped into the silence. Then he boomed as loudly as he could between cupped hands, "Hey, vodka . . . vodka . . . Smirnoff," and began to wave his right arm like a mad metronome over his head. Perhaps it was our willful imaginations, but we thought we saw them waving back. We laughed and laughed at Jim's proficient Russian and his imaginative leap of the political barriers.

The slope we had just skied up was very gradual, gently easing over a mile back down to the Americans' Camp I. The angle of the ski was no problem, but the snow's surface was. Years of alternate baking and melting in the sun had produced an extremely hard névé surface with patches of breakable crust. Skiing over the fragile crust areas would be like walking over a Burmese tiger trap, and the névé, as hard as concrete, would be brutal for setting an edge to turn or stop.

I debated whether or not to take the skins off my skis. An accident here could jeopardize the completion of the circle, and evacuation would be a nightmare. I opted to leave my skins on my skis to control my speed and minimize the number of turns I'd have to make on my descent. Jim decided to do the same. Ned and Rick chided us for being wimps as they tore the glued climbing skins off the slick bases of their skis.

Jim slid down a bit and yelled back a "roll em" from behind the 16-mm camera. I pushed off for a smooth but slow descent, while Rick and Ned went for the gusto. They looked like frisky dogs on ice, slipping and gyrating for control. It wasn't desperate, just funny, but I still wasn't persuaded to take my skins off. As strange as it sounds, I often prefer the feeling of muscles working hard in rhythm on the ascent to the speed of skiing down. My thrill had been reaching the pass first.

My descent was free and effortless. I looked up and over my shoulder at the looming ice and rock masses, and hummed familiar music to myself. I wasn't carrying any weight on my back and my skis were carrying me. I was very content. Happiness smoldered deep inside me like a glowing coal.

Hockey-stop parallel turns weren't possible since the skins held my metal edges off the snow. But the long smooth arc of the ancient telemark was perfect. The telemark turn, named after Telemark, Norway, was used centuries ago in

Scandinavia for turning with 10-foot-long edgeless wooden skis. By sliding one ski ahead of the other and "genuflecting," you arc your skis in a swooping turn.

All during my descent I was entertained by Ned and Rick, who got in some good turns and some bad turns, but also got more serious thrills. As we neared the bottom, I saw that Rick had taken a header into a crevasse. But it was nothing serious, since he went in only waist-deep, and he came up laughing.

We collected at the bottom to pack our gear and skis and lug them back down to Advance Base Camp. The first skiing of the expedition had been a breeze, the weather had cooperated, and we had reached the border. It had almost been too easy. We ribbed each other about style variations and spills. Jim teased, "I don't really think we're going to be able to use this footage for much of anything. If you guys are supposed to look like expert skiers, you sure did a good job of hiding it." Jim's frankness didn't offend anyone—it was hilariously true.

Working together had brought us all closer. Our recent complaints were simply forgotten. We trudged with our gear back down the moraine, past the ghostly ice sailing ships on the glacier, discussing our next plan of action.

Jim and Ned had spotted a peak shy of 23,000 feet and had an itch to climb it. But someone needed to return to Base Camp, sort out another food cache, and load the yaks with our skis for the trip up the East Rongbuk Glacier to the British Advance Camp. It wasn't pleasant duty, so Rick and I decided to do it together, rather than leave only one to shepherd all the supplies for the other three. The peak would be a one-day climb, but a demanding one, and I was just as glad to save my energy for skiing and hauling my load over the two remaining passes, Lhakpa La at 20,000 feet, and Karpo La at 22,000 feet.

Back at Advance Camp we were tired, but contented. Ned's birthday wasn't until May 5, two days later, but we decided to celebrate that night, while the four of us were still together. It was a rather quiet party. We nibbled chocolate and drank a bit of brandy. Everyone laughed when I gave Ned his presents of massage oil and muscle balm for his aging, aching body. But we all knew Ned was hardly the aged weakling—he was the strong man of our trip.

The next morning, we retraced our steps back down the Rongbuk Glacier toward Base Camp and Rick and I wished Ned and Jim luck when they went their separate way. I hoped they were prepared for their climb—they had gathered and packed their gear hastily.

Base Camp was a sorry place without the others and without the British—and with the wind. I dove into my tent to escape the howling gusts and buried my loneliness in a book. But that didn't work, and I decided this was a good chance to get to know Rick better.

"Hey, Rick, what are you doing?" I yelled over the gales.

"Just reading. How about you?"

"The same thing."

We yelled back and forth between the tents for quite a while, explaining to each other what was happening in our respective books. Although it was silly, I didn't suggest reading together in one tent. Rick and I had always functioned in the group of four, never alone, and I think we both felt a little awkward. But the next few days would be a good opportunity to overcome that by working together. Later that evening when I first spotted Jim and Ned walking back into camp, I was afraid something serious had gone wrong, but it turned out that they'd simply forgotten part of their stove. In minutes they were—sheepishly—on their way again.

The next morning, the weather was calm, and Rick and I used this windless pause to pull out the food and sort it yet another time. The wind returned by afternoon, and snow began spitting down.

There was an inch of snow on the ground the next morning when Rick and I scurried around camp to finish getting the loads ready. Then we laid all the gear, including our four pairs of skis, in a heap and motioned to the two yak drivers that we were ready to load and be on our way.

They came over to us waving their arms as if they were pushing something imaginary away and shaking their heads "no." Eventually I got the message that they were telling us to get rid of some of the stuff, that it was too much for their four yaks. Rick and I looked at each other and shrugged. We, of course, had thought we needed everything in the load, but figured we had to do something. We started opening everything up, asking each other if we really needed this or that. We soon got the load down to a more manageable size—provided the two drivers carried small packs as well.

The drivers refused at first, and then began demanding more money to carry the small amount on their backs. I didn't want to delay our departure by quibbling with the two men, and I didn't want to antagonize the only drivers we could get for the next three days. It was worth it to me to make them happy now so that I could establish good rapport with them and enjoy a hassle-free trek to the British Advance Camp. I ran to my tent and pulled out some of my own money and jewelry and offered it to them. They were delighted, and we were on our way.

I wasn't sure what Rick thought about the way I had handled the situation. I wondered if he thought I was too soft because I had not only succumbed to but exceeded their demands. Or if he thought I was overbearing because I had taken charge. But he didn't register any complaint. When we had trekked up the Rongbuk Glacier on our way to the Lho La, we four expedition members had kept our own company, as did the three yak drivers. But now, with our smaller numbers, the four of us worked together as a unit.

By the time we'd stopped for lunch, Rick and I had learned that the drivers' names were Norbu and Turtup. Norbu was a scruffy, wiry old man, and I guessed that Turtup was his son. Norbu thought this language exchange was a good game, so he wasn't the least bit hesitant. At lunch we traded words for simple things like facial features and the clothes we were wearing. When Norbu got to the word "socks" he exposed his own, which were more hole than they were sock. Then he began asking for a new pair with gestures. Rick dug around in his pack and gave him what looked to be a fresh, unused pair.

I was still concerned, though, because Norbu and Turtup seemed to hold all the cards. They could stop the yaks at any moment and demand better wages. I had no cash with me, but after the gift of Rick's socks, they probably figured we had plenty of other extra giveaways in our load. I wasn't sure if being friendly, communicative, and giving was the best way to work with these Tibetans. I didn't know if they would try to take advantage of the fact that Rick and I hadn't kept our distance or taken a hard line with them. I knew that with our Sherpas a close relationship had worked extremely well, but these Tibetans were different—more desperate, perhaps. Some of the yak drivers had been caught stealing by the British, so I was aware that they all weren't trustworthy.

But there was nothing to be done about it now. Our relationship as friends was established, and any attempt to reverse our behavior would only be confusing. We were having fun together and learning from our closer associations with the Tibetans. I decided to stop worrying.

In the early afternoon, Turtup stopped the yaks at a predetermined campsite. The route up the East Rongbuk could be done in one long day hiking alone, but would take us two and a half days at yak rate. Norbu erected the tent we gave him near Rick's and mine. Shortly after we'd settled in, Norbu's face appeared at the door of my tent. His gestures indicated that he wanted something, and we finally figured out that it was scissors and a mirror so he could trim his beard. I had scissors on my Swiss Army knife, and a smudged one-by-two-inch mirror.

Then Turtup appeared, asking for some of our freeze-dried food. I knew that he and Norbu had plenty of *tsampa,* the ground barley that is the staple of their diet at home, but I supposed they wanted to experiment with our funny stuff in the bags, so I gave him a bag of stew.

"I don't know, Jano. These guys are getting pretty greedy," Rick said as we looked at each other after this last request. Still we had to laugh when, in a few minutes, Norbu returned, obviously feeling quite slick and proud of his trim work, brushing his shortened whiskers forward and smiling.

The requests continued all evening for this and that. We had realized that they were simply curious and would ask for anything that caught their eye, and we were no longer afraid they would quit and leave us stranded. If the request wasn't reasonable, we simply said no.

As we trekked on the next day, my thoughts drifted to Ned and Jim. I was hoping to be able to spot them on their peak or cross paths with them, since we would all eventually be heading up the East Rongbuk toward the British Advance Base. I asked Rick if he could make out any traces of their route on the peak as we moved slowly by it.

"It almost looks as if you can see a line that could be footprints diagonaling up the slope." He sounded unsure. I took out a telephoto lens and scanned the area, but couldn't really see anything. I was disappointed that I couldn't see any signs of them, and vaguely anxious.

During our midday break, after Rick and I had eaten some nuts and cheese, I pulled out a small instrument, a wooden recorder in hopes that playing it would help me relax. As I played, Norbu hopped up on a boulder and started to dance what looked like a jig. His expression was intent, and his dark, tattered clothing flapped up and down on his thin, dirty body.

In the early afternoon, we stopped to make camp. I had noticed that since lunch Rick had begun to droop like a plant without water, and I was afraid that coming up in elevation again might be giving him some trouble. While Rick rested, I looked for a spot to put the tent. But as I paused at one site after another, Rick called out some reason the spot wasn't appropriate. When I asked him where he thought the tent should go, he said he wasn't sure.

"Why don't you just wait for a minute, Jan?" I could feel the tension in the air. I didn't want to say that I was eager to put the tent up so he could crawl in.

There was an awkward pause, and then I continued with the tent as if I hadn't heard a thing. I was baffled by Rick's attitude. I thought that maybe he was frustrated at not feeling better. But I didn't want to stop what I was doing, because the activity helped me keep my mind off Jim and Ned.

By that evening, the tension between the two of us had ebbed. After dinner, as the cold curled around our tent, Rick and I laughed and danced inside. We each wore earphones attached to my cassette recorder, and we lay on our backs in the tent, dancing with our stocking feet on the ceiling. Norbu and Turtup must have wondered what on earth we were doing, since they couldn't hear the music but could see our shadows on the tent wall.

The next day our yak train began traveling over mixed rock and snow, and the wind sliced and slapped our faces. I knew we were due to reach the British camp soon, so I stuck with the drivers and yaks to supervise the unloading. I wanted to make sure the movie camera wasn't dropped and, though I'm ashamed to say it, I wanted to make sure nothing "disappeared." Rick lagged behind.

The snow swirling down from the plateau below the East Ridge of Everest stung my eyes. When we finally reached the British camp, we had to push and pull the yaks through the deepening snow to an appropriate unloading site.

Charlie must have heard the drivers' calls, because he came pushing through the frozen flurry. Norbu and Turtup were yanking off the ropes, letting the bags and skis thud in the snow, but I rushed to the yak carrying the camera in time to set the camera gently on the ground. I could see Charlie grinning under his balaclava as he came nearer, then grabbed me for a big hug.

"Charlie, are Ned and Jim here with you?"

"No, I haven't seen them. Joe, Pete, Chris, and Dick are all here, though. They're exhausted and going down to Base for a rest before trying again. They did some amazing climbing and have reached 26,900 feet." Charlie must have sensed my disappointment.

"Are you worried about Ned and Jim?"

"Well, I'm not sure if it's time to worry yet, but they should have climbed a small peak two days ago. I thought they'd be here before Rick and I got here with all the equipment."

"They'll be along. Come in for some tea," he said, apparently unconcerned. Charlie was probably right. "I'll be in in a bit. I've got to pay the drivers and organize our gear." Rick appeared around the corner and Charlie left to greet him. They continued on together into the large canvas cook tent. We were on the edge of the white plateau below Everest, at about 21,000 feet.

I said good-bye to Norbu and Turtup, then stacked and secured the bags. I took one last long, sweeping look toward the glacier we'd come from, hoping to see two figures approaching. When I didn't, I realized how concerned I was.

Inside the tent it was warm, dark, and steamy. As my eyes adjusted to the low light I could see everyone sitting in a semicircle around a large flat rock used as a table. Joe, Pete, Dick, and Chris had been sucking in warm, moist air from their homemade teapot hookahs to soothe their raw throats, and croaked a warm greeting as I opened the door. I gave everyone a hug and a kiss. It felt as though they were old friends I hadn't seen for a long time. We'd brought their mail, which had been delivered to Base Camp, with us—including a letter I had written Dick since he hadn't received any others. Mail from the outside world is invaluable on an expedition, and they were all delighted to get the reminders that family and friends were thinking of them and wishing them well.

The British were planning to reach Base Camp that day, so they left after passing along a few stories from their recent climb. They offered us their large tent for our use, which Rick and I accepted gratefully, since we had only small two-person tents with us.

But once the excitement was over and Rick and I were alone, I began to worry in earnest about Ned and Jim.

16

CLOSING THE CIRCLE

"We've purchased the world's most expensive ski ticket for the world's worst skiing."

Rick Barker

NED: 

On May 4 Jim and I left Base Camp at dawn and headed up the east side of the Rongbuk Glacier. We were restless, and wanted to climb a mountain. During the days near the Lho La we had been attracted to a pretty rock peak that was located on the long ridge extending north from Changtse. The top section ended in a rocky spire that looked challenging. We thought the other side of the mountain might offer a less technically demanding route, and were on our way to try it. Jan and Rick had agreed to stay behind, pack the gear for the next leg of the trek, then accompany the yaks to the head of the East Rongbuk Glacier. Jim and I planned to meet them there.

We walked along a sandy moat between the glacial ice and the hillside for three miles, then left the moat and followed a well-worn path away from the glacier into a small cleft from which a small stream cascaded. We traversed steeply upward in a southeasterly direction to a height where the stream flowed more slowly over bedrock. The rock was striated—evidence that ice had overridden it in the past. Presently the debris-covered snout of a glacier—"like the huge waves of a brown angry sea," as Mallory described it—blocked our progress. We cut upward to our right, still on the path, and came out onto a shelf with a surprising view of a broad valley. Big rock and snow peaks formed the opposite side of the valley. A tumbled river of ice—the East Rongbuk Glacier—curved gently upward to the south. We knew it led directly to the base of the North Col and Northeast Ridge of Everest. This was the line of ascent attempted by all the prewar British expeditions, and the one used by the Chinese for their 1960 success.

Jim and I were just beginning to feel fit, having been at altitude for nearly two weeks. We walked along separately in the cold sunshine, pausing frequently to rest and talk. I was pleased to have the chance to explore the north side of Everest and happy to be moving with a good friend through impressive country carrying only a light pack.

The wind came on in the afternoon, and it began to spit snow. The landscape was wild and threatening. Often we lost the trail while scrambling across scree fields. Occasionally we saw telephone wire or dumps of rusty food cans—signs of the 1980 Japanese expedition, which spent over a million dollars to climb the same route the Chinese had in 1960 and 1975; and the 1981 French military expedition, which was unsuccessful. Ordinarily the residue would have bothered me, but I was wrapped up in the simple joys of the day's walk and my own musings about the history of the area.

As the clouds lowered it became increasingly difficult to orient ourselves to the unnamed peak—Point 22,680 feet on the map—that we hoped to climb. After six hours we pitched the tent on a level, snowy spot at the edge of the glacier. There was plenty of time to read, talk, drink, and eat a leisurely dinner. Our little tent was a profound comfort.

May 5, my birthday, was partly cloudy as we left to climb our peak, which lay behind the shoulder above camp. We scrambled up a snow couloir for 1,000 feet to a vantage point. The peak was there, all right, but the top lay at the end of a long, serrated ridge.

"The top's not worth it," Jim announced after a glance. "Too much danger on that ridge." He headed down to the tent.

I agreed but, enjoying my elevated stance, decided to poke around on the easy terrain that led up to the ridge. I had a fine view of Everest, from which a terrific wind blew a huge plume westward. Looking down, I realized that the ridge to the south was also connected to Point 22,680. The mountain was shaped like a gigantic easy chair whose backrest was the sharply pointed summit. The other ridge looked to be an enjoyable climb, and I hurried down to tell Jim. He was enthusiastic, so, after hot tea, we packed up and moved a mile-and-a-half up the glacier, camping at 20,000 feet at the entrance to an amphitheater. Our peak formed the head of this snowy bowl. During the 1922 expedition, the first time anyone had trekked up the lower East Rongbuk, the British had established Camp II approximately where we were now. The leader of the expedition, General C. G. Bruce, had described our goal as "... a peak of slender beauty, and as the moon rose its crests were silver cords." Shipton's reconnaissance expedition climbed the peak in 1935.

The tent was still in deep shadow when we started the next morning, walking unroped along the top of a thin lateral moraine. The sun hitting the top of the peak turned the central flutings a ruddy yellow, which contrasted sharply with the dark blue sky. Once past a rocky buttress, we angled upward across a long, steep slope leading to the ridge that formed the south "arm" of the "easy chair." The snow was unconsolidated initially, and we worried about avalanche danger; then, within a distance of 10 feet, it thinned. Jim was leading and his crampons ground into hard ice. He had been climbing casually, using one ski pole for balance; but his momentum, such as it was, carried him out onto the hard ice. Suddenly he was in a dangerous position, precariously balanced on the side teeth of his crampons. On guard, he swiveled his feet to dig in his front points. Thus secured, he reached back over his head very carefully to retrieve the ice axe that he had slipped under a pack strap. I did likewise, but from a position in deeper snow. We sidled across the ice for 150 feet, facing inward, moving crampon and axe placements alternately, still unroped. Below, the slope fell away to the seracs of an unnamed glacier.

Once we were on the ridge, which rolled upward, the going was easy for several hundred yards. We crossed a small bergschrund by front-pointing against the far wall, then kicked steps in nonstop rhythm up a sharply angled section of névé. We stopped on a rock outcrop where the backbone of the ridge broke clear from the snow. A series of rock gendarmes rose directly above; to our right, a very steep snow slope ran down into the flutings that marked the East Face of the mountain. The rock looked rotten and the snow unstable—to climb on either one would be dangerous.

Instead, we climbed on both—one foot on rock, the other on snow—thus gaining the advantages of both while minimizing the risk. The air had been sunny, warm, and still; but now, in the matter of a few minutes, powerful gusts wracked us as they funneled through the slots between the rock towers. Soon a vicious snow squall enveloped us. Standing waist-deep in a little hole that was rock on one side and snow on the other, I hurriedly put on my anorak. Jim had left his behind, and his pile jacket was soon woolly with blasted snow.

An eight-foot-high wall of white, lacy ice blocked the channel between the rock and snow, so we had to go across a deep hole, the bottom of which we couldn't see. Jim plunged his axe into the vertical wall on the far side, stepped boldly across, and front-pointed his way up it. Pushed by the nasty storm that raged around us, I followed, pulling myself quickly up the wall. At the top I looked down into the hole I had just confidently climbed over without a safety rope, and was slightly appalled at my own feat. Jim, with his superior technical expertise, remained nonchalant.

We had climbed this far without a rope, and it had been tremendously enjoyable and natural. Freed from the extra link to Jim, I had felt closer to the mountain and climbed in a cocoon of concentration. True, a slip would have had serious consequences. But I had felt a real sense of worthwhile challenge and freedom that produced a far more rewarding day than we would have had, had we assumed every safety precaution. Our risks helped square the odds. Besides, Jim carried the rope, and he had always been ahead on this last technical section!

Now, standing next to him with the rope at hand, I felt different; especially so when, through a break in the clouds, I surveyed the last 100 feet to the summit. We were sheltered in the lee of the final gendarme. The wind roared over the corniced ridge above, and there was no choice but to move out onto the 60-degree snowfield. I asked for the rope. Jim, sensing my concern, quickly uncoiled it and we tied in. Sitting on a ledge at the base of the gendarme, I braced my feet and paid out the rope as he climbed up into the clouds. He signaled me to follow by tugging on the rope three times.

At the top, I nearly climbed over him because his clothing was so caked with snow that he appeared to be part of the snowy environment. The summit was but a sliver; and, for a belay, he rode it like a horse, his legs kicking space. As suddenly as it had started, the squall passed. Gray clouds still swirled overhead. I had the sensation of being submerged in ocean water, peering at the underside of breaking waves. We were perched on the highest point of the ridge that extended north from Changtse. Everest was totally obscured to the south. To the north, beyond the hideous ridge we had tried to climb the day before, we surveyed a maze of brown valleys. To the west, we looked straight down onto the serac-infested surface of the Rongbuk Glacier. To the east, we could see beyond the East Rongbuk to the vast snowfield of the Far East Rongbuk Glacier. More distant views were obscured by the still unsettled weather.

We were *at* the top, but not *on* the top. In China, you need specific permission and must pay a fee to climb any peak. We had not paid to climb this one. So I must dutifully report that we climbed to within one foot of the summit. Unnamed Peak remains unclimbed—at least by us.

A second squall moved in, and we retreated in near whiteout conditions. The sun came out by the time we were on the easy ridge below the bergschrund, and we trotted down toward camp. Jim had a splitting headache. Twice he

Overleaf: *Lamas along an alleyway in Tashilhunpo Monastery*
Top: *The Potala, Lhasa, as seen from the roof of Jokhang temple*
Bottom: *Pilgrims waiting to enter Jokhang temple, Lhasa*
Facing: *Monks in the Great Chanting Hall, Tashilhunpo Monastery, Shigatse*

Top: *Monk wiping gilded bowls from which the spirits are believed to drink*
Bottom: *Sakyamuni Buddha, the holiest image in Tibet, Jokhang temple*
Facing: *The most beautiful woman in Tibet, Lhasa*
Following spread: *Travelers on Tibetan Plateau, near Dzaker Chu*

Facing: *Street vendor, Shigatse*
Top, left: *Pilgrim with prayer wheel and rosaries*
Top, right: *Mother holding child in cradleboard*
Bottom, left: *Pilgrim about to prostrate himself*
Bottom, right: *Prosperous trader on tea break*

Top: *Reading hand-printed scriptures, Tashilhunpo Monastery, Shigatse*
Bottom, left: *Woman waiting to pray in Jokhang temple, Lhasa*
Bottom, right: *Worshipper during daylong vigil in Jokhang temple*
Facing: *Lighting yak-butter candles before the Buddha of the Future, Jokhang temple*
Following spread: *Everest in alpenglow and moonlight, from Rongbuk Base Camp*

Above: *Jim herding our yaks up the Rongbuk Glacier toward Everest and the Lho La*

Top: *Mister Truck and crew—(from left to right) Rick, Ned, Chang, Laba, Jim (on truck) and Losan*
Bottom: *Rhododendrons in Kangshung Valley*
Following spread: *Ice pillars and meltwater on East Rongbuk Glacier*

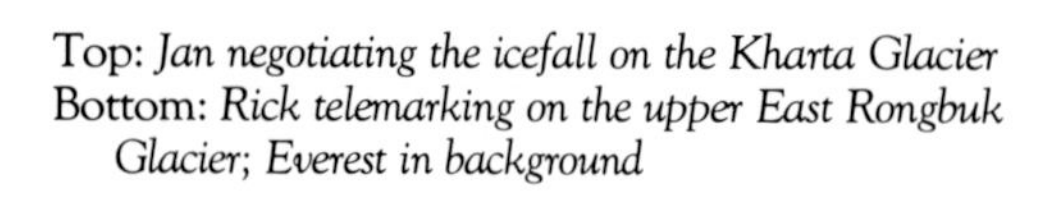

Top: *Jan negotiating the icefall on the Kharta Glacier*
Bottom: *Rick telemarking on the upper East Rongbuk Glacier; Everest in background*

Above: *Lull in the storm below Lhakpa La; Kangchenjunga in far distance*
Following spread: *Rappelling off 20,000-foot Karpo La, our final pass*

Top: *Jan and Jim crossing a frozen lake, Kangshung Valley*
Bottom: *Jan swimming through a rhododendron jungle*
Facing: *Rick (left) and Jan clambering through the boulder battlefield, Kangshung Valley*

Top: *Jan asking directions from surprised Tibetan lumberman near the Karma Chu*
Bottom: *With Chris Bonington and Charlie Clarke on the Langma La; across the Kangshung Valley (left to right) Chomo Lonzo, Pethangtse, Lhotse, and Everest*

broke through into small crevasses, but his hips wedged and he pushed himself free with his arms. He called it "spelunking." While we waited in the tent for the water to boil, we remembered that, near the top, we had considered turning back in the squall. Was the top worth the risk? Climbing Unnamed Peak gave us no glory or public recognition, but it left us immensely satisfied.

The next morning we started toward the head of the East Rongbuk Glacier and Bonington's Advance Base Camp at 21,000 feet, where we planned to meet Jan and Rick. Our immediate problem was fighting our way across the tumbled sea of ice that separated us from the more level central part of the glacier, the line of easiest access. We skidded down a loose gravel bank into a deep boundary trough and skirted three small meltwater ponds. We followed the ditch for several hundred feet in an attempt to discover an easy way to cut through, but there was none, so we simply plunged into the forest of ice pinnacles. An alley led to a little col between two 50-foot-high towers, and we surmounted the slippery surface by climbing on knobs of ice. More than once I thought of the practicality of the hobnailed boots worn on the early expeditions. Once over the wall we were in the interior: a fairyland of bluish white spires, moats, and corridors. "The White Rabbit himself would have been bewildered here," Mallory wrote of traveling across these Tibetan glaciers (Howard-Bury, 1922).

Our journey through these miniature mountain ranges, valleys, and watercourses—with innumerable false starts and retreats at forks and junctions—was exciting but safe work. This was not an icefall, as one would expect on a glacier in Alaska or the Alps. There were no crevasses and no delicately poised seracs, and the pinnacles were firmly based. Melting, not movement, had created them; the black-gravel-covered ice had "sunk" on every side, leaving the spires.

The sun shone, and we were in no hurry to escape the enchanted scene. In half an hour we broke out onto a broad avenue of level ice in the middle of the glacier. This was the "miracle highway," a natural path of access to the North Col discovered by the British in 1922. It was formed by the differential melting under the rock moraine that snaked down from the union of this and the Changtse Glaciers. Jim and I turned right and marched up it.

As we gradually gained altitude, the ceiling lowered and obscured the high peaks on either side of the glacier. Snow flurries developed. The traveling was straightforward but, in the afternoon, Jim and I began to feel listless. Oxygen deprivation, even at moderate altitudes, slowed and weakened us, and dampened our enthusiasm. As we progressed higher, we had less capacity for hard work. We trudged along in the gloomy weather at different paces, so that often we were out of sight of each other.

◆ ◆ ◆

In April 1934, a solitary figure staggered over the same portion of the East Rongbuk Glacier. He had come illegally to climb Everest, but now waged a losing battle against hunger, altitude, and lassitude. His mountaineering expertise was nil.

The man was Maurice Wilson—a tall, powerful 38-year-old ascetic. He had survived the horrors of the trenches in World War I, then wandered

Captain Maurice Wilson, Reprinted from I'll Climb Mount Everest Alone, *by Dennis Roberts.*

aimlessly as one of the "lost generation." Falling seriously ill, he had cured himself by prayer and a drastic fast of 35 days. Fanatically convinced by his miraculous recovery that faith and fasting would make everyone a better person, he set out to climb Everest alone as a means of publicizing his cause.

He made three valiant but inexpert attempts to climb the North Col. He expected "a handrope and steps" from the 1933 expedition to be in place and so hoist himself to the top. He was bitterly disappointed upon finding only ice and snow. He finally died in his tent at the foot of the North Col.

◆ ◆ ◆

We followed the "miracle highway" to the northern buttress of Changtse, where we looked ahead up a long snow slope and saw six figures. It was our British friends descending from their second assault on the East Northeast Ridge and headed for a rest at Base Camp. At extreme altitude the body deteriorates quickly, and it is necessary to go down below 18,000 feet to recover. When we met them in the middle of the slope, we found that they were in good spirits and confident, despite the physical wear and tear. I was appalled at the changes they had undergone since we last saw them. They looked like wizened, hunched old men, and their eyes were wild. Even so, they had a kind of desperate nobility.

They told us about the progress they had made, talking in short sentences through fixed grimaces. They had spent four nights without oxygen at or above their last snow cave at 25,700 feet. The main difficulties of the climb started above at 26,250 feet—higher than all but the 14 tallest peaks in the world. There a ridge narrowed into a knife-edged crest of snow, and progress was barred by a series of rock pinnacles. The ridge ran nearly a half-mile and gained 1,300 feet before joining the original prewar route to the summit.

On May 4 and 5 they had accomplished some of the most difficult climbing ever done at extreme altitude, boldly leading up steep broken rock, ice, and insubstantial snow. They had stopped just short of the top of the first pinnacle at 26,900 feet.

Tired as they were, they still had an appreciation for the beauty of the mountain. "The view from the third snow cave is fantastic," Pete said. "We hang out thousands of feet above the Kangshung Glacier and look at Makalu and Kangchenjunga."

"Why don't you send the party girl down," Joe teased me about Jan, exhibiting a rare flash of humor. The British told us that Jan and Rick had made it to their Advance Base Camp and awaited us there.

Our visit was brief, for it was obvious they had but one thing in mind: the relative luxuries of Base Camp. Charlie tarried a minute after the others moved on. "It's absolutely incredible how they've pushed themselves to the limit," he said. "With such a small team, there are no back-up climbers to relieve them. But there have been problems. Dick had a strange tingling sensation down his left side while climbing at 26,700 feet. He got himself down, but it's very serious. It was a mild stroke. Afterward, Dick lost a crampon. When Chris went to help him, there was a slip and both almost toppled off. The price can be so high up there. Look at Chris. He's very nearly gone. He's 47, and the mountain is eating him up." We shook hands and he left.

Jim turned and started up without a word. The meeting had piqued his inner ambitions—he was a climber, and would have loved to be climbing Everest. I stood several minutes and watched the little band grow smaller in the distance. At that time I didn't know that only two of them would be fit enough for a third assault, and that this was the last time we would see those two.

I plodded upward, intrigued by the encounter with the British. They were top fellows, and we cared deeply for their success and welfare. It was a privilege to share some of the same camps, even though we were on different adventures. On the day of our picnic two weeks before, Chris had told me he thought our circle concept was an intriguing one because of the exciting ground we would cover. "In some ways I envy you," he had said. "You're doing something well within your powers, and avoiding the terror and exhaustion we sometimes face on Everest itself."

As Jim and I continued, a hostile wind blew a fine dust of spindrift against my boots until I could barely see them. By the end of our trek up the East Rongbuk I was more tired than I thought I should be, and Jim was even worse. As we neared 21,000 feet, the tents of the British Advance Base Camp under the east side of Changtse came into sight. Jan had been watching, and hurried down to meet us with mugs of steaming tea. Her hug felt wonderful, but it spilled half the liquid. We sat for a few minutes in the blowing snow and talked. I explained that we were later than she expected because it had taken us two attempts to make the top. Then she carried my pack up to the tents. We cooked a hasty dinner and turned into our sleeping bags for a long sleep.

The next morning, May 8, the wind that careened off the North Col was brutally fickle. It hit the tents in hammer blows that bulged the nylon inward; then, as each gust moved on, the camp was left in calm air. During the quiet we could hear the next gust approaching with a roar. We dozed fitfully through the entire morning, then finally managed to rouse ourselves for brunch in the British mess tent, which we had been given permission to use.

The mess tent was a ramshackle, improvised affair. The basic tent was olive drab, but it bore little resemblance to the single-walled shelter that had first been erected by Bonington and company. Extra tarps had been added to it to reinforce the fabric, stout tie-down lines had been thrown over the roof, and rock walls had been built up along the sides. I could imagine Charlie and Adrian adding to the structure as the wind blew harder each day.

Inside it was dark, dreary, and cluttered with food, stoves, pots and pans, books, and every sort of odd community gear. We sat around a cockeyed center table made of a great slab of rock. The tent jumped and rattled at every gust. Jan was feeling peppy, but Jim and I were tired and mopey. Jan reminded us that we were here to circle Everest, and not to climb every mountain. She was concerned that something could go wrong before the circle was finished, and wanted no part of detours.

Rick was having another bout with altitude sickness. Although he had never shirked any assignment, his difficulty adjusting to the thin air severely dampened his enjoyment of the Tibetan highlands. Still, he didn't complain. He sat across the tent from me slowly spooning up food as if he were eating dirt. The wind was still blowing when we went to bed that night.

The next three days were quite pleasant, despite chilly temperatures and a brisk breeze. Rick felt far stronger, so we did some recreational skiing on the slopes under the North Col. There was little chance for stylish skiing among the closed crevasses and seracs, and we skittered over icy firn and banged down wind-etched, unyielding snow. The occasional island of forgiving snow allowed time for a quick genuflection into a telemark between survival parallel turns. While the rest of us demonstrated a number of buttocks arrests and elegant head-plants, Rick—finally performing his specialty—was masterful. A glint of pleasure had returned to his eyes, and a deep chortle of satisfaction punctuated the last turn of each run.

"There is no doubt," Rick said, "that we've purchased the world's most expensive ski ticket for the world's worst skiing!"

I could only agree: the cementlike snow on which we ground out each hobbled turn with gritted teeth and clinched toes was such an unlikely surface it was almost funny. But I've never said that adventure skiing offered the best conditions, only the most exotic locations. The rock walls of Everest that rose above us were cross-hatched with softening lines of snow.

We were not the first to consider using skis in Tibet. Three pairs were brought along on the 1921 Reconnaissance, although they were never unpacked for use. However, they did fascinate the Tibetans, who, according to C. K. Howard-Bury, had heard of flying machines and thought the long slats were the framework on which the British intended to fly to the tops of mountains.

Nor were we the first to ski in Tibet. On the 1922 expedition George Finch actually slid around on skis on the slopes of the East Rongbuk Glacier. In 1945, Austrian-German mountaineers Heinrich Harrer and Peter Aufschnaiter skied once while en route by foot to Lhasa after escaping internment in war-time India. They made skis out of a couple of birch trunks, but broke their skis on the second day of what the Tibetans called "snow riding." That put an abrupt end to their sport.

During the next couple of days we discovered better snow on the slopes that fanned out from the base of Changtse. Here the consolidated snow had a hint of softness and consistency to it, and we swung down the slopes like real skiers, ecstatic to let go of the "don't make a mistake, don't get hurt" conservatism that is the trademark of expeditions in remote areas. This was one of the few times on the expedition that gravity worked for us instead of against us.

That evening, after a brief snow squall had blotted out Everest and halted our skiing, the purple hues of dusk painted the rocks and snow of the mountains the same color as the sky. A full moon rose along the East Northeast Ridge of Everest. Our location—the beginning of the main route up Everest from the north—had been the site of so many examples of hope and courage, hardship and difficulty, disappointment and success.

On May 12 we woke to a blustery wind that swept spindrift across the featureless surface of the upper East Rongbuk Glacier. It abated by the afternoon, and we packed and departed toward the east at two o'clock, carrying 45-pound packs, with enough food for eight days. This was the final leg of the circle, during which we would have to cross two high passes in order to reach the Kangshung Glacier Valley. The border between Tibet and Nepal runs along the south side of the valley. Our forthcoming travels would pique our sense of adventure not because of the technical difficulties, but because we were about to step into terrain even more remote than the Rongbuk. Only three expeditions had ever traveled in the area we would negotiate, and none since 1938.

Because of the constant wind, the glacier surface was as hard as concrete. As in Nepal, we left our skis behind and wore our double mountaineering boots. The skis were cached at the British Advance Base Camp with Jim's big 16-mm movie camera and other excess gear. We had scheduled the Tibetan yak drivers to retrieve the gear two days hence and deliver it to Losan at Rongbuk Base Camp. An hour's walk across smooth ice brought us to the foot of the Lhakpa La, which means "windy gap," a 22,200-foot pass, where we started up a moderate slope. The wind picked up again and, finding a nook in the terrain that was somewhat protected, we camped a third of the way up the pass. As usual, intermittent blasts of wind alternated with calm spells. It had been pleasant to use the British facilities, but it felt good to be off on our own, cooking on our mountain stoves and living in our dome tents.

We clipped on crampons the next morning and started up about 1,000 vertical feet. There were several small crevasses to step over and a couple of ice patches, but all in all it was a very straightforward hike toward a saddle to the north of a rocky peak. Just below the crest and out of the wind, we halted to enjoy our last view of the Rongbuk area. Below us spread the broad bay of the upper East Rongbuk. To the west we could see Point 22,680, which Jim and I had climbed, and the rocky face of Changtse. Between them, partially obscured by clouds and many miles away, Gyachung Kang rose on the far side of Pumori. The large crevasses and avalanche-prone slopes of the North Col were clearly visible, and what had looked formidable from the British Advance Base now appeared as small features on the low point of the ridge. The Northeast Ridge of Everest reared up from the col in a seemingly endless slope. The massive East Northeast Ridge—Bonington's route—faced us directly. An evil-looking gray plume of clouds billowed from the entire ridge to the east. The highest point on earth rose behind the rocky junction of the two ridges.

We continued up the short distance to the top of the pass. A strong gale was blowing and the clouds were closing in about us from the east. There was just time to catch a glimpse of our descent route to the Kharta Glacier. To the north, still above the clouds, rose Khartaphu, 23,720 feet high, which was first climbed by members of Eric Shipton's 1935 Reconnaissance.

Shipton was opposed to the idea of large expeditions. In a certain way he was even opposed to climbing Everest himself, for his real love lay in the exploration of unknown mountain areas rather than assaulting a particular peak. But Everest gripped him and he found it "hard to stand aside." The 1922, 1924, and 1933 extravaganzas had failed to climb Everest. Shipton decided to attack the mountain in his own style. In 1969 he wrote, ". . . I was anxious for the opportunity to demonstrate that, for one-tenth of the former cost and a fraction of the bother and disruption of the local countryside, a party could be placed on the North Col, adequately equipped to make a strong attempt on the summit."

As the seven-man party trekked toward Everest, Shipton couldn't resist halting for a fortnight to investigate an unknown range and fill in a blank on the map. In the distance he could see that Everest was in ideal condition. But because of the delay, when they reached Everest monsoon storms had closed in and he had lost his chance. Even though the expedition was mandated as a reconnaissance, a dash to the top might have been possible.

Had he been successful, he would have proved once and for all his point about the strengths of small expeditions. In a larger sense, his success might even have changed the entire style in which expeditions approached the Himalayan giants. The massive operations might have been foregone in favor of lighter forays and more sporting ethics—a tactic which has just recently come into acceptance. As it was, Shipton lived with the knowledge that he had missed his one superb opportunity.

JAN: It was a straightforward rappel down a snow slope to the Kharta Glacier. I slipped down first, and when we were all down we collected at the bottom of the rappel and roped up in pairs to cross the glacier, which was laced with crevasses. Hopping the cracks took a lot of concentration, but they gave me something to focus on in the midst of the lowering whiteout.

Even though Ned and I have traveled roped together countless times, our timing isn't perfect. I was walking behind Ned with a small coil of extra rope in my hand to pay out or haul in as needed to keep the rope fairly taut between us.

Ned suddenly began to speed up. We'd been traveling over softer snow for quite some distance, but Ned had just reached a section of firm hardpack that sloped down. This made walking easier for him, but I was still working through deeper stuff behind him. I gradually paid the rope out, over the next few yards, but ran out of buffer coil just as I hit a crevasse. Before I could lift off my feet to jump it, Ned jerked the rope forward—and me with it—and I went right in.

I fell in up to my knees, and Ned got a sharp jerk. "What's the problem back there?" he asked as he was turning around. We could just make each other out vaguely through the cloud curtain. It became obvious to Ned I was sitting on the edge of a crevasse, because there was no other apparent reason to be sitting in the snow.

"I didn't have much choice," I yelled loudly. "It was involuntary crevasse inspection. Take it easy when you're in the clear. Remember, I might still be wading through some junk."

I could hear a faint chuckle as I extracted myself, brushed off the snow, and coiled a bit more rope. We wandered in and out of the white void that afternoon, then camped on the glacier just below 21,000 feet. It had been a long day with heavy loads, and we were all tired. My legs had that dull ache I used to get as a child after a long day of hard running and playing. My mother would comfort me at night and tell me that they were just growing pains. Perhaps that's what they still were.

NED: After we descended from the Lhakpa La, the upper Kharta Glacier cirque had been a maelstrom of wild wind throughout the afternoon. Gusts of 50 miles an hour shoved us along our way and sandblasted spindrift. The blowing snow was so thick that, at times, it felt as though we were in the foam of a breaking ocean wave. Often I was not able to see my feet below or the mountains above that framed the valley. I led the way through deep snow, which soon gave way to bare ice. Navigation was by sight during the periods of less wind and by feel and instinct the rest of the time. Wide crevasses soon began to cut across the glacier, and we were forced to weave a zigzag pattern through them. Each time I turned to monitor the progress of the others or shout a few words, icy pellets stung my face. So I just kept moving on at a steady pace, relying on the tension of the rope between Jan and me to govern my speed. After two hours we discovered a somewhat sheltered spot in the lee of an ice bulge and decided to camp.

We wrestled the tents into position. Even though the worst of the williwaws flew overhead, the tents flapped wildly, and we had to look sharp not to loose our grip on them. Once they were staked out, we flopped inside and began the evening's gymnastics. Not only did we have the usual litter of cooking gear, boots, spare clothing, sleeping bags, and food packets—but it was all jumping about like popcorn in a popper as the wind hit the tent in intermittent blasts. Our "house" had the floor area of a good-sized dining room table. There we had to cook, eat, sleep, and take care of all other functions—including using a plastic bottle as toilet if the weather was stormy. Even if you took pains to be as gracious as possible, there was no way to avoid the belches, farts, nose blows, chewing quirks, snoring, body odor, dandruff, and stinky feet of your partner.

It is one thing to put up with the odors and dribbles of somebody you like, but quite another if egos or feelings are being rubbed raw. Rick and Jim had been total strangers before the trip. I had taken a chance that they would hit it off, but they didn't. They made do as tentmates, but the atmosphere was strained. Each made an effort at preserving the peace but, except for the occasional burst of laughter or encouraging aside, a slight chill hung inside their tent. It reminded me of a dissolving marriage: they were both determined to keep up appearances of civility until the end of the expedition. I felt responsible for the problem, but didn't have a solution.

Somehow, the Tibet half of the circle lacked the energy, spirit, and challenge of the Nepal portion. It felt instead as if we were finishing off a job. I considered our position: we were in spectacular country that was, by today's standards, virtually untraveled. Away from our Chinese liaisons, we were free to wander and climb and explore to our hearts' desire. But we tended to stick to the specific itinerary of the circle. There were reasons. I am goal oriented and, in retrospect, would have done better had I included an equivalent of Pumori in the northern half of the circle, or possibly some unique exploratory strike. Jan tended to vote for the most direct line to finish the circle without detours, Jim was on a trip that was not in his hard-hitting style of assaulting vertical chunks of rock, and Rick was still bothered by altitude and lacked the expeditionary experience to take hold and push in new directions. It is always easy to say what might have been. On the other hand, we had nothing to complain about. We were moving on our own through beautiful, remote country at the foot of the world's highest mountain, had had no major arguments, and had visited one of the world's most exotic cultures. Taken on its own terms, it was a delightful recipe for high mountain trekking.

JAN: Early the next morning, May 14, I heard Jim's voice breaking into my dreams as he unzipped his tent. "What a whiteout out there. It reminds me of watching TV at four o'clock in the morning."

Then I heard Rick in a silly mood, "Hello, campers! Another fine day! Okay, Jim, it's your move. I moved the pee can to the corner, you can move the pads." I was glad that Rick felt well enough to joke—especially since the previous night had been our highest sleep so far.

Before I'd even opened my eyes, I knew we weren't going anywhere. Jim and Rick had to be organizing their tent for down-time because the whiteout was so thick it wasn't safe to move.

I lay in my bag feeling groggy, as the day pulled itself together around me like a mirage becoming real. "Hey, I think I see a patch of blue sky. Oops—it was just some fleece from my jacket floating by." I chuckled myself awake.

I often enjoy being snowed in. My tent becomes a warm, isolated womb, surrounded by the angry weather. Time slows down, and the long day is punctuated only by food and drink. I was happy to have a rest that day, and a chance to finish the spy thriller I was reading. Even so, this storm made me a little anxious because we were so close to completing our circle that I couldn't bear the thought of anything standing in our way.

The wind intermittently blew violent breaths at us that were so hard they seemed to shake our brains. During these bouts, Ned and I would lie on our backs and use our arms and legs as reinforcing rods for our fabric tent. It was difficult to tell if the storm was going to become stronger or go away and leave us alone.

Between the wind blasts, tent life was pleasant and relaxing. I had time to attend to matters that often go neglected on an expedition, like taking my hair down, brushing it out, and braiding it tight again to hide beneath my silk balaclavas. I decided to change my socks as well. Because I like to travel as lightly as possible, I take only two pairs of wool socks. I wear only one pair, keeping the second as an emergency reserve. Because I wear only one pair continually, I slip into my bag at night with damp socks on, but they are dry again by morning. Jim's technique is to alternate days with two pair of socks. He puts the dry ones on to sleep in at night, and dries out the damp ones underneath his armpits in his sleeping bag. And Ned has extra socks dropping and falling out of everywhere.

My socks had been getting pretty ripe, and when I did take them off, I discovered that I had gardens growing between my toes. Quite suddenly, Ned bolted out the door, screaming. Jim unzipped his tent immediately and asked, "Hey, did you guys have a fight?" as Ned lay writhing in the snow, clutching at his throat. "No, Jan just took her socks off. I was being asphyxiated." Everyone, including me, burst into laughter.

We heard soft sounds of thunder through the day, and also had occasional clearings that opened up spectacular views of Makalu, Chomo Lönzo, and Pethangtse. The storm appeared to be moving away, and by the next morning we were in the clear.

Our lethargy of the previous day was still lingering, and it took us until half past 11 to be packed up and ready to move. Our immediate morning challenge was maze maneuvers through the jumble of ice that was the Kharta Glacier. Having relaxed so totally, I had a hard time steeling myself for the task ahead.

Ned had proposed that we skirt along a rock wall on one side of the frozen jumble, but Jim thought the opposite side would prove more negotiable and less frustrating, so we took that one. Ned and I were keenly aware of each other's positions as we worked through the icefall, and occasionally gave belays over small descents and large, gaping crevasses. I looked down one hideous smile of a crack, wondering if I could see its bottom. I couldn't. I'd have to do a decent standing broad jump with a full pack on my back, and land with control so I wouldn't twist an ankle from catching my crampons. "Okay, here we go," I cheered. "Watch me, Ned."

"Wait, Jano, that's a great shot." Ned, who had already hopped the gap, wanted a photo. I accepted my duty to model with chagrin. Just as I took flight, I realized Ned had both hands on the camera and that the rope between us was dangling loose from my waist right in my landing pattern. I grabbed the rope midair, lifted it overhead, and swung it away from the rope-chopping spikes under my boots. Ned shouted, "Hold it" as I was in midflight, as if I had the power to remain fixed in the air. He is a photographer to the bone—he knows his angles and he gets his shots!

The last stretch was a long, gradual slope up to the height of the Karpo La, our last pass in the circle. It was merely a matter of postholing to the top where we paused for water, chocolate, and—in Jim's case—cigarettes. From here on, the only way was down.

NED: The crest of the Karpo La was at 19,960 feet. It had taken two hours to descend the icefall below camp, walk eastward along the Kharta Glacier, then turn sharply to the south and climb up a short, moderate slope to the top of the pass. A vista of magnificent proportions opened before us—the Kangshung Valley, perhaps the wildest, most remote, most pristine valley in the Himalaya. I had the feeling of looking at scenery so spectacular that it was a new sensation. The landscape of cascading glaciers and curving moraines was mottled with snow. Half hidden in clouds that rolled through the valley rose three of the five highest peaks in the world. Everest dominated the head of the Kangshung, its bulky East Face a broad, white wall of hanging glaciers and snow deposited by the prevailing westerlies. Lhotse, its North Face of black rock sneering and defiant, presented one of the last, great unclimbed faces of the Himalaya. Makalu stood as a yellow gray pyramid of frigid granite. In 1982 none of the three had been scaled from the Kangshung side. The smaller peaks of Chomo Lönzo and Pethangtse were perfect towers and pyramids. Incredibly, not one individual peak held the eye. Together, their awesome precipices formed a gigantic bulwark of rock and snow, connected by aretes and shoulders, that was overpowering. At first glance the features of the place looked to be simple, but the eye never tired of tracing the intricacies of astonishing beauty.

Much of the ridgeline on which we stood was heavily corniced, but Jim discovered a spot that dropped directly down ice and snow onto a subsidiary glacier. He made a quick assessment for a descent, then, with hardly a word, began chopping a bollard out of the ice from which to rappel.

The incline below was so steep I wondered about avalanches, and it gave the illusion of being longer than it was. I suppose I should have said nothing, for Jim's mountain judgment is usually unerringly on the mark. But I remembered reading that, in 1921, Mallory and Bullock had climbed the pass from the south with "agreeable exertions" via a ridge outcrop of rocks. I suggested to Jim that we might be wise to scout further and follow Mallory's proven route. Jan agreed, but Rick was noncommittal.

"It's one—at the most, two—rope-lengths to rappel," Jim said curtly. "We'll be down and off in half an hour." He spoke as if we were people blind to the obvious.

Jan agreed with me and took a firm stand that it was worthwhile to scout around. After more and increasingly sharp discussion, Jim tossed one end of the rope down to demonstrate and confirm the length of the rappel. When that didn't bring out a group assent, he threw down his axe and sat down, exasperated. He pressed his lips together and glared at us.

The best leadership on an expedition comes from the team as a whole—individuals taking mutual responsibility for each other. But there is still need for a leader on any trip, even if everyone is an acknowledged expert. I try to be a leader who gives the appearance of encouraging democracy while actually ruling by benign autocracy.

We had mulled things over long enough. I turned to Jim and said, "Okay, let's rappel." He immediately set to work finishing the set-up, backing up the bollard with his ice axe and mine.

I was first over, and slid quickly down the single strand of 9-mm rope, following a shallow groove of milky ice onto the upper section of a broad apron of snow. It seemed stable, so at the end of the rope I cleared out a platform and called for the others to follow. As I waited, I chuckled to myself at how easy the descent had been. The whole to-do had been for nothing. Jan, then Rick came down. Jim pulled up the rope, doubled it, descended halfway, pulled the rope, and climbed down to us. "You were right, Jim," I said. Jan echoed the acknowledgment.

JAN: Jim was adamant that rappelling was the only sane thing to do, considering the time of day. Besides, he'd had enough of snailing with a pack. He had no desire to take a long hike when the same thing could be accomplished with a few rappels.

Ned, on the other hand, had been an Olympic cross-country racer. Endurance and strength are his keys. He felt we could minimize the risk and simply walk down to the moraine. Two men, two points of view. Because my strengths are similar to Ned's, I leaned toward his suggestion, which frustrated Jim. He seemed absolutely amazed that both of us were missing something so apparent to him. Rick didn't say much of anything, so I asked him what he thought.

"I don't really know enough to make a judgment call," he replied.

"Yes, but what do you think?" I just wanted to know what was going on in his brain. But he still refused to declare his preference, which I found irritating. I'm used to saying what I think, whether or not that will affect the outcome of a situation.

Jim had had it with this stalemate and threw his axe into the snow. "Okay, okay, have it your way. We'll walk around but we may end up having to rappel over there anyway."

"This spot here is going to take at least five rappels, Jim. With no anchors, it'll take a fair amount of time to hack that many bollards," Ned cautioned, as he crooked his neck to peer over.

"Look," Jim said as he grabbed the rope and threw it clear of obstruction. The free end landed halfway down the steep part of the slope. "We can do it in two single-line rappels. We don't need to double the rope." We were sold.

Ned rappelled first. He and Jim had used their axes to reinforce the dubious bollard, so I gave Ned my axe just before he took off and he used that to dig himself a platform and anchor himself into the slope. Jim came last. We'd tested the bollard and it held, so Jim removed the axes. He doubled the rope, slid down, anchored in halfway down to us to pull the rope down to him, then continued to the shelf where Rick, Ned, and I stood. One more rappel and we were on a frozen drainage stream surrounded by moraine.

I was ashamed I had been reluctant to rappel, especially in front of Jim. But left to my own devices I would probably always go a longer route to avoid a situation in which I had to depend on equipment rather than on my own two legs.

"Hey, we just won the freeze-dried delight sweepstakes, a trip to the Kangshung," teased Ned. We all laughed with relief. We were off the snow and entering into one of the most splendid, remote valleys on earth, the Kangshung.

Another short rappel brought us onto a slope down which we traversed.

We crossed the glacier, climbed down a short wall of ice at the snout, and camped below on a patch of old moraine at 18,200 feet. The light gray rocks with which we anchored the tents were etched with black spirals. Clumps of dark brown moss, tan sedges, and last year's reddish flowers decorated the campsite.

17

SECOND ESCAPE

"Down is what we want, not up. I'm going to find that bloody trail."

Jim Bridwell

JAN:  The women walking the brilliantly lit ramp were stylish and stunning. The fashion creations they wore were somewhat bizarre, yet attractive. The models sashayed toward me, turned, and posed so that I could see the clever details of their costumes. The hues they wore were so vibrant that they woke me up. I was ecstatic to realize I had color in my dreams again. For a long time my dreams had been vague and muddy, but now that we had descended to 15,000 feet they were vivid and clear. Many times before I had noticed a flood of thoughts and ideas as I descended in elevation. It's as if all the sparse oxygen at higher altitudes had been used for basic reason and muscle output, so that my imagination was starved, and ceased producing until it had sufficient fuel.

I awoke from my dream about ten o'clock in the morning on May 16, the day we would complete our orbit of Everest. The sun was bright, and we laughed and lolled around in the warmth on our stony beach like satisfied seals until early afternoon. We were in no hurry to move, and were savoring the peace that follows urgency. We had heavenly views here in the Kangshung Valley of the Lhotse wall, Pethangtse, Chomo Lönzo, and Makalu. But the East Face of Everest, the only face we had yet to see, was veiled by thick white clouds. The scenery in this valley was so spectacular that I felt as though I had broken through to a new world. We were tiny black specks.

We slid out onto a large frozen lake that separated us from a rocky gully leading to the soft carpet of soil and moss. The ice cracked and groaned slightly as we moved across the lake's surface, but held us above water. We meandered through the rocks and boulders, marveling at the immensity of the stone and snow peaks welling up around us, walling in the valley.

After descending the gully, Ned and I sat together on a large rock, kicking the moss with our toes, matching peaks with names, and picturing where we had been the previous winter, as if we were looking right through Makalu. I felt very close to him as we sat silently absorbing our dream-come-true. The solitary moment was so powerful there was no need to say anything. Only Ned and I had endured every leg of the expedition. We hadn't failed each other. We had done what we set out to do.

Rick and Jim eventually caught up to us and we all chatted, then continued down separately. I was intrigued by the small signs of life—dried horns, animal droppings, and little edelweiss scattered in the fragrant moss. My spirits were high. We stopped to eat some crackers, dehydrated cheese, and chocolate. Now that it was warmer and the ground was bare of snow, our replenishment stops had turned into picnics. Everything was becoming so effortless and pleasant that I had the feeling I had entered a fairy tale.

We chose a comfortable campsite a bit farther down valley, where we caught the sweet scent of the rhododendrons that were blossoming into spring. If the East Face of Everest stubbornly remained clouded through the next day, we might well never see it, which would be a great disappointment. All we could do was hope for clear skies in the morning before we pushed on down the valley toward civilization. Jim woke us early at the turn of day with a delighted shout: "Look at this, Everest is as clear as can be."

When I stuck my sleepy head out the tent door, the view brought me wide awake. The East Face of Everest was massive and intimidating. Avalanches shoved off and tumbled down at irregular intervals. This face looked like a frightening place for climbers to be. (It wouldn't be scaled until 1983, when a group of Americans finally managed to do it.)

NED: The morning air was crisp and quiet. The Scotch mist that had rolled up the Kangshung Valley at dusk the previous evening had dissipated, and the sedges lay bent with frost. Two hundred feet below, our two domed tents nestled in a grassy patch. I continued climbing to a knob lit by the rising sun, then turned to look westward at Everest. The summit lay six miles away, but the amphitheater was so colossal and all the mountain walls so high that even Everest was oddly miniaturized. To the south the peaks forming the Himalayan crest hung like paintings on a museum wall—each dab of ice and rock precisely recorded, each ridge etched against a cobalt sky. Directly across the valley stood the sharp, symmetrical cone of Pethangtse. At just over 22,000 feet and positioned like a pint-size referee, it filled the gap between the Everest-Lhotse massif and the Makalu-Chomo Lönzo massif. It was a dwarf among the giants lining the south side, but its perfection of form and its solitary grace were riveting. I sat motionless on my perch. I had come to take photographs, but just sat looking. The Kangshung was a valley like no other. It opened to spectacular vistas normally reserved for those on mountain tops. After awhile, wispy clouds materialized out of the thin air near the top of Everest.

After breakfast, we packed our gear and started down the north side of the valley. The sunshine brought out the first faint smells of spring from the meadows spreading up the hillsides. A well-worn yak path led down a shallow moat that lay between the Kangshung Glacier's lateral moraine and the hillside. We rested often, lolling on the alpine lawns, and talking of people we knew and plans for the future. The hospitable nature of our surroundings was in marked contrast to the stark, polar vistas of the Rongbuk Glacier from which we had so recently departed.

We meandered down the moat for three miles before it petered out; then we moved along on top of the lateral moraine. Even though we were only 100 vertical feet higher than the moat, we now trekked in an alpine world again. The wind was nippy, dispelling our illusions of spring. To the south spread the Kangshung Glacier—a mile-wide chaos of ice towers and gravel bands—and, beyond, the great mountain walls. It was vast, untraveled country, wild and untamed, with no trace of other Western visitors. It was a place that few knew—certainly one of the most magnificent, unspoiled valleys in all the Himalaya.

At noon we arrived at Pethang Ringmo, a grassy alp at an elevation of 16,400 feet. Tibetans pasture their yaks here during the summer months. The place was deserted, but there were several rings of flat rocks that had once held down the edges of tents. These and circular "bins" built of rock and capped by sod roofs gave us a sense of the yak herders' presence. It was a welcoming spot, a pastoral Shangri-La. We nestled behind some large rocks and picnicked. Then we lay back and gazed up at the immense cliffs of Chomo Lönzo, which towered 9,000 feet above to a three-tiered summit.

"I never thought I'd be in a place," Jim said softly, "where Everest would look like a second-rate peak. Everest may fill up the head of the valley, but a half-dozen of the peaks here are much more striking."

From Pethang Ringmo the trail divided and redivided until there were scores of yak avenues heading generally downhill. Twice we surprised basking marmots. Another time we startled a herd of 16 burrhel, or blue mountain sheep, which thundered off toward high ground and safety. Wolves, foxes, hares, pikas, and voles lived here as well, although we were not lucky enough to see them. Lammergeiers—bearded vultures of the Himalaya—occasionally soared overhead, graceful on their eight-foot wingspan. Raven, red-billed chough, yellow-billed chough, black-eared kite, Himalayan snowcock, chukar partridge, great rose finch, painted snipe, pin-tailed snipe, hill pigeon, and snow pigeon live at elevations above 15,000 feet. Once we thought we saw a gyrfalcon dive to the attack behind a low ridge.

We continued our descent into spring, headed toward a meeting with our Chinese support crew in Kharta, on the east side of Everest. Tiny purple flowers and yellow buttercups bloomed in protected niches. Later, we spied azaleas and pussy willows. The idyllic nature of the place lulled us into an unhurried pace.

Ordinarily, an expedition is constantly mentally stressful and physically demanding. It feels like running half-marathons day after day on unscouted courses, then each night sleeping outside, unshowered and marginally fed. You get worn down and loaded with residual fatigue. Persistence is the key. But now, in the sweet spring sunshine, we eased up and relaxed. We figured we had it made, but our departure was about to take on the urgency of an escape.

As we neared the end of the Kangshung Glacier, we were confronted with the first part of one more test of our persistence: we lost the trail. A massive landslide had torn away an entire mountainside, leaving a three-quarter-mile-wide chaos of giant boulders. The rubble lay across the logical downward path of our progress. We considered crossing to the other side of the valley, but the way was blocked by the snout of the surging Kangdoshung, a subsidiary glacier that had bulled its way into the foot of the landslide. The river looked dangerous—if not impossible—to ford. The muddy current thundered against rocky banks, then emptied into a wicked looking cavern carved under the ice of the glacier and rock of the landslide.

JAN: We faced roaring water, grinding ice, and tumbled rock. Rather than backtrack, we simply tackled the obstacles head on. We began a painstaking traverse across the landslide, a long battlefield of immense boulders which we had to negotiate while encumbered with our loads. The rocks were sharp-edged, and tumbled against each other in such a random manner that there were gaping holes to jump and small ridges to climb. My pack caught and hung up on protrusions, nearly pulling me off balance several times. We all picked our separate lines through this peril, but shouted to each other now and again to make sure everyone was making careful progress. Actually it became a game of attention and analysis. Secretly we were each monitoring the others' progress, playfully measuring our skills and calculations against those of our teammates. Yells of, "Hey, how'd you get there," or, "What's it like on that side?" bounced back and forth. Jim scampered easily through this stone jungle. He said it reminded him of Yosemite.

As soon as we cleared the boulders, we were faced with a waist-high green sea of juniper, which we virtually had to swim through to make any headway. I kept my arms and legs moving. I laughed to think that my feet weren't even touching the ground, but despite how funny our unique mode of travel seemed, we were wearing out fast. The ease of the day before, our first day out of the snow, had vanished. Now we had to tackle increasingly difficult terrain and surging, swelling vegetation as we descended.

I began to wonder if this was the beginning of a new chapter of adventure, like the struggle after we had completed our half-circle in Nepal. Our circle had been well calculated and well executed—but once again it was finding our way back to civilization that provided the severest test. Then I began to see why that was so. When we trekked *into* the mountains, the route was obvious and the peaks visible. But once the climbing was over, we couldn't go out the way we had come in because we had swung a half-circle. We had to search like sleuths for civilization, clue by clue. In a sense this was the true adventure of the expedition: it couldn't be planned for and prepared for; we had to rely on our instincts and our wits.

We stumbled upon a patch of clearing in the juniper and decided it was a perfect place to lay our heads for the night. The clouds began to sprinkle snow lightly down on us. It was beautiful, but wet, so we quickly crawled into our nylon tents and tried to locate ourselves on the map. Our exact position was confusing. We could pinpoint where we had been at midday—Pethang Ringmo—but where we were now and how we got there were vague and perplexing. I thought perhaps tomorrow's light might give us clear minds and possibly a plan for escape from this jungle. Still, I wasn't concerned. It was warm, we were near running water, and we had food, so it couldn't be nearly as draining or brutal as when we had been lost in Nepal in the dead of winter with no food. I slept soundly.

NED: During the night a light snow fell, thinly coating the bare ground. In the morning every stem and leaf and flower was artistically highlighted by the dusting. When the sun rose, water droplets formed, glistening, before evaporating. Chomo Lönzo, perfectly reflected in the serene surface of a tiny lake, was powdered with the fresh snow. Scores of dry-snow avalanches filtered down its sheer ramparts.

The beauty could not hide the fact that we still had a problem. Surrounded by juniper, we had not yet relocated the main trail. We talked over our options. Jan and I recalled our troubled escape from the mountains in Nepal, where the course of the path had not been obvious to the eye. Now we found ourselves in the same situation.

Our immediate destination was the Langma La, an 18,000-foot pass leading from the Kangshung Valley to the Kharta district. The trail over the pass was clearly detailed on our map. It ran six miles farther down the north side of the Karma Chu, the river draining the Kangshung, to a place named Sakytang, which means "pleasant terrace." Then it swung in a great U-shaped bend up and over the pass. From past experience, we knew the map was accurate in its portrayal of geographical features, so we assumed that the trails shown were equally accurate. It appeared that the first thing to do was get to Sakytang. We weren't at all sure what we'd find there. I recalled reading during my research for the expedition that at one time there had been a village there, but a pestilence believed to have been sent by a local demon had wiped out the inhabitants.

Adding confusion was the fact that, high above our campsite, we could see a trail winding up the mountainside. This didn't jibe with the map, so we discounted what we saw as a yak herders' trail leading into a sister valley. Later we learned that it was, in fact, the trail to Kharta. Some of the information for the map had not been updated since it had been compiled during the 1921 British Reconnaissance. Many of the trails were no longer in use, or had been rerouted.

JAN: The day shone with liquid brilliance. All the creases in the rhododendron leaves held drops of melted snow that sparkled in the sun, and the ground was still elegantly dusted with snow. The valley glistened with a pure, clean radiance.

When I went for a quiet walk to absorb the grandeur of the new day, I stumbled on Rick looking into a pool of water. Curious, I went over to see what had caught his attention. I had learned that Rick was an inquisitive, sensitive fellow, and I liked to listen when his imagination roamed, so I asked him why he was peering into the water.

He looked up at me and said, "This must be an underprivileged area. These bugs couldn't afford a good coach. They keep swimming in circles. This place couldn't afford a gardener either. That's why the juniper was so thick on the hill. It's all just a matter of money."

I laughed at the irony of his joke. Money meant nothing in this part of the world. A million dollars was useless, barely enough paper for a good fire. It couldn't provide the comfort and security it was capable of providing in the Western world. Then I realized that I wasn't moving through a fairy tale here in Tibet. I hadn't stepped through the "looking glass" at all. My life in the West was the storybook existence, because there money created empires and made fantasies real. Here in the Kangshung Valley a person could be nothing other than the essence of himself, unaffected and unadorned. He had no wealth or power with which to shape or protect himself. In a simple joke Rick had expressed an entire concept. I admired the way his mind worked.

NED: We spent an hour poking about and following dead-end paths that radiated out from our campsite. When we could find no trail to confirm the data on the map, my instinct was to take the time to check out the well-defined trail above. I took a few minutes to climb onto a knoll to get a better look, then returned to the others.

I found only Jan and Rick waiting. "Jim left," Jan explained. "He seemed impatient. His last words were, 'Down is what we want, not up. I'm going to find that bloody trail.' Then he marched off."

Jim's impetuousity startled and irked me. Now, if we were to stay together as a team, the rest of us had to follow his wild plunge into the bush.

Jan, Rick, and I started down valley. Within a half-mile we reached the end of the maze of faint yak trails, then forged ahead into luxuriant vegetation. The map—and Jim—were leading us straight into an exasperating, seemingly endless series of thickets and bogs. Soon we were battling through a tangle of unyielding juniper, willow, mountain ash, and dwarf birch. We bullied through the brush like battering rams. Often the little trees were so densely packed together that we had to clamber up and over them, airborne on the stiff branches. Elevated, we pranced along like drunken tightrope walkers, our progress won with faltering giant steps. A misstep or too much weight committed to a rotten limb sent us tumbling into prickly shafts. Much flailing and gnashing of teeth accompanied our exits from these vegetable strait jackets.

JAN: Ned, Rick, and I hiked through thick juniper high on the bank of the cascading river for a couple of hours. We crossed tributary streams and drank fresh, cool water under clear skies. Life was easy, even if it was perplexing. But still we found no sign of Jim. I thought it was due time to begin considering that we might not see him for days. I started asking who had what for gear, to determine just what Jim had on his person for support during his solo trek. He and Rick had divided the weight of the tent between them, so Jim had only the material—no poles or rain fly. He had little or no food, because the rest of us had most of it. I knew Jim was tough enough to do without comforts, and there was plenty of water to be found, so he would probably be all right. But I couldn't figure out why he had just taken off.

The next time we crossed a stream, we came to a trail adorned with prayer flags tied to bushes high overhead. I looked at Ned and Rick. An overhead highway that appeared out of nowhere was right in keeping with a day that seemed to get stranger and stranger.

We moved down the wide trail, staying alert for any signs of Jim. We were all wondering if he had found this trail too, and were looking for footprints or other indications that someone had traveled this way before us. The ground was very wet, which made it hard to positively identify the markings we did see. As I bent over about the tenth possible tread mark, something caught my eye a few feet down the trail. It was a crumpled piece of cellophane wrapper from the throat lozenges we'd all been eating to soothe our raw throats.

"Look, you guys!" I called out. "Jim must have been here. Here's one of his wrappers."

"Litterbug," laughed Rick. It was a relief, yet baffling to understand how Jim had come across this trail. We had been traveling somewhat aimlessly for a couple of miles through pathless brush, and had found this trail paralleling the river hundreds of feet up the canyon. It was a strange coincidence that Jim had already passed this way. Down the trail we found a couple more lozenge wrappers, so we were sure that we were on Jim's scent.

The trail stopped abruptly at what appeared to be some kind of campsite—we found fire rings and cut limbs in the matted juniper. We circled like bloodhounds trying to decipher which way the Tibetans might have left camp, but there was no one obvious route. I was finding this whole episode very funny. "Hey, Ned," I said, "let's try heading down and crossing the river. Maybe the going is easier on the other side, so the trail might be there too." Ned ignored the comment. I could see that he was having trouble seeing the humor in this situation and Rick seemed to be bothered too. Rick hadn't been lost in Nepal with us. I wondered if he'd ever been this lost before. I supposed he might be getting a little nervous about our predicament, and it might seem more desperate to him than it really was. I wanted to be more adamant about searching for the trail down lower, but Ned and Rick weren't very receptive, so I let it go. Soon we spied some footprints in a melting patch of snow. Apparently Jim, as confused as we were, had opted to push on in the same direction the trail had been heading. A logical decision. We could follow Jim's prints only through the snow; after that, he was impossible to track, which sent us back to square one again—no trail, no Jim.

Spread in front of us for a mile or so was a large, spongy bog, which would give no clues about which way Jim had gone. But Ned and Rick seemed to prefer snooping around in the moss and moisture to climbing up to the ridge for a scout's view or hiking down to the river in search of a trail. I realized we were floundering in the bog, but held my tongue. Ned and Rick were becoming visibly more tense and uncommunicative. We ambled in every direction out in the mush until I finally got tired of the foolishness. We needed to go up, down, or back, and yes, we could push ahead through the rhododendron forest, although that would be the most difficult, but we had to do something.

"Why don't we just walk back the mile to the last campsite, or head down to the river to look for the disappearing trail?" I offered.

Even this mild question was enough to trigger Rick's anger. "Jan, that's not going to do us any good. Why don't you be quiet." His comment was curt and out of line. He and Ned had been making the decisions, much as Craig and Ned had in Nepal, after Jim had left for the States and the three of us were humping over the passes. It was a repeat scenario. I chalked Rick's comment up to his anxiety, and kept quiet. We gradually pushed forward down the valley in silence. At least we were moving in one direction, so my prodding had accomplished something.

Soon we were swallowed by the 20-foot-high rhododendrons that had been in front of us. The trees were so tightly packed that the only way we could move ahead was to crawl on our bellies, with our packs pushing our faces into the ground. A machete would have been useful, but we hadn't thought to bring one along. Because progress was so slow, we decided to work our way up higher, to see if the forest thinned enough to spot where we were in this river valley. Rick looked at me and ordered, "Ned and I are going up, you stay with the bags." He seemed so tense and distracted that I didn't argue.

I suppose, since I had spent over a year organizing the expedition and had been on every leg of the circle, I might have bristled at having Rick dictate to me. But I couldn't see that anything would be gained by arguing with him while he was in this frame of mind. So I leaned on my pack and relaxed as I listened to Ned and Rick rustle through the forest.

By the time they returned they had decided that the only thing to do was push straight ahead. After an hour or so we came to a fence of criss-crossed rhododendron limbs. The undergrowth was so thick that we couldn't see the obstruction until we were right on top of it. We guessed it was supposed to prevent stray yaks from fighting their way farther up the valley, and decided to follow the fence up the hillside to see if it led somewhere.

Ned and I scrambled over roots and squeezed between trees until we realized we were going nowhere. Rick began cooing to us so that we could locate him and wouldn't fragment our small party again. When we reached him, Rick said that if we gave him a boost he could get up a large tree and might be able to spy a trail, Jim, or perhaps some clearing.

Rick was nimble and was soon up the tree, but his report was negative on all accounts. Darkness was seeping through the forest, and the only sensible thing to do was to follow the fence downhill to the river for fresh water and a campsite. The reality of Jim's separation hit us as the evening began to fold around us, and we thought of him spending the night alone. I missed him and hoped he hadn't encountered any serious trouble. We stopped on the mossy bank of a small tributary shortly before reaching the river bank, and I was listening to Ned and Rick discuss what to do next when I heard two very faint yells.

"Hey, I heard something. A voice. Maybe it's Jim!" I could tell by their expressions that Ned and Rick didn't take me seriously, but I began yelling back anyway and waited for an answer. It came—indistinct but audible. Rick and Ned joined in my calls, and a few minutes later Jim came crashing through the bushes.

"Gorky buddy!" said Rick, and he thrust his hand out to Jim. Rick and Jim had shared reading the mystery thriller *Gorky Park* in their tent, and had had good laughs while doing so. Rick was visibly moved to be reunited with Jim, and I realized how deep his concern had run. Rick's tension and anger seemed to drain away.

"Okay Jim, so where have you been?" I laughed. "We've been trying to track you all day. We followed you as far as the bog."

"I was up on the ridge watching you guys flailing around down there, going in circles. There was no way you could hear me call and I wasn't going back into the bog—that was nowhere. I could hear Rick cooing later on, so I knew you were close. I figured you'd head to the river for water at the end of the day and I'd case the bank until I found you. And here you are."

Ned perked up. "Rick was cooing to Jan and me so we could regroup. Did you see that fence along the hillside? We followed that down to here."

"Yah, and the mad hacker was out there somewhere. Did you notice rhododendron slashed randomly out in the middle of nowhere?"

We all laughed at the strange day we had spent, and laughed in relief at having Jim with us again. He acted very casual about the whole thing, as if it hadn't been a big deal, but I noticed he had a new glint in his eye. The day had probably kindled just the kind of excitement Jim needed, but I thought he was glad that now we were all spending the night together.

I was awakened the next morning by Jim's voice teasing, "I've been touring the countryside, didn't want to miss anything." Then he laughed as he walked past our tent. Rick popped his head in to apologize for having been curt the day before, and I accepted his apology. I was glad to have the air cleared.

After a brief map consultation, we started to think we'd trekked beyond the Langma La, the 18,000-foot pass that led to the nearest villages. It was almost impossible to know if we had, because we couldn't trust the scale of the map. Not far from the river, in what we guessed to be close to our location, was a point labeled Sakytang. Just what Sakytang was—a village? a high country yak pasture?—we didn't know, but we hoped that if it was large enough to make the map then it would have some route of travel in and out of it. We began to wonder if it would be better to look down low for Sakytang, rather than up high for the mysterious Langma La. We decided to travel close to the river bank in hopes of finding easier going, so that meant we'd be looking for Sakytang rather than the pass.

Our route down the river was sandwiched between a swiftly flowing river and a violent tangle of undergrowth on the bank. We jumped rocks on the side of the river and clung to outcroppings and roots on the bank to make our way downstream. One spot demanded that we make a few climbing moves up onto a boulder covered with dirt and gravel, then throw our packs down onto some rocks below to make a dangerous traverse move as the grit slid under our feet on the boulder. Then we were safe to jump down to our packs below. Rick went first and worked out the traverse moves. Now that he was no longer bothered by altitude sickness, he made a point of offering to pioneer.

The going became easier for a bit, so Ned and I traveled together higher on the bank while Jim and Rick stuck to the river. Some movement caught my eye and I grabbed Ned's arm and pointed in the direction of the movement. Before I could explain to Ned why I'd stopped him, a handsome young Tibetan came into full view up ahead of us, and we rushed to greet him.

He was carrying hand-hewn lumber with a rope tumpline over his head. I could see from the expression on his face that he was very excited to see us. He grabbed my hand and held it, then squeezed it in his fist. He was so strong I had to fight to make a fist as well, so he didn't crush my hand with his enthusiasm. Then we began to pump our arms up and down enthusiastically in a handshake.

His skin was smooth and dark, and he had a beautiful piece of turquoise in one ear with a round bit of red coral hanging from it on a string. His smile was broad and genuine.

Ned had been questioning him about Sakytang, and the Tibetan began motioning down river. We couldn't tell him where we'd come from or ask how far we had to go, but at least he recognized the name of the place we were looking for and knew how to find it.

"Hey, look at this!" Jim shouted from the river below. "It's a bridge and a trail. Come on!" I was reluctant to leave the young Tibetan. He was the first person we'd seen since we'd climbed the passes and gotten lost. To me he was security and assurance that we were on the right track. But I was as anxious as the others to be on our way. Ned and I waved to the Tibetan and scurried down the bank to Jim and Rick.

We hiked up the trail only a few hundred yards before we realized this was no trail to Sakytang, but a path leading to a logging operation. As I walked back down the trail looking at my feet, I had a sinking feeling that we'd blown it by saying good-bye to our Tibetan friend, but when I looked up there he was again, motioning aggressively that Sakytang was down the river, not here. Then Ned, Jim, and Rick gathered around the boy, waving money and asking for the Langma La. After this false start on the logging trail the others wanted to be sure we could locate the pass, and forget all this hunting around for mysterious villages. The boy understood, or so it seemed, that we were willing to pay him to accompany us to the Langma La.

He appeared quite interested, but motioned us to sit down and left at a gallop, carrying the blackened pot containing old, wet tea leaves that he'd brought with him. We sat for half an hour smirking and content, almost feeling saved and dreaming of hiring even more Tibetans to carry our packs.

Then from behind us came two Tibetan men carrying full loads of lumber. They weren't quite as jovial and friendly as the boy had been. They stared at us in wonder and were obviously apprehensive. I noticed that they gripped their axes tightly. It was quite probable that they had never seen Westerners before, and here I was with a bright red coat, a pink bandanna around my neck, a blue one over my hair, and dark sunglasses covering my eyes. I could have looked something other than human to the barefoot men with dark skin dressed in black.

Jim was tired of being patient, and wanted to solve this Langma La mystery once and for all. He boldly approached the men and began speaking English very slowly and distinctly, as if they might understand. I began to laugh, which startled the Tibetans. When they realized the laughter meant no harm, they seemed to relax. Jim began drawing the route we'd done around Everest and on out to where we stood now on a scrap of paper, trusting that the Tibetans could follow the idea that this was where we'd come from.

He had repeated the word Langma La enough so that the Tibetans realized that was what we were looking for. Jim pulled out our topographical map, in the faint hope that they might recognize the river on the map and could possibly point out the pass in relation to it. It was a long shot—but why not?

Jim grunted and motioned, and the Tibetans returned the gestures. Jim and Rick went with the Tibetans down the trail to the river, for a clear view and more specific directions. Ned and I stayed put, waiting for the boy to return. When he did arrive, he was visibly less enthusiastic. He had to turn down the money, which seemed neither here nor there to him, but he was obviously disappointed that he couldn't accompany us on our trek and search for the pass. My guess was that the older loggers had cautioned him about strangers, and had informed him that he was here in camp to work, not to go wandering over the hills.

We walked down to meet Jim and Rick, who felt comfortable with their new directions to the pass, then we all crossed the river again to a trail that began on the other side. About a half-mile up we came across the Tibetan loggers' camp. The spot these wooden structures occupied looked to be Sakytang by our map, but not according to the Tibetans. We started calling the map "the gospel" in jest, as we tried to determine whether to believe the map or the Tibetans. We shrugged our shoulders and continued up the trail to a beautiful clear pond and meadow, where we decided to camp among the yellow wildflowers for the night. Late in the quiet night I heard Rick slam his book closed and mutter, "This night life is killing me." I smiled to myself as I heard him settle into his sleeping bag.

When I awoke the next morning, May 20, Rick was already up and gone. The evening before he had spied a trail heading up the hillside and had risen with the sun to make sure the trail was genuine and not another false start. Rick had become "Mr. Eager Beaver" since we'd left the ice and snow.

He returned disappointed. "It just doesn't lead anywhere. It peters out up there." We looked at each other and rolled our eyes in disbelief. While everyone else was packing up, I slipped off for a little exploring myself. Since Rick had eliminated one option, I knew there must be another somewhere. In a grove of trees, I found a path leading out from camp. It was well camouflaged, but obviously well traveled. I was proud to announce to everyone that I had a strong hunch which way we should head. Once we were on the trail, we were convinced that this was it—anything this size couldn't simply disappear. But we lost it at the first large, open meadow we came to. We dumped our packs and scattered to scout for the trail leading out of the pasture. It took almost an hour before Ned cupped his hands and yelled, "I've found it, over here," and began waving to us. We trundled back to our packs and then joined him. From the ridge we could see that the path paralleled the area we had been lost in for the past couple of days, but the trail we were on was much higher above the river. We were heading right back where we'd come from, and could only hope we were headed in the right direction.

We paused for lunch by a brook, and laughed at ourselves and the map. We toyed with the idea that the Langma La might be shown as being farther downstream than it really was. If so, we were headed in the wrong direction. As we chatted, I mentioned that this was the day I had calculated we'd meet the Tibetan porters Chang was sending to meet us—if we were near the Langma La. I wondered if the porters would leave if we weren't in the vicinity of the pass to meet them.

We pushed down the trail until dusk, and put up camp for the night in another high meadow, with a patch of snow we could melt for water. We were up high, above the jungle, even though we were back-tracking. As we were finishing our hot drinks we heard thumping and bumping outside, along with excited voices. Small, smoky black faces appeared in the door of our tent, and after another grunting session we learned these were the Tibetan porters Chang had sent to greet us.

The next morning we discovered that these porters were quite unfamiliar with portering. As they stood and watched us divide our heavy personal packs into light loads for both us and them, we couldn't help but compare them to the Sherpas, who were true professionals in this field. Since we had to pack their loads for them, we weren't on the trail until almost noon. They balked at carrying the reasonable loads we gave them, and we began to think this might well be the first time they'd been hired out to carry loads.

Once on our way to the pass, the porters claimed exhaustion every few hundred yards and asked to take a rest. We would have made much better time without them, but we were sure they knew the way and weren't quite sure that we did. As it turned out, the Langma La was hidden right up until we were almost on it. We trekked along a high valley that looked like a box canyon, but tucked behind some cliffs was a rocky trail leading steeply up and over the pass. High atop the pass the wind blew tattered prayer flags, and the skies were gray and spitting snow.

Rick and I hiked quickly off the pass and into the snowy, rock-walled valley below. We waited for Jim and Ned, but they were nowhere to be seen so we tucked behind a large boulder out of the wind. Finally we started heading back up the pass to see if anything had gone awry. One of the porters had been suffering from the high altitude, so Ned and Jim had divided up his load to carry it over.

We did not stop trekking until six o'clock that night. The next morning we walked into Kharta and a reunion with Chang, Losan, and Laba.

NED: Kharta was a beautiful, exotic, hidden place. We decided to stay a few days and explore it before returning to Lhasa. We established a camp in a lush pasture beside the river. The weather was mild, the region fertile by Tibetan standards, and the people friendly. After the stark landscapes and biting winds of the Rongbuk, Kharta was soothing. Fresh, green sprigs dotted the irrigated fields of barley, potatoes, and mustard, which were bordered by rose and currant bushes. Yellow marsh marigolds and primulas grew beside the watercourses. Stone houses three stories high were built of brown gneiss and looked as solid as fortresses, especially since they had few windows. Juniper lined the edges of the flat roofs, which served as open-air gathering areas. More than once we accepted invitations to climb wooden ladders through dark interiors, and then emerged in sunlight to sit cross-legged and drink chang and rakshi.

We made one mistake. Admiring the brass ladles used in the homes we had visited, we offered to pay or trade for a couple. Soon the word got around, and our Base Camp was inundated by half the village population offering all sorts of household paraphernalia for barter: ladles, baskets, bowls, knives, teapots, and jewelry. One of the items they sought in return was adhesive tape, which they believed had healing properties when applied to an injury.

It didn't take long for things to get out of hand. Intent on selling, the Tibetans would unzip the doorways of our tents and thrust items in at us. They were persistent as magpies. Worse, our expedition gear started to disappear, and we were forced to cordon off the camp. Fortunately, all this hullabaloo didn't lessen our enjoyment of the many walks we took, climbing the crooked paths that connected clusters of houses dotting the hillsides. It was a rare opportunity to wander among the people who inhabit the Tibetan hinterlands. Although the language barrier was enormous, we usually were received with friendly touches and benign curiosity, and felt a kinship with the people bred from a love of the land through which we had traveled and in which they lived.

18

THE SEARCH

"There always is the risk, isn't there?"

Charlie Clarke

NED:  On May 25 a truck lumbered up the narrow road toward our camp. Its appearance surprised me, for motorized vehicles were rare in Kharta. As it drew closer, I recognized Chris Bonington and Charlie Clarke standing in the back. I waved and yelled an exuberant welcome, happy to see our British friends. They stood unmoving, their hands gripping the superstructure of the vehicle. Their odd, frozen attitude was ominous. The truck pulled into camp and stopped. Without a word of greeting, Chris, looking terribly emaciated, said in a hoarse voice, "Joe and Pete are dead."

As the others joined us, he repeated the wrenching words: "Joe and Peter are dead." We were stunned.

Together we walked over to the river's edge. While Chang brewed tea for us, we listened to Chris and Charlie. We asked few questions, but voiced our sympathy. They spoke quietly, as if the words were therapy. It had been a week since things had gone wrong for them. During those days they had built up a tight control around their grief—distancing themselves from the mountain, the men, and the moment. They had had to, for the sake of their own mental preservation. Still, the story was painful for them to tell. We were the first outsiders to hear it. The telling brought a second wave of hard reality and sorrow, but they maintained control. There had been just enough time for them to begin to adjust to the deaths. Their wounds were not as raw now as when they had held each other at the foot of the North Col—rocked by the driving wind and snow—and wept for Joe and Pete.

What had happened? Peter Boardman and Joe Tasker, two of the best climbers in the world, had vanished high on the East Northeast Ridge of Everest in a courageous final effort to reach the summit. They had climbed as a team of two after Dick Renshaw had gone home because of a mild stroke he suffered at 26,700 feet, and Chris had taken himself out because of extreme exhaustion. I remembered Charlie's words when we last saw the British descending the East Rongbuk after their second assault. "The team is stretched to the limit," he had said. Joe and Pete had taken a step farther.

When the third assault had begun, Pete had still been strong, but Joe had been in only fair shape. He had had a very bloody throat, which had led to blood in his stools. Everyone had been fearful of "addling their brains" from the extended exertions at extreme altitude, and the whole project had been in danger of falling apart. But Pete and Joe had desperately wanted to succeed—to complete the new route and break new ground. Nobody had ever tried to climb through such technical difficulties above 8,000 meters; nobody had ever spent so many days so high without oxygen.

On the final assault, Joe and Pete had left Advance Base Camp on May 15 and taken only six hours to reach the second snow cave on the ridge at 23,800 feet. Their speed confirmed the fact that they had recovered a large measure of their strength. The next day they had reached the third snow cave. On May 17 they had started at dawn and quickly reached their previous high point of 26,900 feet. It had taken the rest of the day to run out about four rope-lengths on technical ground. At dusk, after climbing for 14 hours, they had worked their way around the corner of the Second Pinnacle onto the east side of the ridge. In doing this they had vanished from the view of those at Advance Base. There had been no radio contact during the day, not even at the scheduled 6 P.M. call-in.

By the evening of May 20, three days after the last sighting of the two climbers, there could be no doubt that a catastrophe had occurred. Chris later wrote of the inescapable and grim interpretation of the facts: ". . . they were both dead. Either one had fallen, pulling off the other, or perhaps one of those fragile ice flutings had collapsed, sweeping both of them down the huge Kangshung Face" (Bonington and Clarke, 1983).

Charlie, Chris, and Adrian Gordon—those remaining—had been engulfed in tension, tears, and sorrow. "I was washed over by different waves of emotion," Charlie had written in his diary. "I fought with pain because I loved them."

During those anguished days in the East Rongbuk, they had also learned of the death of the American woman climber Marty Hoey on the North Face of Everest. Now Chris and Charlie had come to Kharta to continue the search for Pete and Joe. By now, there could be virtually no hope that they were alive. But there was that infinitesimal chance that the climbers had survived a fall into the Kangshung. Duty to those waiting at home required that the survivors exhaust every possibility.

While Chris and Charlie set up their tents next to ours, I consulted Jan, Jim, and Rick. I proposed that we cancel our plans of leaving for Lhasa and help our friends. They immediately agreed that we should team up with the British and retrace our steps into the Kangshung. We knew the way, and could aid in any rescue effort. Charlie and Chris were pleased and grateful.

Shortly afterward, I noticed Charlie lugging a large, gray, flat oval stone from the truck to the tent area. Curious, I strolled over to him. Inscribed on the rock were half-finished words:

IN MEMORY OF
PETER BOARDMAN
JOE TASKER
MAY 1982

The next morning we set out along the track that wound up through stone-walled villages. Three cheery Tibetans accompanied us as porters. The weather was warm and sunny. We meandered along, trading stories and stopping at several houses for cups of chang. Jan had elected to stay behind—her knees had become so painful that it was nearly impossible for her to carry a pack, and she had an acute case of *giardia.*

Charlie and I pulled ahead of the others. "It's a welcome distraction to be with you, Jim, and Rick," Charlie admitted to me. "Chris and I get along very well, but after the stresses we've undergone over the last three months, we have exhausted all normal bounds of conversation."

We left the main valley and started up toward the Langma La. A band of Tibetan girls followed us, and we teased and joked with them. When they left, the mood again turned serious. Charlie started talking again. "With each expedition I get more anxious about the consequences. It's my kids I worry about. If I died, it would foul up their lives."

The path steepened, and our pace slowed. He was silent and thoughtful, then continued talking haltingly between breaths. "It is incredible that more people don't voluntarily cancel out of their adult lives—like Hemingway did. We all have such wonderful dreams and vitality as youth. Then most of it dissolves and leaves people disillusioned in later life. I used to jump for joy when Pete and Joe came to visit in London. They hadn't lost anything along the way. To them, the risk of the mountains was worth it because that was part of the way they lived life to the fullest."

We stopped to rest. Below us a family of Tibetans moved about a canvas tent that housed them while they tended their yaks in the high pastures. "The expeditions give us far more than summits, don't they?" I said. I thought of the exotic cultures and truly wild places we had visited; the camaraderie we had shared and the integration of mind and body we had experienced. I thought of the outlandish doors of opportunity that had opened and of the extraordinary people we would have met in no other way. We are very lucky to be doing things we love to do. It makes all the risk and hardship seem worthwhile.

"There always is the risk, isn't there?" Charlie was speaking as much to himself as to me. "I learned that in the uphill avalanche during a past expedition. We were walking 500 feet above the valley floor. I thought we were safe. But a giant avalanche poured off the opposite wall, swept across the valley, and nearly got us." He paused. "There is always risk. Joe and Pete had their way of looking at it. Here, read my diary. I wrote this entry when I knew, in my heart, that they were lost." He thrust the open pages toward me.

> They [Pete and Joe] were the personification of what I once wanted to be, but I had not that combination of physique, skill, and drive to push high on great peaks. They courted danger, yes, in the huge scale of the undertaking, but not because they were reckless. . . . For Peter and Joe there was, I feel, that middle way: they believed that hard high-altitude climbing was a reasonable sport within mountaineering. Statistically dangerous, yes, but with care, stealth, and speed, within reason . . . they knew and respected the arena of avalanche, storm, and stonefall. . . . They were wily and sometimes very frightened. They never showed self-indulgent elation when successful.

Jim, Rick, and Chris caught up with us, and the conversation took a lighter turn. Charlie began to talk about a vacation he had taken with his family in the south of France. That evening we camped in a lovely meadow speckled with colorful flowers. Chris was relaxed and looking forward to seeing the storied terrain to the east of Everest. From experience, he knew these were his last days of calm before the storm of returning home.

In the morning Chris and I walked together up the switchbacks toward the top of the pass. "Peter always had a gentle romanticism to him," he said. "There was always the belief that he could make it with Joe." His pace slowed briefly, and his shoulders sagged. "Over the past 10 years I've lost almost all my close friends in the mountains. It's been hard. It's the hardest on the relatives." He squared his shoulders. "While still on an expedition you stay somewhat immune to the real emotions involved in the death of a friend. It isn't until you're out and under the pressures of families and press that you truly feel it." We walked farther, cupped by the peaks of the amphitheater leading to the pass. He looked up at the peaks, and said, "But I'd never give up climbing. I love the mountains too much."

When we reached the top of the Langma La, we found Charlie, Jim, and Rick sitting in the sunshine. The summit ridges of Makalu, Chomo Lönzo, Lhotse, and Everest creased a clear sky. We sat for two hours, eating lunch and enjoying the scenery.

The porters finally caught up with us. At the crest, they chanted "O mani padme hum" beside the prayer flags fluttering in the light breeze. "What do you think of all this prayer?" Chris asked, of no one in particular. "Our men over in the East Rongbuk sent up lots of prayers. But you see how much good it did us."

Later, after we descended from the pass and neared the old campsite in the clearing where we had gotten lost 10 days earlier, Chris spoke with mixed feelings about the East Northeast Ridge. "It's the most elegant line on the mountain. Yet it always frightened me. We were stretched to the limit at all times. We needed more climbers, because it's long enough to be more than just a straight push without oxygen. At that height, your mind is befuddled most of the time. That's the problem."

The next day the five of us hiked up to 17,450 feet, leaving our porters at the campsite. The grandeur of the terrain was undiminished for those of us who were seeing it for the second time. Charlie and Chris were enthralled. Along the way, we found a shallow lake with surprisingly warm water. Charlie, Rick, and I took a swim. We trekked beyond the shrubs and flowers, and camped in a desolate scene of morainal rock and dirty gray ice, within a couple of miles of the great East Face of Everest. The clouds were down on the deck, but we could see lightning flashes to the south. The 1981 American Expedition to the Kangshung Face had left lots of corrugated boxes, and we used them to make a huge, cheering bonfire. It helped lift Chris's and Charlie's spirits, but I could still sense the tension and sadness in them.

We woke early. Everest was clear in the dull predawn light. We mounted on its tripod the 40-power telescope that the British had brought and scanned the snow and rock above. There was no trace of Joe and Pete. After breakfast we started back, wrapped in our private thoughts.

Now there was no choice but to finish carving the memorial to Peter Boardman and Joe Tasker. Chris called them "men of vast humanity." It was a memorial very much like the one this same team had discovered earlier: the stone tablet dedicated to George Leigh Mallory and Andrew Irvine, whose mysterious disappearance nearly 60 years earlier was so tragically similar.

Men for whom we cared deeply had died in the mountains we had come to love. They had accepted risk and hardship while pushing to, and beyond, their limits. Their urge to climb had been joyful. They did what they did because they wanted to. We will miss them, even as we continue to pursue our own goals and dreams.

The trek back to Kharta took two days. At the first village we all stopped for a few cups of chang, talking lightly about past expeditions and future plans. Throughout the search and the sadness, we had all maintained a steadying sense of humor. Now we joked about returning to the Rongbuk Base Camp and finding Joe and Pete safe and sound—berating us for worrying like old maids and delaying another attempt up the mountain. We chuckled about trying to explain to the CAAC—the Chinese airline—that we needed two more seats going home. "You see, sir, we thought they were dead."

Jan was waiting for us at the campsite beside the river in Kharta. The grass was green and speckled with purple and yellow flowers. She welcomed us all with warm embraces, giving Charlie, who looked elfin in his bright red hiking costume, a bear hug that lifted him off the ground. It was good to be together again. Weary, I sauntered over to the river bank, peeled off my stinky shoes and socks, and lowered my feet into the cool water. Jan soon joined me. I told her about the events of the last five days. She listened in silence; then I became silent, simply enjoying her company. In many ways we had been the center of each other's circle during the circumnavigation of Everest. It had been our plan and we had gone the distance together. At times we had gone around and around in our discussions of when, where, who, how, and what. But in the end, although personally determined, we had always been mutually supportive, and the whole thing had worked.

JAN: We threw our gear and ourselves into the back of the truck again for our three-day ride from Kharta back to Lhasa. As we rode, the dust coated us as it had on our way in, and we continued to squabble over who got to wear the headphones to the stereo. But now the ride had a pleasant, calm comfort that had been missing on our ride to the mountain. We'd become a team. On an expedition, weaknesses and holes in character tend to leak—we'd learned how to stop them up in each other.

Released from the intensity of the expedition's physical demands, we were free to laugh and joke, giving each other the fond attention we were too drained to give while working hard up high. Being considerate was easy now.

As we came into Lhasa, Jim stood up high on our baggage behind the cab and began waving in lordly fashion to the people we passed on the street. We laughed at our commander, especially when a strong tree limb stretching across the road caught him off guard, and laid him down in the back of the truck with the rest of us. The luxurious accommodations in Lhasa were a welcome sight, and we arrived just in time for dinner. But when we walked into our suite, all I could see was the big white porcelain bathtub. None of us had washed properly for two months, and I was aching to soak away the caked layers of dust, dirt, and sweat, and to feel warmth all around me. The others literally ran to eat, but food was secondary for me.

I lay back in the tub with my eyes closed and amid the steam, played back the entire trip in my mind. As I watched the brown rings forming around me in the tub, I knew that the trip had been worth it. The bad food, the cold, the strain, the hard work, and the danger were nothing compared to what I had learned, felt, and shared with people who were something more to me than friends. I supposed this was my own answer to why I did it.

NED: Our final moments at the edge of wilderness had a familiar, bittersweet flavor that I had experienced at the end of every expedition. The next day we would depart for the long trip homeward. The circle was already a memory. During the course of the expedition I had often spoken longingly of the luxuries of home, and sometimes had cursed the hardships of altitude and ice, solitude and storm. Now that we had finished, I felt a strong attachment to the experiences and camaraderie of the expedition.

It had been the kind of enterprise I thrive on: an exotic, imaginative venture that combined sport, business, and the arts of photography and writing. And there had been real accomplishment: we'd been the first to go around the "nose tip" of the world. I smiled every time I remembered that it had all begun with an alcohol-fired comment long before in Beijing.

BIBLIOGRAPHY

Ahluwalia, Major H.P.S. *Faces of Everest.* New Delhi: Vikas, 1978.
Allen, Charles. *A Mountain in Tibet.* London: Andre Deutsch, 1982.
Avedon, John. *In Exile from the Land of Snows.* New York: Alfred A. Knopf, 1984.
Ballard, R.D. *Exploring Our Living Planet.* Washington D.C.: National Geographic Society, 1983.
Bell, Sir Charles. *Tibet, Past and Present.* London: Oxford University Press, 1968.
__________. *The People of Tibet.* London: Oxford at the Clarendon Press, 1928.
Bernstein, Jeremy. *The Wildest Dreams of Kew.* New York: Simon and Schuster, 1969.
Bonington, Chris. *Everest: The Hard Way.* New York: Random House, 1976.
__________. *Kongur, China's Elusive Summit.* London: Hodder and Stoughton, 1982.
Bonington, C. & Clarke, Charles. *Everest: The Unclimbed Ridge.* London: Hodder and Stoughton, 1983.
Bruce, Charles G. *The Assault on Mount Everest, 1922.* London: Longmans, Green, 1923.
Cameron, Ian. *Mountains of the Gods.* London: Century Publishing, 1984.
Cronin, Edward Jr. *The Arun.* Boston: Houghton Mifflin, 1979.
David-Neel Alexandra. *Magic and Mystery in Tibet.* New York: Claude Kendall, 1932.
Denman, Earl. *Alone to Everest.* New York: Coward-McCann, 1954.
Dhyrenfurth, G.O. *To the Third Pole: The History of the High Himalaya.* London: Werner Laurie, 1955.
Fairservis, Walter Jr. *Asia, Traditions and Treasures.* New York: Harry N. Abrams, 1981.
Fleming, Peter. *Bayonets to Lhasa.* London: Jonathan Cape, 1961.
Harrer, Heinrich. *Seven Years in Tibet.* New York: E.P. Dutton, 1954.
Hedin, Sven. *Trans-Himalaya: Discoveries and Adventures in Tibet.* London: MacMillan, 1909.
__________. *My Life as an Explorer.* Garden City, N.Y.: Garden City Publishing, 1925.
__________. *A Conquest of Tibet.* New York: E.P. Dutton, 1934.
Hillary, Edmund. *High Adventure.* New York: E.P. Dutton, 1955.
Hillary, E. & Desmond Doig. *High in the Thin Cold Air.* New York: Doubleday, 1962.
Hilton, James. *Lost Horizon.* New York: William Morrow and Co., 1933.
Hopkirk, Peter. *Trespassers on the Roof of the World.* Los Angeles: J.P. Tarcher, 1982.
Howard-Bury, Charles K. *Mount Everest, The Reconnaissance, 1921.* London: Edward Arnold, 1922.
Hunt, Sir John. *The Conquest of Everest.* London: E.P. Dutton, 1954.
Jugoslovenska, Revija. *Tibet.* New York: McGraw-Hill, 1981.
Keay, John. *The Gilgit Game.* Hamden, Conn.: Archon Books, 1979.
__________. *When Men and Mountains Meet.* Hamden, Conn.: Archon Books, 1982.
Lall, J.S. & Moodie, A.D. *The Himalaya, Aspects of Change.* Delhi: Oxford University Press, 1981.
Mariaini, Fosco. *Secret Tibet.* New York: Viking, 1952.
Mason, Kenneth. *Abode of Snow.* London: Rupert Hart-Davis, 1955.
Matthiessen, Peter. *The Snow Leopard.* New York: Bantam, 1978.
McGovern, W.M. *To Lhasa in Disguise.* London: Grosset & Dunlap, 1924.
Nin, Anais. *Diary of Anais Nin.* New York: Swallow, 1966.
Noel, J.B.L. *Through Tibet to Everest.* London: Edward Arnold, 1927.
Norton, E.F. *The Fight for Everest: 1924.* London: Longmans, Green, 1925.
Noyce, Wilfrid. *The Springs of Adventure.* London: John Murray, 1928.

Roberts, Dennis. *I'll Climb Everest Alone: The Story of Maurice Wilson.* London: Robert Hale, 1957.
Rowell, Galen. *Many People Come, Looking, Looking.* Seattle: The Mountaineers, 1980.
___________. *Mountains of the Middle Kingdom.* San Francisco: Sierra Club, 1983.
Ruttledge, Hugh. *Everest, 1933.* London: Hodder & Stoughton, 1934.
___________. *Everest, The Unfinished Adventure.* London: Hodder & Stoughton, 1937.
Salkeld, Audrey. *Mountain 79,* "People." Sheffield, England: Mountain Magazine Ltd, 1980.
Sayre, Woodrow Wilson. *Four Against Everest.* Englewood Cliffs, N.J.: Prentice-Hall, 1968.
Schell, Orville. *In the People's Republic.* New York: Vintage, 1978.
Shipton, E.E. *That Untravelled World.* New York: Charles Scribner's Sons, 1969.
___________. *The Mount Everest Reconnaissance Expedition, 1951.* London: Hodder & Stoughton, 1952.
___________. *The Alpine Journal,* vol XLVIII, "The Mount Everest Reconnaissance, 1935." London: The Alpine Club, 1936.
Skrede, Wilfred. *Across the Roof of the World.* New York: W.W. Norton, 1954.
Snellgrove, David and Richardson, Hugh. *A Cultural History of Tibet.* Boulder, Colo.: Prajna, 1980.
Tasker, Joe. *Everest The Cruel Way.* London: Eyre Methuen, 1981.
Tilman, H.W. *Everest, 1938.* Cambridge: Cambridge at the University Press, 1948.
___________. *Nepal Himalaya.* Cambridge: Cambridge at the University Press, 1952.
Topping, Audrey. *The Splendors of Tibet.* New York: Sino, 1980.
Tucci, Giuseppe. *The Religions of Tibet.* Berkeley: University of California Press, 1980.
Tung, Rosemary. *A Portrait of Lost Tibet.* New York: Holt, Rinehart & Winston, 1980.
Unsworth, Walt. *Everest—A Mountaineering History.* Boston: Houghton Mifflin, 1981.
von Furer-Haimendorf, C. *The Sherpas of Nepal.* New Delhi: Sterling, 1964.
Waddell, L.A. *Tibetan Buddhism.* New York: Dover, 1972.
Younghusband, Sir Francis. *Everest: The Challenge.* London: Thomas Nelson & Sons, 1936.
___________. *The Epic of Mount Everest.* London: Edward Arnold, 1926.